Beyond the Horizon

Beyond the Horizon

Daily Devotions for Seniors

Harry A. Renfree

Edited and Compiled by
Gordon H. Renfree

RESOURCE *Publications* • Eugene, Oregon

BEYOND THE HORIZON
Daily Devotions for Seniors

Copyright © 2016 Gordon H. Renfree. All rights reserved. Except for brief quotations in critical publications or reviews, no part of this book may be reproduced in any manner without prior written permission from the publisher. Write: Permissions, Wipf and Stock Publishers, 199 W. 8th Ave., Suite 3, Eugene, OR 97401.

Resource Publications
An Imprint of Wipf and Stock Publishers
199 W. 8th Ave., Suite 3
Eugene, OR 97401

www.wipfandstock.com

PAPERBACK ISBN: 978-1-4982-3225-8
HARDCOVER ISBN: 978-1-4982-3227-2

Manufactured in the U.S.A.

Scripture taken from the Holy Bible, New International Version®, NIV®

Copyright© 1973, 1978, 1984, 2011 by Biblica, Inc.™

Used by permission of Zondervan. All rights reserved worldwide.

WWW.ZONDERVAN.COM

To my father, whose spiritual legacy carries on
through the lives of his family
and through the pages of this book.

Preface

I come from a family of teachers. I had uncles who were teachers, my grandmother was a teacher, my only two siblings were teachers, my mother was a teacher, my wife was a teacher, and I was a teacher. My father "failed to see the light" and became a minister. Just joking, of course.

Ministers are multi-skilled people, and one of their primary skills is teaching. My father was no exception. There's a joke that says, "Old ministers never die; they just get put out to pastor." This was actually quite true in my father's case. For much of his ministerial life, he worked in leadership positions with his denomination, but when he retired, he made good use of his pastoral skills. In his early retirement years, he led Bible studies and filled in as interim pastor at various churches. In his later retirement years, he presented a series of devotions to a group of seniors at a seniors' complex in White Rock, BC. Those devotions form the basis of this book.

After my father went to his eternal reward, my mother moved to a seniors' complex in Edmonton, Alberta. After one of my visits with her, I went to get my coat from her closet and noticed a lone, small box on the closet floor. Curiosity getting the better of me, I lifted it up to see what it was. Papers written in my father's handwriting filled the box, and I soon became aware that the papers were devotions. I asked and received permission from my mother to take them home so that I could examine them closer.

An adventure was about to begin.

How these devotions made the journey from their initial oral presentation to the publication of this book has indeed been an adventure for me. When I taught school, one of my students' favorite series of books was the "Choose Your Own Adventure" series. Each book is arranged so that the reader is faced with two or three choices, each of which leads to more choices and then to one of many endings. This adventure has been somewhat like that for me. When I first looked at the devotions, I thought I would just read them with the dual goals of filling some spare time and reconnecting with my father. As I read further, I began to realize that the devotions could prove to be a blessing to others besides myself and the people who had been the original recipients of the devotions at the seniors' complex. How could this be accomplished?

I could hire a writer and have him/her put something together, perhaps in a booklet—even a book—but that could have proved costly.

PREFACE

I, myself, could possibly put something together in the way of a coil bound booklet that might be of interest to family, friends, and acquaintances.

I could select some devotions and send them to publishers who put out monthly or quarterly devotion booklets.

I could send some to a religious organization that puts devotions online.

I could do nothing and just enjoy the devotions for what they were.

Or I could try to use my limited writing skills and my even more limited typing skills to put together a book.

I decided to take the more "adventurous" route and attempt to put a book together myself. Who knew where that would end up? I could imagine a lot of different endings—most of them not that positive—but I decided that if the Lord wanted it done, He would open the doors, so I prayed about it and the compiling of a book began.

I found it interesting that the first eight devotions were written in point form, as my father outlined his sermons, but from the ninth on, the devotions were written word for word. To me, it indicated that perhaps my father intended for them to be used later on in some other manner, or perhaps it was just his advancing years that presented memory problems. I like to think it was the former.

I began to type out the devotions. You need to understand that my typing is a very spiritual exercise since I use the biblical method of typing— "seek and ye shall find." I do a lot of seeking before finding the correct keys. The original manuscript turned out to be around 127, 000 words. That was a lot of typing, and for me, that translated into many years. It took additional time to track down and verify some of the stories and to obtain permissions where required. I had to contact people scattered in many different places to accomplish this task. Communicating with those involved in the various stories turned out to be quite rewarding in its own right. The process of contacting publishers, facing rejection, and finally finding the right publisher took quite a while as well. Now here we are with the finished product. I hope that this book proves to be a blessing to you— the reader.

Acknowledgments

I have some special people to thank. Thank you to Rena Fish for her great talents and spiritual insight in the tremendous job she did with the copyediting. I would like to thank those in my family who have directly supported this project: my two brothers, John and Paul, for their encouragement and financial support and a special kudos to Paul for designing the website. And my deepest gratitude to my wife Darlene for her continual support right from the get go. She helped keep me focused when there were times of discouragement. She helped me with the many "computer challenges." She was a great sounding board and supplier of creative ideas. It was through her initiative that I was able to finally find the right publisher after many rejections.

Finally and foremost, to my father who is the author of the book. The book is being published after you, Dad, have passed on to your eternal reward. God does indeed work in mysterious ways. This book underlines the spiritual legacy that each one of us can leave to succeeding generations. Our legacy may not come out in book form, but it will come out in what our children and others learn about our character and the way we live our lives.

> Note: Profits from the sale of this book will be given to a scholarship fund established by my parents for students at a seminary in Cochabamba, Bolivia. More information about this fund and other information concerning the book can be found at the book website, beyond–the–horizon.info.

Gordon Renfree
Compiler/Editor

Fear or Hope?
January 01

John Greenleaf Whittier (1807–1892) was an American poet and staunch advocate of the abolition of slavery in the United States. One of his poems, called "Child Songs," has the message about learning from children and the importance of a childlike heart.

A couple of the verses are as follows:

> We need love's tender lessons taught
> As only weakness can;
> God hath his small interpreters;
> The child must teach the man.
>
> Alone to guileness and love—
> That gate shall open fall;
> The mind of pride is nothingness
> The childlike heart is all![1]

We do not really know what the New Year will bring, but we can proceed by our faith. The Psalmist was musing about some of these things and out of his musings came one of the most magnificent Psalms in the Psalter that of Psalm 8: *"O LORD, our Lord, how majestic is your name in all the earth! You have set your glory above the heavens."* Then this: *"From the lips of children and infants you have ordained praise"* (Psalm 8:1–2a).

Jesus Himself was similarly musing one day during His sojourn on earth. In a prayer, He said to His Father: *"I praise you, Father, Lord of heaven and earth, because you have hidden these things from the wise and learned, and revealed them to little children"* (Matthew 11:25).

The season through which we have just been passing is about a child—the Child. It's primarily for children—young children, as well as for those who, with childlike faith, worship at the manger and then put their hand into the hand of God and move confidently into the New Year.

A Double Future
January 02

The month of January, particularly the first few days of the month, is often felt to be a time to look forward. People make New Year's resolutions which, sad to say, are seldom kept . . . and it's a time for planning. As I am sure most of you know, January is also a time for reflection, a time for looking at what has recently been done. The name of the month January indeed is taken from Janus, the Roman god of beginnings, who is represented as an idol with two bearded heads set back to back—looking backward and forward.

The story is told of a group of people looking back at particularly memorable moments in their lives. One talked of his first job, another of getting through university, another of being discharged from the army, and then a grandfather mentioned that his was becoming a grandparent and realizing something of him was going into the future.

Ours is a double future actually—a future that we make for ourselves and then a future in which we have an influence on others by the way we live. As C.S. Lewis puts it: "The future is something which everyone reaches at the age of sixty minutes an hour, whatever he does, wherever he is."

God's people in the day of the prophet Jeremiah were languishing as virtual slaves in Nebuchadnezzar's Babylon. God gave Jeremiah the message for the exiles, one of the finest moments in Scripture in Jeremiah 29:11: " 'For I know the plans I have for you,' declares the LORD, 'plans to prosper you and not to harm you, plans to give you hope and a future.'" How to ensure that promise? God's message continues in verses 12 and 13: " 'Then you will call upon me and come and pray to me, and I will listen to you. You will seek me and find me when you seek me with all your heart.'"

"Plans to give you hope and a future" . . . your own and those whom you influence.

Something New
January 03

There is an interesting story concerning the history of the Royal Hotel in Calgary in 1892. At that time the Royal Hotel was the area's most imposing structure. It proclaimed itself the finest hotel west of Winnipeg—although they hung blankets from the ceiling in place of walls. In any event, that year, 1892, the hotel became ultramodern. They installed newfangled electric lighting. They also hung a sign which read: "Do not attempt to light the bulbs with a match. Simply turn key on wall by the door. The use of electricity is in no way harmful to health."

We are all a little tentative about something new, whether it's electricity, or the latest in computer technology. We have to prove whether or not it's better than the old way.

Early in his Gospel, Mark tells of reaction to Jesus on perhaps the first trip of His ministry to Capernaum. He taught in their synagogue and startled them with His knowledge and caring . . . he healed a man with an evil spirit. Mark writes: *"The people were amazed at his teaching, because he taught them as one who had authority, not as the teachers of the law"* (Mark 1:22). "Jesus' teaching" was—and is—new.

The old Jewish law was an eye for an eye and a tooth for a tooth. Said Jesus, *"You have heard that it was said, 'Love your neighbor and hate your enemy.' But I tell you: Love your enemies and pray for those who persecute you"* (Matthew 5:43-44).

Indeed as the Apostle Paul puts it, the one who follows His way is a new creation . . . a new person.

Sufficient Grace
January 04

Many of you are familiar with the remarkable life of Helen Keller. As a baby, she went through a terrible illness that deprived her of both sight and hearing, and soon she became mute. When Helen was six, her parents sought the advice of Alexander Graham Bell regarding her education, and as a result, Anne Sullivan became her teacher. Through Miss Sullivan's diligent efforts and the efforts of others, Helen Keller eventually was able to go to college and graduated with honors.

Helen Keller's greatest achievement of course, was the help she was able to give those who were similarly disabled. Her driving force was her Christian faith.

During His three-year ministry, Jesus healed many. He opened blind eyes and cured some who were paralyzed. But He was not able to reach all of Palestine's sick . . . nor were all able to reach Him. God still heals, but not all experience a miracle. Helen Keller's miracle was not that she was given new sight, new hearing, but that despite the handicaps, she was able to accomplish a great deal and, in particular, to greatly help others.

The Apostle Paul, surely one of the finest Christians who ever lived, writes that he asked God three times to heal him of what he called his "thorn in the flesh," and each time God responded: "My grace is sufficient for you" . . . and that grace is offered to each of us as we look up and out to Him. Around us we see many examples of overcoming faith, "the victory that overcomes the world." As God promised the people of Asher in the Old Testament: *"Your strength will equal your days"*

From the Beginning
January 05

In the Old Testament book of Deuteronomy, there is a verse that just fits the beginning of a new year: *"It is a land the LORD your God cares for; the eyes of the LORD your God are continually on it from the beginning of the year to its end"* (Deuteronomy 11:12).

God's people Israel had a centuries-old promise from God that one day they would possess a homeland far beyond their wildest dreams. After languishing for over four hundred years in Egypt, God had seen to their deliverance, and they were on their way to Canaan, the Promised Land. They roamed the wilderness for over forty years before their children stood on the bank of the Jordan River, hesitating before crossing into Canaan.

Here the promise of God rings in, as it were, a marvelous new year: *"The land you are entering to take over is not like the land of Egypt, from which you have come, where you planted your seed and irrigated it by foot as in a vegetable garden. But the land you are crossing the Jordan to take possession of is a land of mountains and valleys that drinks rain from heaven"* (Deuteronomy 11:10-11).

His promise to us in this land as we enter the new year, as surely as we place our faith in Him, is not only an earthly Promised Land, but an eternal one—which is far better. They both have Heavenly spiritual showers of blessing. We are assured that God will be with us continually . . . from beginning to end, here and in eternity, which has no end.

Poet John Oxenham's words seem to chime in for those of us who have a few doubts.

> Not for one single day
> Can I discern my way,
> But this I surely know,—
> Who gives the day,
> Will show the way,
> So I securely go.[2]

Keep Looking
January 06

In the book *Tough Times Never Last, But Tough People Do*, Robert Schuller speaks of his boyhood on a small farm in Iowa. His family was poor, but they managed to get by in an area where the weather was not predictable. One summer the family was particularly devastated when a tornado virtually destroyed their farm. However, they remained grateful that all the family members had escaped unharmed. After the storm, they returned to survey their damaged property. Among the ruins was a sign that used to hang on the kitchen wall. Originally the sign read: "Keep looking to Jesus" ... but after the tornado, broken in two, it simply said: "Keep Looking."[3]

"Keep Looking" ... a marvelous motto for a person at any stage of life particularly as one gets older.

Looking back on his life in the magnificent passage of Philippians 3, the Apostle Paul reflects on the glorious experiences he has had in serving Jesus Christ. Then he says this in verse twelve:

> "Not that I have already obtained all this, or have already been made perfect ... But one thing I do: Forgetting what is behind and straining toward what is ahead, I press on toward the goal to win the prize for which God has called me heavenward in Christ Jesus" (Philippians 3:12a,13b,14).

Then he adds this bit of wisdom for you and me: *All of us who are mature should take such a view of things* (Philippians 3:15a).

In other words: Keep Looking!

Decisions

January 07

I'm sure you have learned to make right decisions. If you are like me, the right decisions you have made have often resulted from lessons learned from wrong decisions you had made previously. Our failures are sometimes better teachers than our successes.

Coming to the end of His ministry on this earth, with the cross looming, the Master faced a crucial decision. The task of spreading the gospel of salvation was to be left to a diverse group of His followers after His resurrection and ascension. The leader of the group, at least the spokesman, was the fisherman Simon Peter. Could he be depended upon? Peter often wavered, uncertain of himself. Jesus knew this and warned Peter that he might fail in the face of personal danger. Peter protested vehemently that he would never fail Jesus. He did . . . three times he denied his Lord before Calvary—denied that he even knew Jesus.

After the resurrection, Jesus faced Peter on the shore of the Sea of Galilee after a group of disciples had spent a fruitless night fishing. Testing him, Jesus asked if Peter really loved him. When Peter replied affirmatively, Jesus pointed out that it would cost Peter to follow through on that promise. Then Jesus said to him: *"Follow me."* Peter hesitated; success or failure was in the balance. But Peter, aware of his failures and sorry for them, bravely faced up to them. He, of course, became Peter the solid rock, who was largely responsible for founding the first churches. So effective was his witness to his faith that after his sermon the day of Pentecost, 3,000 were won to the way of Christ.

Wrong decisions, you see, may well point the way to right decisions. Let us use some of the failures of the past to form the successes of the future.

The Greatest Satisfaction
January 08

In response to the vast human needs of global proportions, Albert Schweitzer and countless others like him have dedicated their lives to relieve suffering and to tell others of the gospel of Jesus Christ. In one of his writings, Schweitzer describes the kind of moment in his life that gave him the greatest satisfaction. A native with intense suffering was brought into his hospital. Dr. Schweitzer calmed the man by relating that he would operate and the man would soon be well and free of pain. After the operation, the caring doctor sat with the man while he was regaining consciousness. Slowly the man opened his eyes and whispered in sheer wonderment: "I have no more pain." That was the moment of Dr. Schweitzer's greatest satisfaction . . . no monetary reward there, but a deep satisfaction.

In response to the vast human need with which He was surrounded, Jesus gave what we call the Sermon on the Mount, found in which are the marvelous Beatitudes. The last few verses of chapter 4 in Matthew set the scene. News about Jesus had spread, and many brought to him people with various diseases, those suffering severe pain, the epileptics, the paralytics, the demon possessed etc., and Jesus healed them. Large crowds from Galilee and beyond followed Him. Chapter 5 begins by indicating that Jesus then went up to a mountainside and began to teach the comforting words of the Beatitudes:

> *Blessed are the poor in spirit,*
>   *for theirs is the Kingdom of heaven.*
> *Blessed are those who mourn,*
>   *for they will be comforted.*
> *Blessed are the meek,*
>   *for they will inherit the earth.*
> *Blessed are those who hunger and thirst for righteousness,*
>   *for they will be filled*

(Matthew 5:3–6).

Jesus remains as concerned about the sufferer today. And so are His followers, whether skilled like Albert Schweitzer or simply able like you and me to share the Master's love and concern.

Trust

January 09

Trust is one of those precious qualities that make life so worthwhile. And yet . . . we have to admit, sorrowfully, that the mark of trust is becoming less obvious in our day. We have to trust, and yet we must be careful as to whom we trust.

God's Word has a good deal to say about trust. For example, of Daniel, who was an administrator in the king's service, the Bible says that his enemies tried to find something in his life for which they could criticize and destroy him. In Daniel 6:4b, these words are found: *"They could find no corruption in him* [Daniel] *because he was trustworthy and neither corrupt, nor negligent."* We wish often that we could have that kind of trust in those who govern us these many centuries later. Some are most trustworthy; others, sadly, are not. We do get an opportunity to choose—at the ballot box.

"Do not trust in deceptive words," writes the prophet Jeremiah. God's people of ancient times were warned not to trust in the pagan power of the pharaoh of Egypt. As the book of 2 Kings 18:21 states: *"Look now, you are depending on Egypt that splintered reed of a staff, which pierces a man's hand and wounds him if he leans on it! Such is Pharaoh king of Egypt to all who depend on him."* God's people trusted Pharaoh against God's expressed order . . . and Pharaoh let them down.

Some do let us down from time to time, but there is always One in whom we can place complete trust. Over twenty times in the Psalms, the Psalmist calls on us to put our trust in the Lord, who is fully trustworthy. He writes: *"In God I trust; I will not be afraid"* (Psalm 56:11a). And from Psalm 62, verse 8: *"Trust in him at all times, O people; pour out your hearts to him, for God is our refuge."*

It is marvelous to enjoy trust in one another, but surer still is the trust in our God who will never, never let us down . . . in time or eternity.

Immortality
January 10

Napoleon was visiting the Louvre gallery when a painting caught his eye. He said to the director of the Louvre, Baron Denon, who was accompanying him, "That is a noble picture, Denon."

"Immortal," was the reply.

"How long," asked Napoleon, "will this picture last?"

Denon replied that with care, it might last five hundred years.

"And how long," said Napoleon, "will a statue last?"

"Perhaps," replied Denon, "five thousand years."

"And this," replied Napoleon, sharply, "—this you call immortality!"[4]

Five thousand years is a long time for something crafted by man, but hardly a long time by God's standards and certainly not immortal.

In 2 Peter 3:8, we read: "*With the Lord a day is like a thousand years, and a thousand years are like a day.*" Time and space merge with God, and the immortality of the human soul is also timeless.

Peter in his first epistle amplifies this thought as he ponders the love of God to you and me.

> *Praise be to the God and Father of our Lord Jesus Christ! In his great mercy he has given us new birth into a living hope through the resurrection of Jesus from the dead, and into an inheritance that can never perish, spoil or fade—kept in heaven for you, who through faith are shielded by God's power until the coming of the salvation that is ready to be revealed in the last time. In this you greatly rejoice, though now for a little while you may have had to suffer grief in all kinds of trials* (1 Peter 1:3–6).

Living for immortality.

Walking With God
January 11

One weekend as I was walking through the parking lot of a university campus, I came upon something that immediately caught my attention. The parking lot was only partially occupied, but in that lot was a husky young man having the time of his life by manipulating a tiny radio-controlled car. With his handheld control, he sent the car back and forth, weaving, turning, speeding, and slowing—all over the lot. He was obviously enjoying the fun and the sense of power for when I came back twenty minutes later, he was still there.

It seems to me that one might see such a scene as a parallel of life. We, like the little model car, are spinning all over the world, sometimes with purpose, sometimes without—going, coming, eating, sleeping, working, and enjoying recreation. All the while, up there is a power that watches over us so that we won't smash up.

There's a difference of course. We would not like it if God controlled us like the young man handled his model. We feel much better when God lets us run our own show. But most of us, in the back of our minds, want to believe that in the last analysis, God will step in if there's a crisis.

This attitude could, I think, be described as "taking God for granted." But I seem to hear the crashing interjection of the prophet Micah: *"He has showed you, O man, what is good. And what does the LORD require of you? To act justly and to love mercy and to walk humbly with your God"* (Micah 6:8).

God does not want to manipulate us or to be ignored by us. He wants to walk with us. The choice is ours.

A Glorious Vista

January 12

Joseph Mallord Turner, one of the finest and most famous of British artists, lived from 1775 to 1851. Turner was something of a prodigy as a painter, and his father, a barber, is said to have sold some of the lad's sketches when he was twelve. Turner is best known for the brilliant and lavish colors of his landscapes and seascapes.

One day, so the story goes, a lady approached Turner, objecting that she did not see such brilliant colors occurring in nature. The artist's simple but perceptive reply was, "Don't you wish you did, Madam?"

The Apostle Paul expresses similar sentiments in a brief prayer recorded in Ephesians 1:18: "*I pray also that the eyes of your heart may be enlightened in order that you may know the hope to which he* [i.e. Jesus] *has called you, the riches of his glorious inheritance in the saints.*" Paul later adds this similar prayer: "*And I pray that you, being rooted and established in love, may have power . . . to grasp how wide and long and high and deep is the love of Christ*" (Ephesians 3: 17b–18). Paul is painting the spiritual landscape for his fellow Christians, and it contains all the colors of the rainbow.

God loves His children with an abundant, abounding love that truly passes understanding.

Simply put, God loves you and God loves me.

Have Patience
January 13

Sometimes having patience is one of the most difficult things in life. That's why it's called a virtue. As we age, patience becomes even more of a virtue, it seems, as there are issues we have to deal with unique to the aging process.

In the twelfth chapter of Romans, verse 12, the Apostle Paul calls for a type of patience many aging Christians that I know have shown in their daily living. He writes: *"Be joyful in hope, patient in affliction, faithful in prayer."*

In Ephesians chapter 4, verses 1 and 2, the apostle adds this: *"I urge you to live a life worthy of the calling you have received. Be completely humble and gentle; be patient, bearing with one another in love."*

The fortieth chapter of the prophet Isaiah concludes with words which are encouraging when we may come to those moments where we want to give up, to quit—"to throw in the towel" as is done in boxing. Isaiah writes: *"Those who hope in the Lord will renew their strength. They will soar on wings like eagles; they will run and not grow weary, they will walk and not be faint"* (Isaiah 40:31).

Some days we just don't feel like soaring, or running, or even walking, but the key to renewal, writes the prophet, is simply hope in the Heavenly Father. He understands, even when we feel like quitting. *"Cast your cares* [or burdens] *on the Lord,"* the Psalmist David writes, *"and he will sustain you."*

The Ways of God
January 14

While on an overseas trip, I heard an intriguing story told to me by a proprietor of a tiny shop in Kowloon. He told me about a friend of his in northern India who had passed his academic examinations with flying colors and then accepted a good position in Calcutta, 36 hours by train from his home. On his first journey, the young man's parents decided to accompany him.

Waiting to board the train, the young man became restless, pacing back and forth. Then he stopped to watch an elderly man squatting in a corner... apparently in quiet meditation. For a long time the old man didn't move. Intrigued, the young man went over and said, "If you want to pray, why don't you go to the God–House?"

"But God is everywhere," was the simple reply.

So interested did the young man become with the praying person that when he finally looked around, the train was gone—with his parents on board. Bewildered, he berated the old man. "Why did you talk to me so long that I missed my train?"

"Do not fret, my son," said the man. "All will be well."

The youth didn't think so as he was sending a wire to his parents to get off at the next city. But he did have cause for sober reflection when he later learned that a number of miles beyond the place his parents got off, a bridge was out. The speeding train had gone into a gorge, killing many. His plans and his life were changed because he stopped to watch a man pray.

His [God's] *eyes are on the ways of men; he sees their every step,* says Job's friend Elihu in the thirty-fourth chapter of Job. We dare not say that God is responsible for all that goes on in our world. Men build unsafe and poorly constructed bridges and buildings. These are simply facts of human life, as are other man–made tragedies.

The thirteenth chapter of Luke tells us that some in the crowd Jesus was addressing told Him of a group of Galileans in Jerusalem that had somehow run afoul of the Roman procurator, Pontius Pilate, the man who later sent Jesus to the Cross. Pilate ordered the execution of those Galileans. Those in the crowd who mentioned this story to Jesus thought their execution must have been due to some exceptional wickedness in their lives for God to allow such a tragedy to happen. "*I tell you, no!*" said Jesus; they were no more or less wicked than others of their compatriots at the time. He seemed to be saying, "Anyone can be killed... only God's grace allows any to live." Then he added this warning: *"But unless you repent, you too will all perish."* [Jesus meant eternally.]

What about the youth who missed his train and saved his life while an elderly man prayed? We don't know completely the mind of God. God does answer prayer, and a man was praying. Perhaps God had a special job for a special person along the way and this young man was marked to do it. We don't know all the answers now, but some wonderful day we'll understand.

Good Sportsmanship
January 15

The Olympic Games have become probably the greatest sports event in the world. The winter and summer versions are held every four years in various parts of this planet. They are seen by thousands in person and by many millions more on television. Not nearly as well-known are the Special Olympics that involve athletes who are mentally disabled.

An incident occurred in the Special Olympics held in Seattle that surely involved good sportsmanship. It happened in the 100 meter dash. The nine contestants took off at the sound of the gun and headed for the finish line. One boy, however, stumbled and fell to the ground, tears coming down his face. The other eight heard the boy cry and paused. Then all of them ran back, consoled the boy, linked arms, and all nine walked together to the finish line. The stadium erupted with a sustained standing ovation at this display of sportsmanship.

In the second book of Timothy, Paul, writing to his younger co-worker of that name, says: *"If anyone competes as an athlete, he does not receive the victor's crown unless he competes according to the rules"* (2 Timothy 2:5). Those disabled young people were competing that day according to the highest rule in the world, that of love.

"Love one another," said Jesus to his disciples. *"Greater love has no one than this, that he lay down his life for his friends"* (John 15:13) . . . or even his prospect of victory in the race or in the race of life. Adds Paul: *"Knowledge puffs up, but love builds up"* (1 Corinthians 8:1b).

Here for all of us is a lesson in a loving concern for another, which triumphed over the very natural desire to win the race. Berton Braley, author of the poem, "The Prayer of a Sportsman," once said it another way: "If I should lose, let me stand by the road and cheer as the winners go by."

That, too, is good sportsmanship.

Dependable Promises
January 16

One of the simplest definitions of theology is "a body of doctrines concerning God" . . . and what we believe about how God shapes our lives. The promises of God are absolutely and completely dependable, not only for the future of the world but also for our future. In fact, those who follow the Savior are called *"children of the promise"* by Paul in the ninth chapter of Romans . . . that promise being new life now and in the life to come—supreme joy.

The Bible is simply packed with God's promises to His people. For those needing comfort, Jesus promised peace. *"Peace I leave with you; my peace I give you. I do not give to you as the world gives. Do not let your hearts be troubled and do not be afraid"* (John 14:27). To a woman whose life was barren and dry, He promised the water of life: *"Whoever drinks the water I give him will never thirst. Indeed, the water I give him will become in him a spring of water welling up to eternal life"* (John 4:14). For those wondering about tomorrow, the book of Hebrews records these words of the Heavenly Father: *"Never will I leave you; never will I forsake you."*

Then we find this marvelous invitation and promise from the Master. *"Come to me, all you who are weary and burdened, and I will give you rest. Take my yoke upon you and learn from me, for I am gentle and humble in heart, and you will find rest for your souls"* (Matthew 11:28–29).

These are just a few of the many marvelous promises of God, and like all good theology, they relieve, comfort, calm, and give peace, the peace that only God can give.

Reminded
January 17

You've all discovered, I am sure, that the simple act of remembering becomes a little more difficult year by year as we become older. Names slip from us. Even a short list of things we have memorized and then intended to get at the store might be forgotten by the time we get there. Sometimes we need to be reminded.

God's Word, the Bible, is probably life's greatest reminder. Yes, without any doubt, it is. In his second epistle, the Apostle Peter opens the letter with an appeal to his readers and hearers to make one's calling certain. He writes about being certain of one's faith and making sure that one's Christian faith shows itself in goodness, knowledge, self-control, perseverance, godliness, brotherly kindness, and love—qualities of life that indicate true Christian character.

Then Peter adds: "*For if you do those things, you will never fall, and you will receive a rich welcome into the eternal kingdom of our Lord and Savior Jesus Christ*" (2 Peter 1:10b–11). And as a kind of footnote in verses 12 and 15, he writes: "*So I will always remind you of these things . . . and I will make every effort to see that after my departure you will always be able to remember these things.*"

David, in the one hundred third Psalm, writes, "*Praise the LORD, O my soul, and forget not all his benefits.*" And he goes on to list just a few of God's benefits to us.

It is good, I think, to be reminded of the many benefits we receive every day at the hand of our Heavenly Father.

A Singing Light
January 18

A life dedicated to God and changed through the power of the Savior may, and every so often does, make an impact upon the secular world. Such was the case with Mahalia Jackson, famed operatic singer.

Her voice was first recognized nationally in her American homeland in the 1930s when she sang "He's Got the Whole World in His Hands" during a cross-country gospel tour. She resisted offers for fame and fortune singing secular music, instead concentrating on gospel music. Her records sold in the millions. She became a symbol of the Civil Rights Movement in the United States in singing the theme song, "We Shall Overcome." Before she passed away, Mahalia Jackson had sung almost prophetically in the movie "Imitation of Life:" "Soon I will be done with the troubles of this world." She now is, and this is also true of the millions upon millions who have found their rest in Jesus.

Jesus expressed in the following way the opportunity we all have to demonstrate His light: *"Let your light shine before men, that they may see your good deeds and praise your Father in heaven"* (Matthew 5:16).

In the New Testament, one of the fine descriptions of Christians is *children of light*, suggesting that followers of Jesus, the Light of the World, are also lights—lights to penetrate the darkness of our world. Speaking of Himself, just before He went to the cross, Jesus put the Christian's responsibility plainly before them: *"You are going to have the light just a little while longer,"* [that is Jesus was soon going to go to the cross]. Then He added, *"Walk while you have the light, before darkness overtakes you. The man who walks in the dark does not know where he is going."* (John 12:35). Paul picks up this theme in Ephesians 5:8: *"For you were once darkness, but now you are light in the Lord. Live as children of light."*

Found on a baby's monument in an old cemetery was this epitaph: "There is not darkness enough in all the world to put out the light of one little candle."

That's so vitally true, as Mahalia Jackson proved, and we can too . . . by living as children of light.

Misunderstood
January 19

Charlie Harvey, whom I know personally, was a missionary to Africa for many years. Among his many talents, he's a good writer. In one of his books, he tells of entering a contest that required him, as a robust boy, to have a bath every day for a month. Back in the 1930s and 40s, such a ritual was almost unheard of, particularly on a New Brunswick farm.

Fittingly, the contest was sponsored by the Lifebuoy Soap Company, and contestants in that health and hygiene campaign were required to keep careful record of the hours they slept, the food they ate, and whether or not they brushed their teeth. "Then," as he writes, "there was the one great obstacle." With a free cake of Lifebuoy soap, they were supposed to take a bath every evening of the week. There was only one bathroom and one bath with running water in the entire village of Maugerville, New Brunswick, and unfortunately, not in their house. "It already," he said, "took a lot of planning to accommodate the Saturday night baths for a family of six." Since it was Charlie's task to pump and carry in the water, his mother agreed to the contest, and the big red cake of soap was pressed into hygienic action every night. Charlie writes: "It was crazy and unheard of, but I did it."

Unfortunately, when the ten-year-old boy took his completed chart to school, absolutely no one believed that he had done it—not even the teacher who was overseeing the contest, and the prize was given to someone else.

Charlie Harvey must have had very even-tempered parents, for some I know would have raised quite a ruckus at the teacher's failure to treat their son fairly. However, Charlie says that although many years have gone by, he remembers that he had a bath every day and that he told the truth.[5]

Each one of us suffers the same difficulty from time to time: a truth we say is not believed, or we are misunderstood or even misinterpreted. Jesus Himself was not believed, but was misunderstood and misinterpreted. And for that, He died on the cross. In His Sermon on the Mount, Jesus said that His followers would suffer similarly. *"Blessed are you,"* He said to His disciples, *"when people insult you, persecute you and falsely say all kinds of evil against you because of me. Rejoice and be glad, because great is your reward in heaven"* (Matthew 5:11–12a).

That's the only struggle that really counts.

Can We Change?

January 20

Many of you, I know, have read about—or at least heard about—one of the most controversial figures of the United States during the Nixon years—Charles W. Colson. "Chuck" Colson, as he was popularly known, was one of the most powerful members of President Nixon's staff and played a part in the Watergate Scandal. Colson, as well as others, spent time in prison for their involvement in the scandal that caused Mr. Nixon's resignation.

In the early 1970s, when the Watergate revelations mushroomed across the media, Colson was undergoing a spiritual crisis. He wrote that he experienced a terrible deadness inside, not only because of involvement in "Watergate's dirty tricks, but the deep sin within me, the hidden evil that lies in every human heart."

One day a visit to a friend changed his life. The friend was Tom Philips, a prominent businessman who had become a Christian. Colson writes: "But while Tom's explanation that he had 'accepted Jesus Christ' shocked and baffled me, it also made me curious. He was at peace with himself, something I surely wasn't."[6] That night Charles Colson, too, became a Christian, began a new life, and went on to become a powerful witness for his Lord and Savior.

"Therefore," writes the Apostle Paul in his letter to the Christians at Corinth: "*If anyone is in Christ, he is a new creation; the old has gone, the new has come!*" (2 Corinthians 5:17). To a seeking and puzzled member of the Jewish high council, the Sanhedrin, who had timidly come to Jesus under cover of darkness, the Master Himself put it to him straight from the shoulder: "*I tell you the truth,*" Jesus declared, "*no one can see the kingdom of God unless he is born again*" (John 3:3). Then Jesus soon added the words that have become the Bible's "golden text": "*For God so loved the world that he gave his one and only Son, that whoever believes in Him shall not perish but have eternal life*" (John 3:16).

Any one of us can change or, rather, be changed.

The Fruit of My Labor
January 21

The Roman Emperor, Hadrian, who reigned soon after the New Testament era, saw in his travels one day an old man planting olive trees. Knowing that olives are one of the slowest growing trees, the Emperor said to the bent and frail man, "Those trees you plant will not bear olives for years to come. Do you expect to live long enough to enjoy the rewards of your labor?"

The toiling man looked up and replied, "If deity will, I shall, and if not, my sons will eat of the fruit of my labor. My father and his father before him planted olive trees that I might have their fruit. It is now my duty to help provide for those who will come after I have gone."[7]

God's Word points on a number of occasions to the very special status we can secure as Christians. Jesus Himself said: "*I am the vine; you are the branches. If a man* [or woman] *remains in me and I in him, he will bear much fruit.*" (John 15:5a). The Apostle Paul in Romans 8:17a writes: "*Now if we are children, then we are heirs—heirs of God and co-heirs with Christ.*" Indeed, as the Apostle Peter points out in 1 Peter 3:7b, we are "*. . . heirs . . . of the gracious gift of life.*" Not only the gift of life, but also the gift of new life.

Should we not then plant some olive trees with olive branches so that those who follow may know the same peace . . . the peace that passes all understanding?

What About Tomorrow?
January 22

In an interview broadcast on the CBC national news soon after the devastating earthquake that rocked southern California in January of 1994, a CBC reporter was vividly describing some of the damage around the Los Angeles area. She mentioned the loss of life and said that residents were very uneasy in their homes, some of them arranging to sleep outside for fear of aftershocks.

Then the host newscaster asked her reporter, "What about tomorrow?" The response was, "That's the question on everyone's lips."

To be truthful, that's a question on the lips of more than a few people. And usually it is asked against a background of fear or uncertainty . . . for various kinds of earth-shattering events are happening as well as "natural" earthquakes.

"What about tomorrow?" is a very natural question to ask at this juncture in history.

Jesus had something to say about it in the solid pages of teaching in Matthew 5, 6, and 7—part of what is called the Sermon on the Mount. Jesus had just made reference to very simple things like food and clothing and the fact that God cares for the plants and the animals.

> *"Seek first his kingdom and his righteousness, and all these things will be given to you as well"* (Matthew 6:33).

Then He made this incisive statement:

> *"Therefore do not worry about tomorrow, for tomorrow will worry about itself. Each day has enough trouble of its own"* (Matthew 6:34).

It is our privilege to trust God for tomorrow.

An Honest Servant
January 23

Many years before his martyrdom, Hugh Latimer had preached rather forthrightly before Henry VIII. The king was offended, ordered Latimer to preach the next Sunday and to make an apology for the offence he had given. Latimer searched his soul but truly believed he needed to remain faithful to his message. Then he repeated the sermon he had preached to the king the Sunday before. The king asked him how he could be so bold as to preach to the king in that way. Latimer replied that he merely discharged his duty and followed his conscience. The king embraced him and reportedly said, "Blessed be God, I have so honest a servant."

Not many preachers, nor any other Christians, find themselves in such a situation of personal danger in this day and age—at least not in the Western world. It certainly happened in the former Soviet Union, in China, and in other repressive areas of our world . . . and is still happening.

Ask the question: "What is the cost of being a real Christian?" The answer is simple—

"Everything." Didn't Jesus Himself open the possibility? He said to His followers: *"Remember the words I spoke to you: 'No servant is greater than his master.' If they persecuted me, they will persecute you also. If they obeyed my teaching, they will obey yours also. They will treat you this way because of my name, for they do not know the One who sent me"* (John 15:20–21).

Two among the followers who tested the principle were Peter and John. After the resurrection, they were involved in the healing of a crippled beggar and soon found themselves before the Jewish authorities. Boldly, Peter explained the situation, stating that the miracle had been performed in the name of Jesus. Acts 4:13 tells us: *"When they* [that is the authorities] *saw the courage of Peter and John and realized that they were unschooled, ordinary men, they were astonished and they took note that these men had been with Jesus."*

Just as they took note of Hugh Latimer and even of you and me as we stand firm.

Favorites
January 24

Do you try to treat others with complete fairness, or do you find yourself treating people according to who they are? From time to time, all of us, as much as we hate to admit it, treat people according to who they are. And we likely feel fully justified in doing so. We prefer some folk to others, and the ones we prefer, we usually favor. If we decide to have guests over for dinner, we certainly favor the ones we like and would likely invite them to come. Perhaps we favor some people in life because they are wealthy, others because they are famous, still others because they are successful, or even because they are super intelligent; maybe they are people who could help us out along the way.

Jesus went to eat one Sabbath at the home of a prominent Pharisee, and as He nearly always did, He drew a number of lessons from the occasion. One lesson had to do with showing favors to important people. Jesus said to his host:

> *When you give a luncheon or dinner, do not invite your friends, your brothers or relatives, or your rich neighbors; if you do, they may invite you back and so you will be repaid. But when you give a banquet, invite the poor, the crippled, the lame, the blind, and you will be blessed. Although they cannot repay you, you will be repaid at the resurrection of the righteous* (Luke 14:12–14).

I don't think that Jesus is using this principle for every occasion, saying that you can't have your friends, relatives, and neighbors for lunch. He is stressing, I believe, that the poor and the disadvantaged should not be left out of your planning. "*God does not show favoritism,*" Paul writes in his letter to the Romans. We would be wise to follow the example of our Lord in this area.

Every Christian Has a Cross
January 25

In his book *Storm Warning*, Billy Graham tells of an incident that occurred while he was traveling in an Eastern European country, then under Communist domination.

Traveling with him was an Orthodox priest. One day while the usual swarm of media representatives surrounded them, the Orthodox priest said to Dr. Graham, "Every believer has a cross. I know what ours is. But I wondered what yours was." Then looking out over the crowd of reporters standing before Dr. Graham, the priest said simply, "Now I know."[8]

"Every believer has a cross." That seems to fly in the face of the idea that when one becomes a Christian, all difficulties are over. Not so. Jesus Himself said—to his followers—*"In this world you will have trouble."*

When Saul of Tarsus, later called Paul, met Jesus face to face on the Damascus road, Ananias of Damascus was directed to be a messenger of healing to the blinded Saul. *"The Lord said to Ananias 'Go! This man is my chosen instrument to carry my name before the Gentiles . . . I will show him how much he must suffer for my name'"* (Acts 9:15–16).

Yes, as the priest said, "Every believer has a cross."

Didn't Jesus say, *"If anyone would come after me, he must deny himself and take up his cross and follow me"* (Matthew 16:24). The purpose is found in the second half of the verse in John that I referred to earlier. Jesus did say, *"In this world you will have trouble,"* but then He added: *"But take heart! I have overcome the world"* (John 16:33b, c).

"Indeed," writes Paul, *"we share in his [Christ's] sufferings in order that we may also share in his glory"* (Romans 8:17b).

Looking to the Creator
January 26

As I'm sure you can appreciate, walking through a jungle can be a very dangerous activity. I read somewhere of an ingenious way some of the natives have devised to keep tigers from sneaking up from behind them in a jungle environment, which tigers are prone to do. They simply wear a facemask on the back of their heads.

None of us really wants to act two-faced or be seen by others as two-faced, but it would be handy, from time to time, to have a pair of eyes in the back of your head.

This very month of January, of course, suggests it. January was named for the old Roman god of beginnings, Janus, who was represented with two bearded heads set back to back—one looking forward, the other behind. However, a major difficulty we experience in this life when we look back is the realization that although we can look back, we cannot go back, and when we look ahead, we simply cannot see around the corner. May I suggest that there is another place to look that is better by far.

The prophet Isaiah was out looking at a changing sky one darkening night:

> *Lift up your eyes and look to the heavens: Who created all these? He who brings out the starry host one by one, and calls them each by name . . . Do you not know? Have you not heard? The LORD is the everlasting God, the Creator of the ends of the earth.* [And this] *Those who hope in the LORD will renew their strength. They will soar on wings like eagles; they will run and not grow weary, they will walk and not be faint* (Isaiah 40:26, 28, 31).

The Wings of a Dove
January 27

No doubt, you have heard of the adage that says, "You cannot make a silk purse out of a sow's ear." This is true, but you can make good out of seeming disaster.

It happened to an unnamed artist. The story goes something like this. The artist, a painter, was just adding the finishing touches to his masterpiece when he inadvertently made some disfiguring blots on the sky. Instead of going into a rage, he calmly added a beak to each blot, then wings, until they became birds—in flight.

David the Psalmist was meditating and in prayer one day. He was in deep trouble . . . he describes himself as distraught.

> *"My heart is in anguish within me;"* he writes in Psalm 55, adding, *"Fear and trembling have beset me; horror has overwhelmed me."* Then he made this cry: *"Oh, that I had the wings of a dove! I would fly far away and be at rest—I would flee far away and stay in the desert; I would hurry to my place of shelter, far from the tempest and storm"* (Psalm 55: 4–8).

A little bit later in the chapter, verses 16 and 17, comes this: *"But I call to God, and the LORD saves me. Evening, morning and noon I cry out in distress, and he hears my voice."*

This cry from the heart of the Psalmist has an echoing call from your heart and mine when the troubles we face seem to overwhelm us. David's advice to all who face life's troubles (and we all have them) is found in the same Psalm. You have likely heard it many times. *"Cast your cares on the LORD, and he will sustain you."*

Give your cares the wings of God. They too will fly away.

A Tax on Sunshine

January 28

One of the most ridiculous taxes ever imposed was the window tax that was imposed on people in London, England, from 1695 to 1851. Every house with more than six windows was liable to a tax for the extras. Many people simply boarded up their windows to avoid the tax. In effect, the government had put a tax on sunshine.

Quite a few windows are still being boarded up these days—not by boards or brick or mortar, but by human regulation, often at various levels of government. And they are not set up to keep out the light of the sun, but rather the light of spiritual life. There are repressive governments in the world that prevent people from worshipping God and preaching the gospel of Christ.

Lest we forget, there are similar happenings right in our own backyard. It's getting increasingly difficult, for example, for the Gideons to distribute Bibles in the schools anymore. Teachers have to be very careful what they say concerning spiritual matters. And referring to the Christmas season, where can you put up a replica of the manger scene in a public place?

In that long, one hundred nineteenth Psalm, verse 105, the Psalmist writes: *"Your word is a lamp to my feet and a light for my path."* Any country that bans that Word or subverts it does so at that country's peril. Take away the Word of God, and the light and lamp of life goes out, and all is darkness.

As the book of Hebrews puts it: *"The word of God is living and active. Sharper than any double-edged sword, it penetrates even to dividing soul and spirit, joints and marrow; it judges the thoughts and attitudes of the heart. Nothing in all creation is hidden from God's sight."* (Hebrews 4:12–13a).

You might attempt to block out the windows . . . even the windows of the soul. But you cannot hide from God—*"to whom* [as the book of Hebrews puts it] *we must give account"* to avoid the tax. God's light penetrates.

Enlightened Eyes
January 29

Have you ever looked at the world through tinted glasses? What do we see when we look out on the world of today? We often, as someone has put it, "let others do our seeing for us." Television is a prime example of this. Certainly we often see a much-distorted picture of the world in which we live.

In his letter to the Ephesian Christians, the Apostle Paul included this prayer: *"I pray also that the eyes of your heart may be enlightened in order that you may know the hope to which he [God] has called you, the riches of his glorious inheritance. . ."* (Ephesians 1:18). The eyes of faith, the eyes of the heart and understanding, give us "second sight," as it were, to look beyond to the eternal world of Almighty God.

The prophet Elisha was a very godly and powerful man, so powerful that Israel's enemies of the time, the Arameans, sent a strong force to capture him. The force arrived during the night, surrounding the city where Elisha was living. Looking out in the early morning, Elisha's servant saw an army with horses and chariots. The servant rushed back to the prophet, crying, "What shall we do?" Calmly, Elisha replied: *"Don't be afraid: Those who are with us are more than those who are with them"* (2 Kings 6:15b–16). Then further in verse 17a, Elisha prayed: *"O LORD, open his eyes so he may see."* The servant's eyes were opened, and he saw the hills full of horses and chariots of fire—the force of the Almighty. Then, as the enemy army closed in on him, Elisha prayed: *"Strike these people with blindness"* (2 Kings 6:18b). The unseeing enemy army was led the by the prophet to the capital, Samaria, where their sight was restored. The King of Israel, following advice from Elisha, set a banquet table before them instead of killing them and then sent them home—no longer to trouble Israel or Elisha.

Elisha was looking through the eyes of the heart . . . the soul . . . the understanding. Thus we are best served with double vision—to see with our natural eyes the beauties of God's nature and then to see the rich wonders of the inner life of faith and eternal glory. And we don't need any colored glasses.

Is Your Life Flat?

January 30

A choir competing in a music festival was singing flat. The accompanist soon became aware of it and, at a suitable point, transposed to a key or semitone lower. Unfortunately, the tendency continued, and the accompanist changed the key no less than three times. As the piece came to a close, the choir hoped for the best in the judgment of their piece. Saying nothing, the adjudicator simply went to the piano and played the chord that the choir ought to have been singing, a tone and a half higher.

Where are we singing? Flat? Perhaps too sharp? These are questions to be asked not only by musicians, but also by each one of us from time to time—for it's not always easy to stay on key. And on the score of life, close doesn't count.

There's a notion abroad in our day that when God, as the Great Adjudicator, judges our lives, He counts all the good things and then all the bad things. If the good outnumber the bad, we're in; if the bad are more than the good, we don't make it.

I'm afraid that philosophy is off-key. Why? Because that way of looking on life and eternity indicates our belief that everything depends on us and that there is no need of God. We make the choice as to whether we go flat, sharp, or stay on key. That very temptation caused our first parents to fall and to fail in the Garden of Eden. Said the Tempter to Eve concerning the forbidden fruit: *"For God knows that when you eat of it your eyes will be opened, and you will be like God"* (Genesis 3:5). The two ate; they sinned and were cast from the Garden because they thought they didn't need God to tell them how to live—how to keep their lives on key.

The Apostle Paul looks at this situation in Romans 3:23 when he writes: *"For all have sinned and fall short of the glory of God."* Then he adds this wonderful promise in verse 24. *"And* [all] *are justified* [or made just] *freely by his* [God's] *grace through the redemption that came by Christ Jesus."* We cannot "earn" our way to Heaven by the "brownie points" that we accumulate. Our salvation is by the forgiveness of God . . . the free grace of God through the redemption of His Son on the cross. Then our good works are of vital importance because they glorify God and not ourselves.

The importance of being on the right key in life cannot really be overemphasized.

Houses and Homes
January 31

You may be surprised to hear that prefabricated houses have been with us for a long time. In 1908 the Sears Roebuck catalogue started to sell ready-to-assemble materials for erecting houses. Very few materials had to be bought locally. Apparently the prefab houses were sent by train and came with an instruction book.

Most of us have rich memories of the houses in which we lived earlier in our lives. It does not really matter who built them, how they were erected, or if somebody else lived in them before us; they were simply home. The words of the book of Proverbs are particularly meaningful when it comes to our childhood homes.

> *When I was a boy* [or girl] *in my father's house, still tender, and an only child of my mother, he taught me and said, "Lay hold of my words with all your heart; keep my commands and you will live. Get wisdom, get understanding; do not forget my words or swerve from them. Do not forsake wisdom, and she will protect you; love her, and she will watch over you"* (Proverbs 4:3-6).

That home-spun, down-to-earth advice came to many of us and has been the means of our living meaningful, fruitful lives, ones which leave us now with many rich memories and anticipation of a splendid welcome to the Father's house. Jesus Himself puts it this way: *"In my Father's house are many rooms; if it were not so, I would have told you. I am going there to prepare a place for you"* (John 14:2).

What a wonderful comfort to know that our heavenly Father is waiting for us with the door open.

Knowing Everybody but God
February 01

Samuel Clemens, the American author and humorist, had been a riverboat pilot on the Mississippi for many years. He chose his pen name from the phrase "mark twain," which is a river man's phrase for water found to be at a depth of two fathoms. A short while after he had become famous, he was traveling in Europe with his young daughter. Everywhere they went, royalty, as well as well-known artists and scientists, honored Mark Twain. Near the end of their travels, the writer's daughter said to him, "Papa, you know everybody but God, don't you?" History doesn't seem to record Mark Twain's response, but I am sure he was caused "furiously to think," as it is sometimes put.

It is possible to know a whole host of the rich and famous, leaders of the country, even leaders of the world, and yet to be unacquainted with God.

Jesus asked a very pointed question: *"What good is it for a man to gain the whole world, yet forfeit his soul? Or what can a man give in exchange for his soul?"* (Mark 8:36–37). Fame can be very barren in that context.

Paul has this definitive word in writing to his young co-worker, Timothy: *"For we brought nothing into the world, and we can take nothing out of it"* (1 Timothy 6:7). Paul is referring to THINGS of course.

We can take a noble character, one made new by the salvation of Jesus Christ—for we know God, and even more importantly He knows us.

Reaching for the Stars
February 02

Do you like to shoot for the stars? Here's a sobering thought. The nearest star is 4.3 light years away. In other words, if you were able to travel at the speed of light, which is approximately 186,000 miles/second, and you went this speed every second of every day, it would take over four years to get there. Yet, I suppose there is nothing wrong with reaching for the stars as long as you realize you won't get there—not in this life in any event.

A person's reach should always exceed one's grasp. How was it the rhyming couplet put it? "Two men looked out from prison bars; one man saw mud . . . the other stars." It is always better, especially when experiencing difficulty, to look up rather than look down. The Apostle Paul writes to those at Philippi: *"I know what it is to be in need, and I know what it is to have plenty."* And he goes on, *"I have learned the secret of being content in any and every situation, whether well fed or hungry, whether living in plenty or in want."* Then he reaches out and up: *"I can do everything through him who gives me strength"* (Philippians 4:12–13).

In the same epistle, the Apostle wrote these memorable words after telling of his personal yearnings to be like his Master: *"One thing I do: Forgetting what is behind and straining toward what is ahead, I press on toward the goal to win the prize for which God has called me heavenward in Christ Jesus"* (Philippians 3:13–14).

There's a man who caught a glimpse of the stars, and by God's grace he made it. So may you and I.

The Central Figure
February 03

I once read a thought—provoking description of Leonardo da Vinci's famous painting "The Last Supper" by an art critic. The critic, in writing about the unity of the painting, is warm and fairly detailed in his praise of the artist's skill in having everything point to the central figure, but not once does he name who the central figure is. Leonardo da Vinci knows, and so do many others that it was Jesus with His apostles at their "Last Supper" before their Master's crucifixion. Even Judas was still in the picture. He had not yet slipped out into the night.

I wonder how many people wouldn't have any idea what the painting is about as they face it for the first time—let alone recognize the central figure.

There is a long, gripping story in the Old Testament of Jacob, his 12 sons, and their families, who had settled in Egypt after one of those sons, Joseph, had become a dominant factor in Egypt. This new Israelite nation prospered until, as Exodus 1:8 says, *"Then a new king, who did not know about Joseph, came to power in Egypt."* The Israelites were then oppressed and made slaves.

I'm afraid that in our day, a generation is arising that knows not Jesus, who are oppressed by sin, made slaves to sin, and do not know how to escape. That gives each one of us who does know Jesus cause to say that we do indeed know Him. The Apostle Peter puts it this way: *"Always be prepared to give an answer to everyone who asks you to give the reason for the hope that you have"* (1 Peter 3:15b)

What Is Love?
February 04

The concept of love can be a complex one. The word love has only four letters, but we can find all sorts of baffling definitions and examples for love. For instance, a person might say, "I love chocolate." We might say, "I love my country, or city, or countryside." Someone has asked, "Can we feel it in our hands? Does it know how to speak? Is it only written on the heart?"

Greek was the language of the original New Testament. The Greek language is rich in words meaning love. The problem with English is that we really only have one word . . . that's why people love all sorts of things. There are about five words for love in Greek. Two of them are prominent in the New Testament—agape and philia. Agape is God's love toward us, and it is the love we have for God (or should have) and also the highest love we can have for one another. Philia describes only human affection, and it too is a good word. Brotherly love, indeed the name of Philadelphia, "the city of brotherly love," is derived from the Greek philia.

The great love chapter of the Bible, the thirteenth chapter of First Corinthians, centers on the Greek agape and concludes this way. "*And now these three remain: faith, hope and love. But the greatest of these is love.*" And of course the greatest demonstration of love—agape love—was that of Jesus in going to the cross, dying for us so that we could be freed from the bonds of sin and live with Him eternally.

"Why Don't You Come in, All of You?"
February 05

Margaret Bottome, founder of a women's movement known as the King's Daughters, tells of an interesting incident in her life that illustrates what total commitment is.

She was walking along the beach one day when a young friend in a small sailboat passed by. He asked if she was interested in a boat ride and, when she agreed, brought his boat alongside. In trying to step into the boat, Margaret touched the side with her left foot and the boat skidded away. The boat was brought back, and she tried again—this time with her right foot, with the same result. Finally, the young fellow came back for the third time, saying to Margaret, "Why don't you come in, all of you?"[1]

It seems to me that there's a plea here for something we might describe as total commitment rather than tentative sampling, a plea for really being "all out."

Recorded in Luke is an interesting conversation that Jesus had with three men as He, His disciples, and others trudged a dusty Middle Eastern road.

The first man began the conversation by saying to Jesus: *"'I will follow you wherever you go.' Jesus replied: 'Foxes have holes and birds of the air have nests, but the Son of Man has no place to lay his head'"* (Luke 9:57–58). That seemed to end that conversation. The way with Jesus was going to be too tough.

Jesus initiated the conversation with the second man by saying, *"Follow me."* But the man indicated that his father had passed away and he was needed to look after the burial arrangements. The third man indicated that he would follow Jesus, but first he wanted to go back home and say good-bye, to which the Master responded: *"No one who puts his hand to the plow and looks back is fit for service in the kingdom of God"* (Luke 9:62).

Jesus was not being harsh, but he was simply indicating that with the call to His kingdom, there is no place for tentativeness.

The call of Jesus does come from within, with an enthusiasm to live life on the very highest plane of dedication or, again, as the young man put it, "Why don't you come in, all of you.

A Superior Woman
(Part One)

February 06

There is very touching story of answered prayer in the Old Testament concerning Hannah.

After many years of marriage, Hannah had no children and seemed unable to bear children, despite her longing for them. In a society where children were particularly cherished—both for their own sakes and to build up the nation—her state of childlessness became almost unbearable. Constantly, Hannah traveled to the house of the Lord to pray . . . and to cry . . . for she was being mocked about her condition. One day while praying in the Lord's house, Hannah made a vow. If God would give her a son, she would dedicate him to the Lord. So earnest were her prayers and so copious her tears that Eli, the priest-in-charge, chided her for being drunk—her lips were moving, but no sound was coming. *"'Not so, my Lord,' Hannah replied, 'I am a woman who is deeply troubled. I have not been drinking wine or beer; I was pouring out my soul to the LORD'"* (1Samuel 1:15).

"Eli answered, 'Go in peace, and may the God of Israel grant you what you have asked of him'" (1 Samuel 1:17).

God did. And she named her son Samuel, meaning "heard of God" in Hebrew.

True to her word, Hannah took the boy back to God's house as soon as he was weaned and there presented him to Eli the priest for service to the Lord God. *"I prayed for this child, and the LORD has granted me what I asked of him. So now I give him to the LORD. For his whole life he will be given over to the LORD. And he worshiped the LORD there"* (1 Samuel 1:27–28).

Samuel, of course, became one of Israel's greatest prophets.

Some of us have prayed for many years for some dream to come to pass or for someone near and dear to us to be touched by God. God still answers prayer.

A Superior Woman
(Part Two)
February 07

Continuing yesterday's devotion about Hannah, let us notice her song of triumph (really a prayer) found in the second chapter of the first book of Samuel. The song and prayer of Mary, the mother of Jesus, following His birth a thousand years later, has similarities indicating that Mary obviously knew of Hannah's Song.

In that song, Hannah prayed for those who stumble and for the hungry; she thanked God for supplying food and for His help, as she sang, *"And lifts the needy from the ash heap."*

Every year during Samuel's growing period, Hannah made him a coat or a robe to fit the office Samuel gradually assumed in God's sanctuary. Hannah was a practical, loving, caring, prayerful mother. After Samuel, Hannah had five more children, three sons and two daughters.

Many of us were fortunate to have had practical, loving, caring, and prayerful mothers— mothers worthy of praise. We may be doubly fortunate to have had these praiseworthy women as wives and also as mothers to our own children.

The book of Proverbs has an epilogue to end the final, the thirty–first chapter. It is made up of 22 verses and is titled *"The Wife of Noble Character,"* one of the finest tributes to womanhood in all of literature. The last few lines go like this:

> *Charm is deceptive, and beauty is fleeting;*
>
> *But a woman who fears the LORD is to be praised.*
>
> *Give her the reward she has earned,*
>
> *And let her works bring her praise at the city gate.*

Fortunately, those fine qualities that fitted Hannah are still present in many of the women of today.

Spiritual Signs
February 08

Signs are very prevalent in our lives. They are all around us. In all sizes and colors. They tell us where to eat, what to buy, where to buy it, how to proceed in our cars, and so on. Then there are less tangible signs, like the signs of nature that show us spring is coming or the worry lines on someone's face.

There are also spiritual signs. The Pharisees approached Jesus on one occasion and asked Him to show them a sign from heaven. Matthew, the Gospel writer, intimated that the Pharisees, who had made themselves Jesus' enemies, asked for this sign to test Him.

In any event, Jesus turned their request into a very ordinary statement of amateur weather forecasting and signs that were very familiar day after day. *He replied, "When evening comes, you say, 'it will be fair weather, for the sky is red,' and in the morning, 'Today it will be stormy, for the sky is red and overcast.' You know how to interpret the appearance of the sky,"* He went on to say, *"but you cannot interpret the signs of the times."* Then He added this terrible condemnation: *"A wicked and adulterous generation looks for a miraculous sign, but none will be given it except the sign of Jonah"* (Matthew 16:2–4a). He left them puzzled.

They should not have been so puzzled. Earlier Jesus had said to another group of Pharisees who sought a sign: *"As Jonah was three days and three nights in the belly of a huge fish, so the Son of Man will be three days and three nights in the heart of the earth"* (Matthew 12:40). He was making explicit reference, of course, to the very death that even then His enemies were planning for Him—death on the cross. But after His death, He arose, marking that first Easter and the defeat of death. A sign of wonder, grace, and glory . . . a sign of forgiveness, salvation, and eternal life.

The signs in our world direct us on our way in the world. God's signs direct us on our way to eternal life

The Bible . . . God's Word
February 09

Over the years, many interesting and perceptive comments have been made about the Bible. Here are a couple of examples.

Woodrow Wilson, president of Princeton University and later twenty-eighth President of the United States, made this comment:

"The Bible is the Word of life. I beg you will read it and find out for yourself. . . . You will not only find it full of real men and women, but also of things you have wondered about and been troubled about all your life, . . . and the more you read, the more it will become plain to you what things are worthwhile and what are not."[2]

Henry Ward Beecher, nineteenth century American Preacher and Writer said this:

"The Bible is God's chart for you to steer by, to keep you from the bottom of the sea, and to show you where the harbor is, and how to reach it without running on rocks or bars."[3]

Writing to his co-worker Timothy about the Word of God, the Apostle Paul says: *You have known the holy scriptures, which are able to make you wise for salvation through faith in Christ Jesus. All scripture,* Paul says further, *is God-breathed.* (2Timothy 3:15–16a).

Many years earlier the Psalmist had written, *All your words are true* (Psalm 119:160a).

Also wrote the Psalmist: *Your word is a lamp to my feet, and a light for my path* (Psalm 119:105).

The final, underlying thought about God's Word is that of Jesus: "Blessed . . . are those that hear the Word of God, and obey it" (Luke 11:28).

Time and Eternity
February 10

A little word about time and one's aging caught my attention and is significant for those in their senior years. William Dean Howells wrote: "You'll find as you grow older that you weren't born such a great while ago after all. The time shortens up."

When we think about time . . . the time we have and do not have . . . our thoughts can be aided by the verses of Ecclesiastes in the Old Testament.

> *There is a time for everything and a season for every activity under heaven:*
>
> *a time to be born and a time to die,*
>
> *a time to plant and a time to uproot,*
>
> *a time to kill and a time to heal,*
>
> *a time to tear down and a time to build,*
>
> *a time to weep and a time to laugh,*
>
> *a time to mourn and a time to dance,*
>
> *a time to scatter stones and a time to gather them,*
>
> *a time to embrace and a time to refrain,*
>
> *a time to search and a time to give up,*
>
> *a time to keep and a time to throw away,*
>
> *a time to tear and a time to mend,*
>
> *a time to be silent and a time to speak,*
>
> *a time to love and a time to hate,*
>
> *a time for war and a time for peace.*

(Ecclesiastes 3:1–8).

He has also set eternity in the hearts of men. (Ecclesiastes 3:11b).

These verses from God's Word have a dual focus—they are about time and eternity. *Time* has many definitions. One definition I read calls *time* "a definite portion of duration" . . . about as simple as you can get. *Eternity* on the other hand is "reality or existence without time." In other words, it's timeless. For us, time is counted by heartbeats. However, eternity for us is that longing that a loving Heavenly Father has set in our hearts—a heavenly anticipation, if you like.

There are many ways to use our allotted time. Let us use it wisely in the service of our Master in whatever ways we are able.

Out of the Blue Comes the Whitest Wash

February 11

A prevalent and penetrating aspect of our lives is advertising, all based on the fact that advertising sells, i.e., good advertising. Advertising is found in many different kinds of media and is directed at every segment of society. And all of the senses are attacked or teased.

What is the best ad that you have ever seen or heard? In my estimation, the best was a full-page magazine ad from a long time ago, showing a graceful sailboat under full sail, scudding over a beautiful blue lake with the sailboat leaving in its wake waves of purest white. The single caption, all the printing on the page except for the advertiser's name, in small letters at the foot was this: "Out of the blue comes the whitest wash." The advertiser, Reckett's Blue, sold little bags of bluing that were dropped into the washing to whiten clothes.

Strange, isn't it, that blue should make white things whiter . . . dull things brighter. "Out of the blue comes the whitest wash."

That's what James had in mind when he wrote: *"Consider it pure joy, my brothers, whenever you face trials of many kinds, because you know that the testing of your faith develops perseverance"* (James 1:2–3).

In his first epistle, Peter writes: *"In this you greatly rejoice, though now for a little while you may have had to suffer grief in all kinds of trials. These have come so that your faith . . . may be proved . . . "* (1 Peter 1:6–7).

The Psalmist adds this comforting thought:

"Weeping may remain for a night, but rejoicing comes in the morning" (Psalm 30:5b).

"Out of the blue comes the whitest wash."

Reverence
February 12

In the thinking of many in our day and age, God has been relegated to a minor position in His own creation. To countless people, man, not God, is the measure of all things. Some seemingly religious persons go a dangerous step further, saying that we human beings are really gods ourselves. Many believe that we have the power within ourselves to solve all our own—and the world's—problems.

Just pick up a newspaper or watch TV news, and you will readily conclude that with all our technological knowledge and whatever superior qualities we think we possess, the world is in a greater mess than perhaps at any other time in history.

David, the psalmist, though he was Israel's greatest king and probably its most skilful general, was one who was very reverent and humbly respectful of God and His creation. He was likely outside one night, looking up . . . and the awesome experience impelled him to write the Psalm, which we designate, the eighth.

> *When I consider your heavens, the work of your fingers,*
> *the moon and the stars, which you have set in place,*
> *what is man that you are mindful of him,*
> *the son of man that you care for him?*
> *You made him a little lower than the heavenly beings*
> *and crowned him with glory and honor*

(Psalm 8:3–5).

After adding further to the list of humankind's God-given blessings, he reverently concludes in the last verse of the Psalm: *O LORD, our Lord, how majestic is your name in all the earth!*

That puts the whole matter in proper perspective.

The Footsteps of Thy Soul
February 13

Robert Browning and his wife Elizabeth Barrett Browning were both eminent British poets of the nineteenth century.

One morning in their home, Elizabeth slipped a manuscript into her husband's pocket saying: "Please read this; if you don't like it, tear it up." Then she fled back upstairs while Robert Browning sat down to read one of the noblest love sequences ever written by a woman to the man of her choice. Hidden in one of these "Sonnets from the Portuguese" is this line: "The face of all the world is changed, I think, since first I heard the footsteps of thy soul."

Fine sentiments as we approach Valentine's Day.

For most of us, these words have a rich, deep meaning on a human level. Beyond that, they have a vibrant meaning on a spiritual level. Indeed, true human love has a significantly spiritual aspect about it.

The true love we show all mankind is really reflected love from God. *"We love because he first loved us"* (1 John 4:19). In 1 John 3:11 we read: *"This is the message you heard from the beginning: We should love one another."* And in the great love chapter of the Bible,

1 Corinthians 13, Paul writes: *"Love is patient, love is kind. It does not envy, it does not boast, it is not proud. Love never fails . . . And now these three remain: faith, hope and love. But the greatest of these is love."*

And you and I can say of our master (paraphrasing Elizabeth Barrett Browning): "The face of all the world is changed, since first I heard the footsteps of Thy soul." God is love.

St. Valentine's Day

February 14

Pansies are a beautiful flower and are said to be the emblem of love. Today, of course, is the day of love, St. Valentine's Day. Indeed another name for pansy is heartsease.

The origin of St. Valentine's Day is a bit obscure. Apparently, it can be traced back to one or two St. Valentines. Seemingly, the sending of cards and flowers such as pansies has no relation to the saints or any incidents in their lives.

I can see, however, one single connection between the day we celebrate—February 14—and the Christian faith of the saints, and that is the emphasis on love. Yet the meaning of love is quite different.

"*God is love,*" writes the Apostle John in his first epistle, and he goes on to describe love. "*There is no fear in love. But perfect love drives out fear . . . The one who fears is not made perfect in love.*" Then he adds: "*We love because he first loved us*" (1 John 4:18–19). John had written earlier: "*No one has seen God, but if we love one another, God lives in us and his love is made complete in us*" (1 John 4:12).

An expert in Jewish law, a Pharisee, approached Jesus one day with this question: "*Teacher,*" he said, "*which is the greatest commandment in the Law?*"

Jesus responded very directly: "*'Love the Lord your God with all your heart and with all your soul and with all your mind.' This is the first and greatest commandment. And the second is like it: 'Love your neighbor as yourself.' All the Law and the Prophets hang on these two commandments*" (Matthew 22:36–40).

In other words, these two statements—love for God and love for each other—are at the heart of all the other commandments, including the Ten Commandments and many more.

Hopefully, this sort of love—our love for God, God's love for us, and our love for one another—will dominate our thinking this St. Valentine's Day.

Sharing Similarities
February 15

You no doubt have heard about the striking similarities between the lives and deaths of US presidents Abraham Lincoln and John F. Kennedy. Mr. Lincoln was elected to the US Congress in 1846, Mr. Kennedy in 1946. Lincoln became president in 1860, Kennedy in 1960. Both were succeeded by vice presidents with the name of Johnson. Lincoln's assassin shot him in a theatre and fled to a warehouse. Kennedy's assassin shot him from a warehouse and fled to a theatre. Both assassins were themselves killed before they could come to trial. There were other similarities as well.

We human beings share many similarities with one another, whether we are presidents, paupers, or anything in between. Some say that we all come into the world with nothing. That isn't exactly true—we all come into the world with potential, possibilities for a great and meaningful life. And we don't leave with nothing. We can't take anything of the world around us with us—money, things we have accumulated, even fame—that's true; however, we can take the rewards of time—long or short time spent in God's service.

> *"Do not store up for yourselves treasures on earth, where moth and rust destroy, and where thieves break in and steal. But store up for yourselves treasures in heaven, where moth and rust do not destroy, and where thieves do not break in and steal. For where your treasure is, there your heart will be also"* (Matthew 6:19–21).

What the Master of Life says applies to all of us—whether presidents or parcel carriers, young, middle-aged, or seniors.

Going off the Map
February 16

Alexander the Great was arguably the ancient world's greatest general. Alexander's troops had seized, at one point, all of Asia Minor including Egypt and had overthrown the Persian empire of Darius III. Pushing right on into India, his men refused to go farther. Faced with barriers like the Himalayas, they discovered that they had literally marched off the map. The only maps they had were Greek maps, showing only a part of Asia Minor. The rest was blank space. There were no guideposts to the way ahead.

Have you ever gone off the map? Have you come to a crossroads in a strange place and didn't know which way to turn? We all have, at some time or other, I'm sure. I well remember an experience while driving with a friend in a mountainous part of Kentucky where we came to one of those crossroads. There were two road signs, neither of which meant anything to me. One was marked "Pleasant Valley" and the other "Gunpowder." Quite a choice! Fortunately, I didn't have to make the choice since my friend knew which road to take.

Isn't it like that on life's road? When you come to a fork in the way or when you go off the map into the unknown, you would be completely lost without such a friend. Many do have such a Friend—His name is Jesus.

Jesus put the way of life in perspective for all people in all times: *"I am the way the truth and the life"* (John 14:6a).

You cannot go off the map of life. Jesus is the map.

How Do You Stop a Volcano?
February 17

Dr. Harold Bosley of New York City was one of the better-known preachers of the United States some years ago. I heard him preach in Toronto and remember one striking illustration he used. His wife said to him that their fourteen-year-old son was going to have a party in their home and was inviting twenty of his friends. What do you do with that many fourteen-year-old boys? Bosley thought a good film might help. He finally located one that he judged would entertain the boys— *The Birth of a Volcano* —and it did. It showed the beginnings of a devastating volcano erupting in Mexico. Before it blew, a peasant was shown working in the fields as the mountain began to warm up and heave. In the middle of the picture, a little girl was seen running in terror from the molten lava. At that point, Bosley's son turned to him and said, "Can't you stop it, Dad?"

And Bosley mused, "How do you stop a volcano?"

How do you stop a volcano?

In effect, that's the question being asked by the thinking leaders of our world . . . for surely the mountain is beginning to heat up and heave, and at any time the lava could flow.

See how the following Scripture fits. Looking down the avenue of time, Paul writes in a letter to Timothy: "*There will be terrible times . . . People will be lovers of themselves, lovers of money, boastful, proud, abusive, disobedient to their parents, ungrateful, unholy, without love, unforgiving, slanderous, without self-control, brutal, not lovers of the good*" (2 Timothy 3:1–3).

And the list goes on.

How do you stop a volcano? Human beings cannot—obviously. Yet as I was pondering that question, it came to me that the Easter story had begun with an earthquake, a violent one as Matthew describes it. "*After the Sabbath, at dawn on the first day of the week, Mary Magdalene and the other Mary went to look at the tomb. There was a violent earthquake, for an angel of the Lord came down from heaven and, going to the tomb, rolled back the stone . . . The angel said to the women, "Do not be afraid, for I know that you are looking for Jesus, who was crucified. He is not here; he has risen, just as he said*" (Matthew 28:1–2, 5–6a).

How encouraging for today. He lives!

Try Something You Can't Do
February 18

Dr. E. Stanley Jones, famous long time missionary of yesteryear to India, was asked how he maintained his spiritual life—what was his secret? Dr. Jones' reply essentially came down to two things. One was by keeping up his prayer time, and the second was by taking on a task that he could not do—deliberately so—and thus having to rely on the resources of God.

The secret of a serene and successful spiritual life then is twofold. There is first a definite need for prayer.

Abraham Lincoln, one of America's greatest Presidents, said: "I have been drawn many times to my knees by the overwhelming conviction that I had nowhere else to go. My own wisdom, and that of all about me, seemed insufficient for the day."[4]

David the psalmist writes: "*The LORD is near to all who call on him, to all who call on him in truth. He fulfills the desires of those who fear him; he hears their cry and saves them*" (Psalm 145:18–19).

Remember the second phase of E. Stanley Jones' secret for maintaining a meaningful spiritual life: try a task you know you cannot do. If you cannot do it, God can and will empower you to do it. That's the secret, you see: dependence on God.

As Jesus prayed in the Garden of Gethsemane on the night before the cross, He said to His Heavenly Father: "*I have brought you glory on earth by completing the work you gave me to do*" (John 17:4).

And as Paul wrote to the Christians at Corinth: "*God is able to make all grace abound to you, so that in all things at all times, having all that you need, you will abound in every good work*" (2 Corinthians 9:8).

The secret of successful living is as follows: prayer and attempting tasks for God that you cannot do but God can through you.

Why Not Ask?
February 19

Sometimes in life, and particularly more as we get older, we become negative. We too often assume that things aren't going to work out, so there is no sense in trying. We sometimes forget that we can accomplish great things with God's help. We do need to ask, however, and we do need to have the right motives when we ask.

The epistle of James sometimes seems a little blunt. James speaks and writes straight from the shoulder. *"You do not have,"* he states, *"because you do not ask God. When you ask, you do not receive, because you ask with wrong motives"* (James 4:2d–3a). Jesus Himself writes: *"Ask and it will be given to you; seek and you will find; knock and the door will be opened to you. For everyone who asks receives; he who seeks finds; and to him who knocks, the door will be opened"* (Matthew 7:7–8).

There are numerous references in the Psalms about seeking the Lord's help. Here's a sampling.

> *"I sought the LORD and he answered me."*
>
> *"This poor man called, and the LORD heard him."*
>
> *"Wait for the LORD, and keep his way."*
>
> *"Hear my prayer, O LORD; Let my cry for help come to you."*

Indeed, Lord. Hear our prayers today.

Calmed Fears

February 20

Sometimes we may feel, as we go through life's trials and tribulations that God has left us alone to deal with them. We may fear, in fact, that God has abandoned us. The prophet Isaiah offers some very pertinent thoughts on this subject. Isaiah quotes God as saying to His people some ten times, "Fear not," as the King James Version translates the Hebrew, or "Do not fear," as the more modern versions have it.

For those of us who are sometimes afraid of the future, let us look more closely at what Isaiah has to say. *"Say to those with fearful hearts, 'Be strong, do not fear; your God will come'"* (Isaiah 35:4a). *"So do not fear, for I am with you; do not be dismayed, for I am your God. I will strengthen you and help you; I will uphold you with my righteous right hand"* (Isaiah 41:10).

Later on, Isaiah says in chapter 43, verse 5: *"Do not be afraid, for I am with you."* And again he says in chapter 41, verse 13: *"For I am the LORD, your God, who takes hold of your right hand and says to you, Do not fear; I will help you."*

And finally Isaiah says in chapter 43: *"Fear not, for I have redeemed you; I have summoned you by name; you are mine. When you pass through the waters, I will be with you."* (Isaiah 43: 1b–2a).

When we are facing the trials and difficulties in life that we all face from time to time, it is comforting to know that God is right here with us and we need not fear.

Open Your Hand
February 21

A child playing one day caught his hand in a vase. The mother and then the father tried to get the boy's hand out, but failed. At last his father said, "Now, son, one more try. Open your hand, stretch your fingers out straight, and then pull."

It was then the little boy said, "Oh, no, daddy, if I pull my fingers out straight like that, I'll lose my quarter."

Sometimes we hang on to things in the most difficult and sometimes dangerous situations.

In the parable of the rich fool, Jesus told about a wealthy farmer who had a particularly good crop—so big that his barns wouldn't hold it. So his single solution was to hang on—still clutching his "quarter." Said he: "'*I have no place to store my crops . . . This is what I'll do. I will tear down my barns and build bigger ones, and there I will store all my grain and my goods. And I'll say to myself, You have plenty of good things laid up for many years. Take life easy; eat, drink and be merry*'" (Luke 12:17–19).

This is obviously a self-centered attitude on the part of the farmer, without the least concern for others or even for his own spiritual welfare. Jesus' comment contained language stronger than He usually expressed. *"But God said to him, 'You fool! This very night your life will be demanded from you. Then who will get what you have prepared for yourself?'"* (Luke 12:20).

There comes a time when the quarter in the vase and the full barns are of no value.

Introducing the parable of the rich fool, Jesus said to the crowd he was addressing: "*Watch out! Be on your guard against all kinds of greed; a man's life does not consist in the abundance of his possessions*" (Luke 12:15). Later on in the same chapter of Luke, Jesus concludes: "*Do not be afraid, little flock, for your Father has been pleased to give you the kingdom. Sell your possessions and give to the poor. Provide purses for yourselves that will not wear out, a treasure in heaven . . . For where your treasure is, there your heart will be also.*" (Luke 12:32–34).

Sometimes folks have to loosen their fingers from the quarter in order really to live.

Our Advocate
February 22

In the early days of the Salvation Army, when many English judges thought that the Army was nothing but a nuisance, the story is told of an Army lass who was in court on the charge of obstructing traffic. At the time, Frank Crossley was one of the panel of judges in Manchester police court, but he was not going to act in this particular case because the district in which the so-called offense took place was not within his jurisdiction.

When the girl's case came up, however, that brilliant and renowned man got up from his eminent seat on the bench and walked over to the lonely, forlorn girl and stood beside her until her trial was finished.

In his first epistle, the apostle John asks of Christians that we avoid sin. "*But if anybody does sin, we have one who speaks to the Father in our defense—Jesus Christ the Righteous One. He is the atoning sacrifice for our sins, and not only for ours but also for the sins of the whole world*" (1John 2:1b–2).

I do not know what the final judgment was in the Salvation Army girl's case, but any judge would have found it difficult to convict her with his fellow judge, the great Frank Crossley, standing alongside her.

Even so, in the court of eternity, the Lord Jesus stands alongside those who have committed their lives to Him. "I died," He says, "that they may be forgiven." Jesus, in a prayer for all believers, in part said this: "*Righteous Father, though the world does not know you, I know you, and they know that you have sent me. I have made you known to them, and will continue to make you known in order that the love you have for me may be in them and that I myself may be in them*" (John17: 25–26).

That's the kind of an Advocate we have standing alongside.

Trustworthy—Absolutely

February 23

The story of Daniel is always thrilling. He got into deep trouble, strangely enough, just because he was trustworthy, a man of absolute integrity. That's actually why he was thrown into the den of lions.

As a youth, he was taken captive from Jerusalem to Babylon. Through his sheer strength of character, he was conscripted into the service of the Babylonian king and soon rose to the top— the chief administrator of the country. When the Medes conquered Babylonia and Darius became ruler, Daniel was again given charge of the land. Some of his fellow administrators, his juniors, were jealous and furious that this foreigner should be their chief, so they plotted against him.

But as the Bible says in Daniel 6:4b, "*They could find no corruption in him, because he was trustworthy.*" Daniel's enemies knew that the only way they could "get him" would involve "*something to do with the law of his God*" (Daniel 6:5b). So they convinced the pagan Darius to decree that for thirty days everyone was prohibited from praying to any god or man, except to the emperor. Daniel, of course, still trustworthy, a man of integrity, could not do this, and he continued to pray regularly to the God of heaven. And his windows were open; he could be seen. The windows were not open to defy anyone, but to continue Daniel's prayers to God as he had always done.

Daniel had to go to the lion's den although the king did everything he could to prevent it. God closed the mouths of the lions, and Daniel came out unscathed . . . to resume his responsibilities.

Daniel, a man of God, a man of absolute integrity, no matter what it cost—he was a hero and a man who has greatly influenced succeeding generations.

Targets

February 24

The story is told of a young girl who, shortly after the end of World War II when target practice with a rifle was still in vogue, decided to try it. After the girl had fired a number of rounds, her instructor stopped her and said, "Young woman, you are coming perilously close to that light bulb." (A lamp was hanging some distance above the target.)

"Why," was the girl's simple response, "that's what I have been trying to hit."

This incident might be seen as a kind of parable describing our world. Actually, the young girl's aim was not really the problem, but the problem was that she didn't know what or where the target was.

Many people of today are firing off in multiple directions in life, seemingly oblivious as to what or where the target or goal of life is. And what is worse—not bothering to ask the Instructor.

The Apostle Paul, in his letter to the Philippians, sums up perfectly his version of life's goal or target. His was a marvelous target, and his aim was good. He says:

> *I want to know Christ and the power of His resurrection and the fellowship of sharing in his sufferings, becoming like him in his death, and so, somehow, to attain to the resurrection from the dead. Not that I have already obtained all this, or have already been made perfect, but I press on to take hold of that for which Christ Jesus took hold of me. Brothers, I do not consider myself yet to have taken hold of it. But one thing I do: Forgetting what is behind and straining toward what is ahead, I press on toward the goal* [or target] *to win the prize for which God has called me heavenward in Christ Jesus* (Philippians 3:10–14).

Paul places his faith completely in Jesus Christ, and hand in hand with Christ, he finds that the target or goal God has set for him is now within reach. He is going to keep pressing on, sure of reaching it.

A fine example for any who find himself shooting at light bulbs.

Work to Do
February 25

In the battle of life, stalemate is an all—too—prevalent state of affairs. In chess, a stalemate is a situation that results in a drawn game. No one can move effectively. The game has come to a standstill. So does life for some.

Paul had a sort of soliloquy in writing the early part of his letter to the Philippians. Like others, this letter was written while Paul was in prison—chained like a common criminal. Although he had enjoyed a fruitful life, it had not been easy—marked as it was by beatings, stonings, shipwrecks, incarcerations, and sometimes even the opposition of his friends. He could well have felt by that time that it was someone else's turn. I'm sure all of these thoughts were passing through his mind as he wrote:

> *For to me, to live is Christ and to die is gain. If I am to go on living in the body, this will mean fruitful labor for me. Yet what shall I choose? I do not know! I am torn between the two: I desire to depart and be with Christ, which is better by far; but it is more necessary for you that I remain in the body. Convinced of this, I know that I will remain, and I will continue with all of you for your progress and joy in the faith* (Philippians 1:21–25).

Some of us may feel that we don't have any more to offer. We've reached a kind of stalemate. Actually, we have quite a bit to contribute to the oncoming generations. We lived in the world where marriage and the family were cherished, where good manners and courtesy were esteemed, and where violence was decried. We can do as the Lord revealed to Jeremiah: "*Stand at the crossroads and look; ask for the ancient paths, ask where the good way is, and walk in it*" (Jeremiah 6:16a,b). Or we can simply tell it quietly to a younger friend.

There is still work to do.

Discipleship
February 26

Living a disciplined life can at times be difficult. In fact, when it comes right down to it, many of us don't like discipline, whether it comes from the outside or from within. Sometimes we even resent discipline. Indeed, looking back on our childhood, we can easily relate to the words of the book of Proverbs: *"How I hated discipline! How my heart spurned correction! I would not obey my teachers or listen to my instructors"* (Proverbs 5:12–13).

As we get a little older, we realize the value of the discipline we have received . . . a guide in the daily round of life. Solomon sets the theme of the remarkable book of Proverbs in chapter one, verses two and three: *"For attaining wisdom and discipline; for understanding words of insight; for acquiring a disciplined and prudent life, doing what is right and just and fair."*

Have you ever thought that the word disciple comes from the same root as discipline? A disciple is a man or woman under the discipline of a master. You and I have the opportunity and privilege of being disciples of the greatest Master of all, Jesus. Jesus put it this way: *"If you hold to my teaching, you are really my disciples. Then you will know the truth, and the truth will set you free"* (John 8:31–32). The proof of that discipleship is our love for one another. Jesus said again: *"All men will know that you are my disciples if you love one another."*

Real Steeple chasing
February 27

Have you gone steeplechasing recently? The question is in reference to the spiritual kind. There is an actual organized sport called "steeple chasing" that involves horse and rider racing over a set turf course, jumping over barriers and water hazards along the way. Originally, steeplechasing involved real church steeples, with people on horseback racing across open fields and farmlands and the steeples of the churches used as markers for the races.

Someone has called steeples "fingers pointed toward heaven," and it is significant that from the earliest times, church builders called for this strong vertical feature. As well as giving monumental character to a church building, many steeples contain the church bell that calls the congregation to worship and to prayer. In days gone by, especially in rural areas, the steeple was often the highest point in a community and signified the spiritual home of a community.

Nowadays, church steeples in an urban setting are likely to be dwarfed by the more modern commercial buildings, especially the skyscrapers. That's a pity and suggests that the interests of commerce, sports, and pleasure have become all important in our society. And all the while our culture is on the downward slide. Perhaps it's time for the world to look again to the steeple. As the writer of the book of Hebrews puts it: *"Let us not give up meeting together, as some are in the habit of doing, but let us encourage one another"* (Hebrews 10:25a).

Time again for real "steeplechasing."

Do It for Somebody Else
February 28

I once read the story of a philanthropist who took a great interest in a shoe-shine boy, so much so that he paid the way for the lad's education at university and medical school. Years later the young man had become a successful doctor and attempted to pay the philanthropist back. The philanthropist, upon receiving a check from the doctor, returned it to him with the instruction for the doctor to do the same for someone else.

Just what is our responsibility toward others? The apostle helps answer this important question when he writes in Philippians 2:4: *"Each of you should look not only to your own interests, but also to the interests of others."*

Why? He goes on to say why:

> *Your attitude should be the same as that of Christ Jesus: Who, being in very nature God, did not consider equality with God something to be grasped, but made himself nothing, taking the very nature of a servant, being made in human likeness. And being found in appearance as a man, he humbled himself and became obedient to death—even death on a cross!* (Philippians 2:5–8).

The loving sacrifice of the Savior calls from us a responding love. John in his epistle says: *"This is love: not that we loved God, but that he loved us and sent his Son as an atoning sacrifice for our sins"* (1 John 4:10). Then John adds in verses 11 and 12: *"Dear friends, since God so loved us, we also ought to love one another. No one has ever seen God; but if we love one another, God lives in us and his love is made complete in us"*

Our prayer today should be for our Lord to make us an instrument of His peace.

Sacrifice
February 29

A young woman was persuaded to teach a class of junior boys—one of the very tough tasks in the Sunday school. She had never made a full commitment to Christ herself and soon asked to be relieved of her position, claiming that she didn't know where she was going herself. However, she was persuaded not to give up the class but to make a full surrender.

A new experience came into her life and a new note into her teaching. She began to give her all for her class. As a result, many of the boys in her class were led to make a profession of faith.

The major element of sacrifice in the Christian way causes some of us to back off.

Sacrifice was and is a hallmark of the Jewish faith, and the Old Testament is teeming with examples—sacrifice both for God and for one another. Perhaps the finest example of both is an incident in the life of David, just after he had become Israel's King. The forces against him were mighty, both within and without. Without were the Philistines, who were in control of parts of Israel including Bethlehem. Fighting them from the fortified cave of Adullam, David was overheard to muse to no one in particular on a hot and stressful day, *"Oh, that someone would get me a drink of water from the well near the gate of Bethlehem,"* which was the place of his birth. He did not expect to be heard, but three of his mightiest soldiers set out at once, somehow broke through Philistine lines at Bethlehem, and brought back to their beloved master a jug of that water.

In the face of such devotion, David was so overwhelmed he could not drink the water. Instead, he poured it out as a sacrificial offering to God.

Jesus said this: *"Greater love has no one than this, that he lay down his life for his friends"* (John 15:13). Yet His own love was immeasurably greater. He died not only for his friends, but also for His enemies.

As for us—for you and for me—His sacrifice still stands. Let us not forget it.

Believing Impossible Things
March 01

There is an incident in the book *Through the Looking Glass,* by Lewis Carroll where the White Queen is trying to get Alice to believe that she is 101 years, 5 months, and a day old. Alice cannot accept that, so the Queen tells her to draw a long breath, shut her eyes, and try. "There's no use trying," said Alice. "One can't believe impossible things."

The Queen responds, "Why sometimes I've believed as many as six impossible things before breakfast."[1]

When we watch athletic events, such as the Olympics, that require great skill, the competitors seem to do impossible things. They are, of course, not doing the impossible but stretching the limits of the possible through better training and better equipment.

When Jesus was on the Mountain of Transfiguration with three of His apostles, the rest of the twelve were down below, working with the crowd that nearly always followed the Master. In the crowd were a father and his epileptic son. The son was continually racked by terrible seizures. The father brought his boy to those nine apostles for healing, but they couldn't heal him. Later, the apostles asked Jesus why they had been unable to cure the boy. Jesus replied: *"Because you have so little faith. I tell you the truth, if you have faith as small as a mustard seed, you can say to this mountain, 'Move from here to there' and it will move. Nothing will be impossible for you' "* (Matthew 17:20).

Have you moved many mountains lately . . . mountains of doubt . . . mountains of fear . . . mountains of frustration . . . mountains of stress?

As Jesus puts it on another occasion: *"What is impossible with men is possible with God."* You and God.

Then Jesus Came
March 02

What a difference the coming of one single person has made in the life of the world.

Johannes Gutenberg invented movable type in the 15th century and made the widespread publishing of books (and knowledge) possible. Thomas Edison's coming made possible the phonograph, incandescent lamp, and many other inventions. Sir Alexander Fleming discovered penicillin. Ludwig Van Beethoven gave the world such magnificent musical works. The list goes on and on.

Then, of course, in our own lives are individuals who have made a difference to us—family members, friends, mentors etc.

Then there's Jesus.

In Jerusalem near the Sheep Gate, there was a pool called Bethesda, whose waters held healing properties briefly when agitated. Alongside many of the disabled, there was a man so crippled that he could never make it to the healing waters in time. He had been an invalid for 38 years. **Then Jesus came**.

Lazarus, beloved brother of Mary and Martha of Bethany, was desperately sick. A friend of many in the community, Lazarus was deeply mourned by all, especially his beloved sisters, when he suddenly passed away.

Then Jesus came.

On the evening of the first Easter day, a little group of Christian disciples huddled in a Jerusalem home . . . doors locked in fear. They were uncertain, perplexed, and confused.

Then Jesus came.

"*The Son of Man*," Jesus said of himself, *"did not come to be served, but to serve, and to give his life as a ransom for many"* (Matthew 20:28).

He came and He did.

Against Wind and Tide
March 03

There's an impression being spread in some Christian circles that being a Christian guarantees you a somewhat lavish, carefree lifestyle . . . in short almost all your troubles are over. The whole idea is bothersome because it bears hardly any resemblance to a cross and smacks of conformity to the world rather than to the One who said, *"If anyone would come after me, he must deny himself and take up his cross and follow me"* (Matthew 16:24).

Jesus indeed indicates that we are likely to receive no applause at all from those on the streets of life. The apostle John quotes Him: *"If the world hates you, keep in mind that it hated me first. If you belonged to the world, it would love you as its own. As it is, you do not belong to the world, but I have chosen you out of the world. That is why the world hates you"* (John 15:18–19). Not much applause there. A little later Jesus adds: *"If they persecuted me, they will persecute you also"* (John 15:20b).

Just before his crucifixion, Jesus said: *"In this world you will have trouble."* Then he gave this promise: *"But take heart! I have overcome the world"* (John 16:33b).

God does not promise that life will be a bed of roses, free from trials, without any pain. But He does promise strength to overcome. Annie Johnson Flint's poetry, which became the words for the hymn "What God Hath Promised," tells us about some of God's promises. The first verses and refrain are as follows:

> God hath not promised skies always blue,
>> Flower–strewn pathways all our lives through;
> God hath not promised sun without rain,
>> Joy without sorrow, peace without pain.
>
> But God hath promised strength for the day,
>> Rest for the labor, light for the way,
> Grace for the trials, help from above,
>> Unfailing sympathy, undying love.[2]

Our Duty
March 04

Lord Baden Powell, as is well known, founded the Boy Scouts organization. To be a Scout, a boy must promise, on his honor, to do his duty to both God and country, to help others at every opportunity, and to obey the Scout law. Lord Baden Powell chose a fine motto for the Scouts: "Be prepared" is a fine precept indeed, even for those of us who are quite a bit older.

It is rather unfortunate, I think, that the whole concept of duty seems to be out of favor in so many quarters in our day and age. Duty, of course, carries with it the idea of responsibility and obligation, and somehow many feel that they don't owe anything—even to God.

If we think about it, we owe a great deal to our God. He is our Creator. He made us. God supplies us the very air we breathe—the sunshine, the rain, the fertile soil.

With familiar phrases, the final chapter of the book of Ecclesiastes also speaks of a word that is prominent in the code of the Boy Scouts—duty: *"Remember your Creator in the days of your youth, before the days of trouble come and the years approach when you will say, 'I find no pleasure in them'"* (Ecclesiastes 12:1). And we find these words in verse 13 of the same chapter: *"Now all has been heard; here is the conclusion of the matter: Fear God and keep his commandments for this is the whole duty of man."*

Like good Boy Scouts, we have a duty to our Heavenly Father.

Cocoons
March 05

Someone has said, "No one helps a caterpillar become a butterfly." Indeed, if you try to help, the result may be a badly injured butterfly . . . or none at all. God has so designed the caterpillar that it knows instinctively when it must spin a cocoon. Within that cocoon, the caterpillar, through the remarkable processes of nature, turns into a beautiful butterfly, bearing no resemblance to the creepy, crawly creature we all love to hate.

We humans don't do very well when, as it were, we make our own cocoons and climb in. Some like cocoons because they have the whole place to themselves. We have no need to talk to others. We have no need for outside relationships. Sometimes this withdrawal is caused by some pain or hurt we've received, but we soon find that the pain of loneliness is much greater.

We need relationships, friends with whom we can laugh . . . and cry. When we have the courage to break out of the cocoon, our cocoon, and accept the fact that in life we have sorrow and pain as well as the feelings of comfort and well-being, we'll be able to face the future well.

God is within and surrounding us with His love and care—if we only ask.

The prophet Isaiah reveals a marvelous promise from the Heavenly Father to those facing difficulties in life and feeling perhaps that they should withdraw into a cocoon. "*Fear not,* [God promises], for *I have redeemed you; I have summoned you by name; you are mine. When you pass through the waters, I will be with you; and when you pass through the rivers, they will not sweep over you. When you walk through the fire, you will not be burned; the flames will not set you ablaze. For I am the LORD your God*" (Isaiah 43:1b–3a).

We have the promises of God. Trust Him. Don't bother about cocoons.

Self–Made
March 06

In an interview of a rather notable person, published in the papers some years ago, the reporter stated: "I understand, sir, that you are a self-made man."

"Well," was the rather slow response, "I suppose I might be called a self-made man." And he paused, then added somewhat ruefully: "But if I had it to do over again, I think I'd call in a little help."

We live in the kind of world where self-made people are greatly admired. Starting with very little and often under difficult conditions, they have accomplished a great deal in the world's eyes. That's the secular world, and the attainments are great wealth, great position, and great power. These things alone never quite spell peace and contentment. As life nears its conclusion, these attainments become increasingly meaningless.

That's why Jesus' conversation with his apostles about the vine and the branches is so very significant. The setting was just before the crucifixion. Following the Last Supper in a Jerusalem upper room, the eleven (Judas had slipped away to commit his terrible act of betrayal) met to talk with Jesus in His final, solemn hours.

"I am the vine," Jesus said, *"You are the branches. If a man remains in me and I in him, he will bear much fruit; apart from me you can do nothing"* (John 15:5). No self-made persons there. The wonder of it all is that we are not self-made but God-made . . . the One who made us in creation is the One who makes us in re-creation—new birth, if you like.

Like the branch in the vine or in the tree, as long as we remain attached to our Master, we will grow, be successful, and produce much fruit—God-made men and women.

Dreams . . . and God
March 07

What sort of dreams do you have? Perhaps you don't dream at all . . . or not very often. Most of us, I believe, have quite a few dreams, and sometimes they are very odd.

In Old Testament times, God used dreams many times for sending His messages to people. In the New Testament, however, this method of reaching people came almost to a halt. Joseph, in a dream, was told of the coming of the Christ child and directed to take Mary as his wife. Joseph was also told to flee to Egypt after Jesus' birth in order to escape the wrath of King Herod. He was later told by a dream when to return to his homeland and by another to go to live in Nazareth.

When Jesus was on trial for His life before Pontius Pilate, Pilate's wife sent a message to her husband: *"Don't have anything to do with that innocent man, for I have suffered a great deal today in a dream because of him"* (Matthew 27:19). And except for one repetition of a prophecy of the Old Testament concerning dreams, that's all there is about dreams in the New Testament.

There were, of course, visions, and I believe the main difference between the two is that visions still contain a direct word from God, whereas God seems to have discontinued using ordinary dreams as a means of carrying His message. His Holy Spirit, sent on the day of Pentecost, now speaks to individuals. Indeed, the Holy Spirit of God and God's Word, the Bible, as well as prayer, are our sources of spiritual life, although I cannot completely rule out the possibility of God's using a dream or a vision in our day.

Sometimes we are fearful of our dreams. Perhaps we have nightmares. Our fears about dreams or nightmares can become less powerful, less fearsome, when we discover that we share them with quite a few other people. In addition, they become much less troublesome when we share them with our Heavenly Father. Our greatest assurance is that we cannot drift beyond the Heavenly Father's love and care. He will listen to our fears always and at any time.

Many ages ago, God spoke directly to Isaac, and His promise still stands: *"Do not be afraid, for I am with you; I will bless you."*

A Quiet and Holy People
March 08

Cyprian of Carthage, North Africa, became a martyr for his faith under the Roman Emperor Valerian in 285 AD. Among his many writings was a simple letter to his friend, Donatus, and although written many centuries ago, it really speaks to our times.

> This seems a cheerful world, Donatus, when I view it from this fair garden, under the shadow of these vines. But if I climbed some great mountain and looked over the wide lands, you know very well what I would see—brigands on the high roads; pirates on the seas; in the amphitheaters men murdered to please applauding crowds; under all roofs misery and selfishness. It is really a bad world, Donatus, an incredibly bad world. Yet in the midst of it, I have found a quiet and holy people. They have discovered a joy which is a thousand times better than any pleasures of this sinful life. They are despised and persecuted, but they care not. They have overcome the world. These people, Donatus, are the Christians—and I am one of them."[3]

Some things are just as bad . . . some worse since that writing. There are still brigands on our highways, and we still read of pirates on the seas. I don't know of any amphitheaters where men are murdered to please applauding crowds, but we do have cruel mayhem in the wrestling ring and in the bullring for the same purpose. There are certainly many murders in our modern world. Under many roofs, there is misery and selfishness. We have a veneer of sophistication that was lacking in those early centuries, but human nature has not really changed that much. We have learned a host of new ways to gain the pleasures of this sinful life.

Yet in the midst of these troubling times, there continues to be a quiet and holy people who "have discovered a joy which is a thousand times better than any pleasure of this sinful life. They have overcome the world."

Jesus Himself showed the way. In forty days of desperate temptation at the outset of His ministry, He was offered, among other temptations, "*all the kingdoms of the world and their splendor*" (Matthew 4:8). He was offered this if He would bow down before the Evil One, but He refused. And He led and taught His little handful of quiet and holy people.

As Cyprian wrote so long ago: "These people, Donatus, are the Christians—and I am one of them." May that be our testimony too.

My Brother
March 09

A church member was driving his pastor along a busy freeway when they came upon an accident scene. A car was overturned on the center strip, and a man was standing by the overturned car, dazed—his face smeared in blood. A police officer directed traffic by the scene. All this was taken in at a glance as the two drove slowly by the scene. After traveling several hundred yards past the scene, the driver suddenly braked, pulled over, and stopped, saying, "Holy smoke, pastor, that was my brother."

Sometimes as we go barreling down the highway of life, we fail to notice those by the roadside who are hurting.

Jesus told the parable of four men involved in a similar drama, which we call "The Good Samaritan." It was not a super highway, but it was a highway. The highway was a lonely road from Jerusalem to Jericho. A traveler was on his way to Jericho when robbers set upon him, beat him terribly, and took everything he had. Three other men, also traveling alone, came upon the scene. Two of the lone travelers, seeing the desperately hurt man at two separate times, didn't want to be involved and passed by on the other side. They didn't want to be involved, but they were. They saw him . . . and they left him.

Finally the third man came along—a foreigner, a hated Samaritan. He stopped, bound up the victim's wounds, put him on his own beast, took him to the nearest inn, cared for him overnight, and left money with the innkeeper to continue the man's care. He also promised the innkeeper to reimburse him for any further expense when he returned.

That's brotherhood.

A Sign of Spring
March 10

We all love to see the signs of spring, particularly after a long, cold winter. When the snow melts, trees begin to bud, blossoms start appearing, grass begins to "green up," and other early signs of spring occur. We eagerly anticipate the coming of spring.

Some of Jesus' enemies came to Him on one occasion and asked Him to show them a sign from heaven, some indication that He really was who He said He was—the Messiah. Jesus immediately referred to an old weather forecaster's sign. *"When evening comes,"* noted Jesus, *"you say, 'It will be fair weather, for the sky is red,' and in the morning, 'Today it will be stormy, for the sky is red and overcast.' You know how to interpret the appearance of the sky, but you cannot interpret the signs of the times"* (Matthew 16: 2–3). Then He added that the only sign they would receive would be the sign of Jonah.

At that, of course, they drew a blank. The salvation of Nineveh depended on the prophet Jonah, but a great fish had swallowed him. However, God delivered him, and Nineveh was saved. As Jesus put it on another occasion, *"For as Jonah was three days and three nights in the belly of a huge fish, so the Son of man will be three days and three nights in the heart of the earth"* (Matthew 12:40).

Jonah's experience was a sign of salvation to Nineveh, so the cross of Jesus and the empty tomb become signs of salvation to a needy world—signs of spring, if you like.

Out of Ashes, a New Life
March 11

The wonders of nature never cease to amaze. God has designed such harmony and balance in the natural world. A prime example of this is the lodgepole pine tree, which is found extensively in British Columbia and the Northwest United States. The lodgepole pine belongs to what is called a "fire origin species." When the cones of the lodgepole pine fall to the ground, they are sealed shut so that the seeds do not germinate in response to water and sun. The pine cones rest on the forest floor, sometimes for decades, until a forest fire sweeps through and the heat from the fire melts the seal; then the seeds fall out and germinate.

Metaphorically speaking, you've likely known people who are "fire origin species." Perhaps you are one yourself—one who has been badly burned in life and who, out of the ashes, has started out again to build a new life. The fires of life have not destroyed you; they have made you even more experienced to face the battles ahead.

A few verses from the forty-third chapter of Isaiah fit this description: "*But now, this is what the LORD says . . .* "*When you pass through the waters, I will be with you; and when you pass through the rivers, they will not sweep over you. When you walk through the fire, you will not be burned; the flames will not set you ablaze*" (Isaiah 43:1a–2).

Isaiah, looking forward to the coming of the Messiah also writes: "*The spirit of the Sovereign LORD is on me, because the LORD has anointed me to preach good news to the poor. He has sent me to bind up the brokenhearted . . . to comfort all who mourn . . . to bestow on them a crown of beauty instead of ashes, the oil of gladness instead of mourning*" (Isaiah 61:1–3b).

"*A crown of beauty instead of ashes.*" Out of the burnt things of life, the ashes, God promises a crown of beauty.

Just like the lodgepole pine reforests the devastated land.

A Woman Called Deborah
March 12

There is a great story in the book of Judges in the Old Testament, a story of a woman named Deborah.

Joshua, who had followed Moses as leader of the people of Israel from slavery in Egypt to the border of the land promised by God, brought them into that land, where he died. Having reached their goal, the generation that had made it possible passed away as well. A new generation arose who, as the Bible puts it, *"knew neither the LORD nor what he had done for Israel."* They began to worship the idols of their pagan neighbors. Troubles began to turn on them and make them a subject people. The people of Israel groaned under the bondage.

The story of the book of Judges is the story of twelve judges or leaders God raised up over many years to deliver His people from that bondage. However, each time after they had been freed, the Israelites would slip back into the same old ways, facing a similar situation time after time. This continued until after the death of Samson, the last of the twelve judges.

Deborah was the fourth of the twelve judges. She burned with anger at the oppression of her people. For twenty years, Jabin, King of Canaan, had oppressed the nation of Israel. Their vineyards had been destroyed, their women shamed, and their children killed. The chief of the Canaanite army, Sisera, had the military might of nine hundred iron chariots, whereas Israel had none.

Deborah had the wisdom—and courage—to summon one of Israel's most capable military leaders, Barak, asking him to take ten thousand men and attack Sisera. Barak was reluctant to face nine hundred chariots with only foot soldiers. He would go only if Deborah accompanied him. *"'Very well,' Deborah said, 'I will go with you. But because of the way you are going about this, the honor will not be yours, for the LORD will hand Sisera over to a woman'"* (Judges 4:9). God did. Barak's army, empowered by God, decimated Sisera's forces.

The fifth chapter of the book of Judges is Deborah's song following the annihilation of Sisera and the Canaanite army. It is a song of praise to the Lord God. The chapter ends with, *"Then the land had peace forty years."*

Relationships
March 13

Each of us has many different relationships in life. For example, there are the relationships of grandparent/grandchild, parent/child, aunt or uncle/nephew or niece, employer/employee, etc. For Christians, in all of our relationships, we should show that Christ is within us—that we are doing our part to ensure that He is always present in our relationships.

Parents of growing children have a double duty of discipline and encouragement in their relationship with their children. Similarly, in our relationship with God as our Heavenly Father, God exercises that dual responsibility of discipline and encouragement. The writer of the book of Hebrews says this: *"We have all had human fathers who disciplined us and we respected them for it. How much more should we submit to the Father of our spirits and live! Our fathers disciplined us for a little while, as they thought best; but God disciplines us for our good, that we may share in his holiness"* (Hebrews 12:9–10).

Paul writes of the encouragement side of God's grace in the second letter to Thessalonians. It is in the form of a prayer: *"May our Lord Jesus Christ himself and God our Father, who loved us and by his grace gave us eternal encouragement and good hope, encourage your hearts and strengthen you in every good deed and word"* (2 Thessalonians 2:16–17).

Thus, in our relationships with each other, may they be based on mutual or reciprocal obligations, treating others as we would have them treat us, often going the second mile. May we too accept the discipline of our Heavenly Father, realizing that He is maturing us, and if we fall, He will pick us up . . . for God is the perfect Father.

We Would See Jesus
March 14

Many years ago, I was asked to preach in Olivet Baptist Church, New Westminster, British Columbia. I have not forgotten that initial experience. It was sobering.

Tucked at the back of the pulpit, where only the preacher could see it, there was a small metallic notice bearing just five words: "Sir, we would see Jesus." Those words brought me up short on that occasion. I asked myself, "What am I doing up here?"

"Sir, we would see Jesus" were words first asked by a group of foreigners who had come to worship with the Jews at their celebration of the Feast of the Passover. Obviously, they were God–fearing men. They were a group of Greeks who had heard of the activities of Christ, including the raising of Lazarus. Learning of His presence nearby, they wanted to meet Him. Coming up to Philip, one of the apostles, they made the request: "Sir, we would see Jesus." Moving in toward his Master, Philip passed on the request to Andrew, and the two of them went on to Jesus.

It was a significant moment in Jesus' life and ministry. First, He had come as Messiah . . . Savior . . . to His own people. Now, *"The hour has come,"* He responded to Philip and Andrew. A little later in John 12:32, He added, *"But I, when I am lifted up from the earth, will draw all men to myself"*—just as those Greeks had been drawn. Salvation, which Jesus offers, is for all.

Back to the little sign. Those words mean that when we stand up to share God's good news, our hearers don't want to see or hear us, but the One whose ambassador we are trying to be—Jesus. Sometimes, even as Christians, our lives loom so large that our Master cannot be seen or heard. We Christians are really to be channels that lead to Christ.

Care and Prayer
March 15

Eight years after graduating as a Doctor, Sheila Cassidy went to work in Chile. In 1975 during the military dictatorship of General Pinochet, a priest asked her to treat a wounded revolutionary, an act of compassion which led to her arrest and torture. After two months in prison she was deported and returned to the UK where she was immediately drawn into a life of frenetic human rights lecturing. In 1980 after trying her vocation as a nun, she returned to the practice of medicine and in 1982 was appointed as medical director of Plymouth's new hospice— St Luke's.

"In my spare time," said Dr. Cassidy, "I do a bit of religious broadcasting and preach in churches and cathedrals, often on suffering and prayer. My belief in God gives me enormous strength and joy, and underpins everything I do. Daily prayer is as important to me as food."[4]

Two words fastened themselves in my mind about her life—"care" and "prayer." There was a young woman who loved enough, cared enough, to give her life and her skills in medicine to unknown patients in a slum hospital in a foreign, third world land. No wonder, with all the danger and the senseless torture by the secret police, she indicated that daily prayer was as important to her as food.

"For the eyes of the Lord are on the righteous and his ears are attentive to their prayer," writes the apostle Peter in his first epistle, chapter 3, verse 12a. Peter continues in verse 13: *"Who is going to harm you if you are eager to do good?"* Apparently some evil men are, as Dr. Cassidy discovered. Then Peter adds this significant sentence in verse 14a: *"But even if you should suffer for what is right, you are blessed."* Peter knew a good deal about caring as well. That's what Jesus directed him to do—to care for Christ's sheep and lambs in that time–stopping moment following the Resurrection when Jesus faced and restored a broken Peter who had denied Him three times before Calvary. After suggesting to Peter what it would cost him to care, Jesus invited him, *"Follow me."* It did eventually cost Peter his life, but what a magnificent life, as Peter passionately followed the example of his Master in caring.

Of course, to care like that, you have to pray daily and fervently.

The Importance of Little Things
March 16

Little things can be very important to our daily lives. Something happened during an American presidential debate that underscores that fact. On September 23, 1976, U.S. presidential candidates Jimmy Carter and Gerald Ford were debating, each vying for the support of millions of listeners over the NBC network. Suddenly, as the broadcast got underway, there was almost deafening silence. For twenty-seven minutes, nothing was heard from the two candidates. What would cause a monumental break at such a historic juncture?

We were living in Calgary at the time, and the director of religious programming for NBC and her film crew were in Canada. They had come to Calgary to do a broadcast tape of an institution with which I was involved. I asked the director if she knew what had happened that night. "Yes," she said, "there was a short circuit in a tiny capacitor—a $1 part about the size of a cigarette filter- which knocked out the only amplifier . . . and there wasn't a backup nearby."

You can draw all sorts of lessons from that one . . . how the world's most important leaders are powerless under some circumstances . . . how important backups are . . . how some people fail to carry out their responsibilities ... how we all make mistakes . . . and so on.

I'd like to point out the importance of little things . . . just like that tiny capacitor.

For example, a little faith. Talking about that, Jesus put it this way: "*If you have faith as small as a mustard seed, you can say to the mountain, 'Move from here to there' and it will move*" (Matthew 17:20b). And it need not be a physical mountain. It may be a mountain of fear . . . a mountain of despair . . . a mountain of doubt. But a tiny bit of faith is needed to make the connection. That's your part. The rest of the miracle is up to our Heavenly Father.

Confused by Grace
March 17

A story is told of a gentleman who had the letters B A I K embroidered on his shirt. Someone who noticed the letters asked what they meant. "Simple," was the reply. "Boy Am I Confused."

"But confused is not spelled with a K," retorted the enquirer.

"That shows you how confused I am," replied the gentleman.

Confusion is apparent in the parable of the landowner with a large vineyard ready to harvest. Early in the morning, the vineyard owner went to the town market and was able to find a group of men ready to work. He offered them a denarius a day, so they went to work. But more workers were needed, so at nine o'clock the owner went to the market and hired more. He didn't say what he would pay this time but promised fair compensation. Then he went out again at noon, three o'clock, and for the last time at five o'clock, following the same procedure.

At the end of the day at six o'clock, all the men came to pick up their pay—and that's when confusion set in. The employer first paid a denarius to each of the group that had worked the shortest time. When all groups were paid a denarius, there was much grumbling and confusion, especially from those who had worked the longest. "Not fair," they said.

"Did not I promise you one denarius and you agreed? Do not I have the right to be generous with my own money?" the owner replied.

A parable is a story with a moral or lesson; and the moral of the story is about God's grace. God does not owe anyone anything, and that which He gives any one of us is given through His grace. Grace is unmerited favor. That which He gives is eternal life, and it doesn't depend on how many years we serve. Grace was exactly what was promised to the penitent thief on the cross beside Jesus, and he had no hours left to work.

Many good folks are confused in believing that they can work for their own salvation. May we be ever so thankful for God's marvelous Grace—His free gift.

Seeds
March 18

There was a strange and interesting discovery made in badly blitzed London, England, after World War II. Those who examined the many bomb craters were amazed to find flowers growing in the gaping holes. Apparently, the explosions had unearthed long-dormant seeds of bygone days, and the bombs themselves had put nitrates into the soil, fertilizing the flowers. Life that had been dormant came to bloom in beauty in the midst of destruction.

The Master's best-known parable, the parable of the sower told in the first three Gospels, concerns seed. In the spring season, a sower went out to place his seed on the land. Scattering by hand was the method of the day. The ground on which the seed fell was not all equal. As the sower scattered, some seed fell on the hard path along the edge. The birds soon gathered that up. Some fell on a stony place where there was very limited soil and little moisture, so when the hot sun came up, the seed sprang into life quickly but soon withered and died. A third portion of seed fell among thorn bushes, which choked the new growth. Then thankfully, the remaining seed reached good soil and resulted in a magnificent harvest.

The lesson? Jesus Himself provided the interpretation. The Word of God is the seed, and we are the various types of soil into which God's Word falls. Some hear the Word, and it is immediately snatched away because of evil interests. In others, the Word springs into life but quickly fades because it is not well rooted. With others, the interests and cares of the world choke out the Word, while the final group hears the Word, accepts it, and produces a fine crop with Christian character. I think Jesus would allow for yet another group, perhaps small—the folks who are like the soil in which the dormant seeds in London's bomb craters settled for a long, long time.

Gentle Peace
March 19

Remember the old fable about the argument the wind and sun were having as to which was the more effective? To put the argument to the test, they decided to each try to get the coat off an elderly man who was passing by. The wind went first and blew fiercely, huffing and puffing, and the man just pulled his coat tighter about him. Finally, the wind gave up, and the sun came out with all its radiance; the man became warmer and warmer until he soon took his coat off. What fierceness and bluster could not accomplish, gentle warmth very easily achieved.

That is one way of saying that more and better things are accomplished in our world by kindness and gentleness than by force.

Speaking to an obstinate nation of Israel, forever rebelling, always "stirring the pot" (as it were), the great prophet Isaiah wrote: *"This is what the Sovereign LORD, the Holy One of Israel, says: 'In repentance and rest is your salvation, in quietness and trust is your strength.'"* (Isaiah 30:15). A couple of chapters later, this further word is given: *"The fruit of righteousness will be peace; the effect of righteousness will be quietness and confidence forever"* (Isaiah 32:17).

This is a message a quarrelling world needs . . . that disputes are not really solved by noise, nor are difficulties overcome by force. Too many shouts, too many loud noises, the clatter of arms—oh, for a spell of quietness, thoughtfulness, meditation, and a lowering of the decibels.

Just before He went to the cross, surrounded by a hateful, rabble-rousing crowd calling for His blood, Jesus spoke to his close followers. *"Peace I leave with you,"* He promised; *"My peace I give you. I do not give to you as the world gives. Do not let your hearts be troubled and do not be afraid"* (John 14:27).

God offers that peace that passes understanding—yes, to nations and also to individuals—to you and to me.

Knowing God
March 20

There is a mystery about God's ways, about God Himself, about prayer, about worship. We cannot fully explain how God has set the seasons, the opening of a flower, or the flight of birds. We can never fully understand all of God's ways this side of eternity. Does this make our faith in God bogus? Of course not. We know Him.

The reason we know God is not that we have seen Him. John writes in chapter one, verse 18 of his Gospel. *"No one has ever seen God, but God the One and Only* [Jesus], *who is at the Father's side, has made him known."*

Just before His cross, Jesus was asked by one of His apostles, Philip, *"Lord, show us the Father."*

Jesus answered: *"Don't you know me, Philip, even after I have been among you such a long time? Anyone who has seen me has seen the Father . . . Don't you believe that I am in the Father and that the Father is in me? The words that I say to you are not just my own. Rather, it is the Father, living in me, who is doing his work"* (John 14:9–10).

What of the Father do we see in Jesus? We see outpouring love. The apostle John, who lived with Jesus day after day for three years, puts it like this in his first epistle: *"How great is the love the Father has lavished on us, that we should be called children of God"* (1 John 3:1a).

We are reminded specifically on Good Friday that Jesus died on a cross, as a common criminal, to show you and to show me God's love, God's forgiveness, and to offer eternal life.

We don't know all there is to know about our Heavenly Father. But by faith, we know we can reach Him at any time. We know that He loves us and forgives us when we ask. We know that He gives us eternal life. That is more than enough to make life worth living—living abundantly, in fact.

Come, Let Us Bow Down
March 21

A great deal of poetry has spring as its theme, but few verses are more compelling than those of the author of the Song of Songs.

> *See! The winter is past;*
>   *the rains are over and gone.*
> *Flowers appear on the earth;*
>   *the season of singing has come,*
> *The cooing of doves*
>   *is heard in our land.*
> *The fig tree forms its early fruit;*
>   *the blossoming vines spread their fragrance.*

(Song of Songs 2:11–13a)

On the first full day of spring, the vernal equinox, when we experience equal day and equal night, we in this part of the world may not notice many fig trees showing early fruit, nor have we seen the end of rain, but we are able to feel a kindred spirit with the writer. And if we like to sing, we sing.

At the beginning of spring, it is also beneficial to turn to one of the Psalms.

> *Come, let us sing for joy to the LORD;*
> *Let us shout aloud to the Rock of our salvation.*
> *Let us come before him with thanksgiving*
> *and extol him with music and song.*
>
> *For the LORD is the great God,*
> *the great King above all gods.*
> *In his hands are the depths of the earth,*
> *and the mountain peaks belong to him.*
> *The sea is his, for he made it,*
> *and his hands formed the dry land*

(Psalm 95:1–5).

Today let us worship the King of kings and rejoice in all that He has given us.

Facing Problems
March 22

The people of Israel, during the time of Moses, had all sorts of problems. Moses, their great leader, had led them from four hundred years of slavery in Egypt to the borders of a new land that God had promised them. Moses would sit as a judge to listen to the problems and difficulties among his people from morning until evening. Moses' father-in-law, Jethro, watched Moses in action, solving problems . . . and wearing himself out in the process. He suggested Moses appoint a representative from every tribe to judge and to reserve only the tough questions for their leader. Moses followed this good advice, and the situation improved.

It's a given, of course, that our own problems are much worse than those of our neighbors and friends. There's a story told of a lady who decided to test that theory. She arranged for what she called a "problem exchange party." As each of the partiers arrived, they put their problems (they had recorded them on paper) into a pile. They then discussed all the problems that had been tossed on the pile. When the party ended, each guest was to select the paper containing the problems they wished to take home with them. Lo and behold, each person picked his or her own problems, leaving with exactly the same troubles with which they had come.

They had learned a valuable lesson. Their problems were no worse than someone else's, and indeed, all felt better equipped to handle their own.

What do you do when your problems become a burden too heavy to bear? David the Psalmist writes: *"Praise be to the Lord, to God our Savior, who daily bears our burdens"* (Psalm 68:19).

The apostle Peter writes in his first epistle, *"Cast all your anxiety on him because he cares for you"* (1Peter 5:7).

The problems don't generally disappear instantly, but God gives the strength to face them and, finally, to solve them. Moses' solution of calling on others to share the burden often helps too.

The Ten Commandments
March 23

A ruthless businessman from Boston once told the author and humorist Mark Twain: "Before I die, I mean to make a pilgrimage to the Holy Land. I will climb Mount Sinai and read the Ten Commandments aloud at the top."

"I have a better idea," replied Twain. "You could stay in Boston and keep them."

Actually, we live in a world where "commandments" are out of favor. It has been offered, in fact, that if God were to give them again in this generation, they should be "Ten Suggestions" or "Ten Recommendations." It's as if many in our world see the commands of God as optional. You can take them or leave them, do them or ignore them.

Jesus had a very different attitude.

> *"'Do not think,' He said, 'that I have come to abolish the Law or the Prophets; I have Not come to abolish them but to fulfill them. I tell you the truth, until heaven and earth disappear, not the smallest letter, not the least stroke of a pen, will by any means disappear from the Law until everything is accomplished.'"* (Matthew 5:17–18).

On one occasion, the Jewish leaders tested Jesus by asking, "Which is the greatest commandment?" Jesus responded: *"Love the Lord your God with all your heart and with all your soul and with all your mind. This is the first and greatest commandment."* And then He added: *"And the second is like it: Love your neighbor as yourself. All the Law and the Prophets hang on these two commandments"* (Matthew 22:37–40).

The New Testament writer James in his epistle echoes Mark Twain's trenchant remark to the Boston businessman. *"Do not merely listen to the word, and so deceive yourselves. Do what it says"* (James 1:22).

Not Always What They Seem to Be
March 24

An old adage says that the camera never lies. I suppose on the surface that is correct, although I once ran across a perfect example of a very clever distortion by the one operating the camera.

A few of us, after attending a meeting in Vancouver, decided to take a walk along Spanish Banks. The sun was just setting over the mountains, spreading its multicolored hues.

We stopped to watch a photographer taking some very interesting shots against the glorious background. In front of him was a little model airplane hanging by a slim wire from an arm jutting out from a wooden stand, and he was shooting pictures of the tiny model plane against the gloriously colored sky. Then he asked if we would like to see his album of similar photos. There he had dozens of pictures taken in similar settings: beautiful, seemingly realistic shots of planes in flight. He had made all the models himself.

Things aren't always what they seem to be . . . and high soaring flight is far more mundane than it appears. Some of the beautiful, attractive ads that promote the wonders of high living fail to disclose the other ninth-tenths of an often sordid story.

"'Watch out for false prophets,' Jesus said; 'They come to you in sheep's clothing, but inwardly they are ferocious wolves. By their fruit you will recognize them'" (Matthew 7:15–16a). In the times we live in, there are many voices calling "Come this way," and they can be overpowering unless we recognize the truth.

Looking at it the other way, we often fail to recognize the finest things in life or take advantage of the opportunities when they are right alongside. The two followers of Jesus who were overtaken on the road to Emmaus by their risen Master did not recognize Him because their eyes were downcast, their hearts were heavy, and their minds had not accepted that He was alive.

Regarding the prints taken by the camera, I'm sure the eyes of an expert—one who knew the real planes well—could quickly have picked up the difference. That's true in life also. We should pray for discernment—to tell the difference between truth and delusion.

Cheerful Music
March 25

A friend of composer Franz Joseph Hayden (1732-1809) remarked to him that his church music was usually cheerful. Haydn's reply was, "I cannot make it otherwise. I write according to the thoughts I feel; when I think upon my God, my heart is so full of joy that the notes dance and leap from my pen; and since God has given me a cheerful heart, I can do no other than serve Him with a cheerful spirit."[5]

The Psalmist is also found with a cheerful heart. He too finds it most difficult not to praise God out of that full heart. He too was a musician. In the one hundred seventh Psalm, the Psalmist begins with overflowing with praise to God. *"Give thanks to the LORD for he is good; his love endures forever. Let the redeemed of the LORD say this—those he redeemed from the hand of the foe, those he gathered from the lands, from east and west, from north and south."*

Then the Psalmist allows his mind to go back to the wonders God has performed in the lives of multitudes. Some had wandered in the desert. Hungry and thirsty, they cried out to God, and He delivered them. Some were in prison; they cried out to God, and He broke their chains. Others, sailing the high seas, ran into a terrible tempest that threatened to swamp them. They cried to God—as did Jesus many years later—and God settled the storm.

We may feel that life is sometimes a desert, leaving us parched; or we sense, on occasion, that prison-like doors have closed on us, and there we are in chains. We may even feel that the tempests of life are threatening to overwhelm us. Cry out to God, as the Psalmist describes, and your voice will be heard, you will be delivered, the chains will be broken, and the storm will be settled.

For He was the Psalmist's God and Franz Haydn's God. Now He is, or can be, your God. And the music of your soul will be cheerful.

Surprised by Joy
March 26

Some of you may recognize the name of Frances R. Havergal, English poet and hymn writer. Frances was a precocious child. She was reading by age four and began writing verse at age seven. She was the author of such well-known hymns as "Like a River Glorious" and "Take My Life and Let It Be."

Early in her life, Frances Havergal was not a "happy" Christian. She simply lacked the joy that every born-again child of God should experience. However, one day God surprised her and vitally changed her outlook.

Frances writes, "I was shown that, 'the blood of Jesus Christ his Son cleanseth us from all sin,' and then it was made plain to me that He who had thus cleansed me had power to keep me clean."[6]

She had read 1 John 1:7, where the second part of the verse in the King James Version states, *"the blood of Jesus Christ his Son cleanseth us from all sin."* The tense of the verb "cleanseth" in the Greek signifies "keeps on cleansing"—and so the verse may be translated, "the blood of Jesus Christ his Son keeps on cleansing us from all sin."

A dramatic change came into her formerly lackluster life. In words that C.S. Lewis used for the title of one of his many books, she was "surprised by joy."

Sometimes, as it were, the bloom comes off the rose a bit as the years stretch on, and we may be faced with a touch of the blues from time to time.

Just before His crucifixion, Jesus invited his followers to, *"Ask, and you will receive, and your joy will be complete"* (John 16:24b).

Frances Havergal put her similar thoughts in verse:

> I am trusting Thee, Lord Jesus
>
> Trusting only Thee;
>
> Trusting Thee for full salvation,
>
> Great and free.[7]

Surprised by joy.

Darkness and Light
March 27

On the first Palm Sunday in Jerusalem, there was great excitement. Vast crowds were there for it was feast time, the greatest celebration on the Jewish calendar. The Feast of the Passover commemorates the day when the angel of death passed over the enslaved Israelites in Egypt but took a deadly toll on their slave masters. And the Israelites were free.

On that day we call Palm Sunday, there was restlessness among the crowd. The rumor was floating about that an important person was about to arrive. Then they heard the noise of a procession coming into the city. "Who is it? Who is it?"

"It is Jesus, the prophet of Nazareth in Galilee," came the answer from the incoming throng. Pretty heady stuff!

But Jesus went to the temple to worship and to pray. They wanted more of His miracles. They would even have made him King, but he wanted none of it. He wanted simply to rule in their hearts—to bring light into their darkened souls.

That's why, many years after Calvary, the apostle John was to write the following words very early in the Gospel that bears his name: "*He* [Jesus] *was in the world, and though the world was made through him, the world did not recognize him. He came to that which was his own* [his own people], *but his own did not receive him*" (John 1:10–11).

The days of Holy Week are days of contrast—celebration and questioning, high hopes and tunnel vision, support and betrayal, light and darkness.

"*Yet to all who received him,*" John continues in verse 12, "*to those who believed in his name, he gave the right to become children of God.*"

The cross was in one sense the blackest moment in human history, the story of man's greatest failure. And yet from God's side . . . and His Son's side, it was the brightest of lights, the dawning of a new day.

Redeemed
March 28

> "The chief priests and elders of the people assembled in the palace of the high priest, whose name was Caiaphas, and they plotted to arrest Jesus in some sly way and kill him. 'But not during the Feast,' they said, 'or there may be a riot among the people'" (Matthew 26: 3–5).

> "Then one of the Twelve—the one called Judas Iscariot—went to the chief Priests and asked, 'What are you willing to give me if I hand him over to you?' So they counted out for him thirty silver coins. From then on Judas watched for an opportunity to hand him over" (Matthew 26: 14–16).

Three truths stand out starkly from the account of that Wednesday in Scripture.

First, the Jewish leaders, meeting in the palace of Caiaphas the High Priest, renewed their earlier decision that the time had come to get rid of Jesus, and they began to make actual plans to do so.

Secondly, a seemingly devoted follower of Jesus—one of His twelve particularly chosen apostles—became a betrayer, making it easy for the leaders to carry forward their devilish plan.

Thirdly, Jesus knew both the activities of the Jewish leaders and the treachery of Judas Iscariot, yet He moved on inexorably to the cross for one reason—because He loved us so.

The price paid to redeem a slave in the Jewish economy was thirty pieces of silver. That's exactly what the leaders paid—and Judas accepted—to crucify Jesus. The price of a slave for the Savior—that's what the world paid, but to our Savior, the price was everything. Yet He paid it so that you and I might be redeemed. His cross is very dimly lit in most minds in our world today.

May it be our prayer that it may become more luminous until it dominates the world.

Jesus or Judas
March 29

The evening before the monstrous events surrounding His death, Jesus and the twelve apostles met for the Last Supper in an upper room in Jerusalem. Yes, there were twelve. Judas had the insolence to participate, though he had earlier arranged to betray his Master for thirty miserable pieces of silver. The Last Supper is also called Communion, Holy Communion, Eucharist, or the Mass by Christians. In the twenty-sixth verse of 1 Corinthians, chapter 11, Jesus said: *"For whenever you eat this bread and drink this cup, you proclaim the Lord's death until he comes."*

Very ordinary people, all of them . . . so like the rest of humanity. Except for the betrayer who took his own life, these were to be the ones who, fired by the resurrection and the Spirit of God, would set their world on fire and become the means of inaugurating and spreading the church.

There is an interesting story surrounding the models used for the famous painting of the Last Supper by Leonardo da Vinci. It might be a legend because, apparently, there is no historical evidence behind the story, but it does illustrate a point. When beginning the Last Supper, Leonardo searched for a model he could use to portray Jesus. Leonardo finally found a man whose countenance showed innocence, not having the scars of a sinful life, to represent Christ and proceeded to paint most of the picture. Some years passed with the painting not quite finished. Jesus and eleven of the apostles had been completed . . . but no Judas.

Once again, the artist searched for the right model. He looked for a man of treachery, one whose evil heart was expressed in his face. Finally, he found one. As da Vinci finished the painting, the model made a startling revelation about his identity. He was the same one who, years earlier, had posed as Jesus. A life of sin and crime had changed the man's countenance so much so that da Vinci had not recognized him.

We humans are changeable that way—from the best to the basest . . . and from the basest to the best. The ultimate question is, Whom do we model? Jesus or Judas? The cross makes the difference in our answer.

Caring to a Careless World
March 30

One of the most significant things you can say about that first Good Friday is that Jesus cares. He paid the supreme price to show His caring to a careless world.

At the close of Thursday evening's Last Supper, after Judas had gone out into the night to betray Him, Jesus spoke the magnificent words of the hereafter found in the fourteenth chapter of John.

> *Do not let your hearts be troubled. Trust in God; trust also in me. In my Father's house are many rooms; if it were not so, I would have told you. I am going there to prepare a place for you. And if I go and prepare a place for you, I will come back and take you to be with me that you also may be where I am. You know the way to the place where I am going.*

Then He went with the disciples to the Garden of Gethsemane, where He poured out His soul in agonizing prayer.

Events then moved swiftly. Judas, with a large band of armed men, arrived and seized Jesus; rushed Him first to Annas, the former high priest; and then to Caiaphas, the current one; then to Pilate, the Roman Governor; to King Herod; and back to Pilate. Washing his hands as if to absolve himself from guilt, Pilate sentenced Jesus to be crucified. And after Roman soldiers had mocked Jesus and placed a crown of thorns on His brow, Jesus, bearing His own cross, was led to Calvary, where soldiers nailed Him to the cross and gambled for His clothing.

And on that cross, that Good Friday, Jesus died for our sins . . . yours and mine . . . because He cared supremely.

Last Words?
March 31

As Christ hung there on the cross, the Gospel writers recorded that He spoke very briefly. Each of the seven last words or phrases packed a wealth of meaning.

The first is a phrase of mercy and deep understanding. Found in Luke 23:34a, it reads: *"Father, forgive them, for they do not know what they are doing."* As Jesus prayed that prayer, the soldiers gambled for His clothes, passersby reviled Him, and the chief priests mocked him.

The second word or phrase was a promise of forgiveness to one of the thieves on either side of Him. One continued to mock with the mockers, but the other, now penitent, called out to Jesus to be remembered when Christ entered His kingdom. Jesus' reply was a comfort for all penitents: *"I tell you the truth, today you will be with me in paradise"* (Luke 23:43).

Third are the words recorded in the nineteenth chapter of John. Realizing His mother's deep needs, Jesus called out to her, referring to John who was standing nearby. *"Dear woman,"* He said, *"here is your son."* And to John: *"Here is your mother."* The Scripture notes that from that time on, John took her into his household.

The fourth word, that of loneliness, is found in Matthew's account of the crucifixion. Jesus, bearing the sins of the world, felt a terrible weight of loss . . . He could not even reach His Heavenly Father. In that moment of utter blackness, He cried out: *"My God, my God, why have you forsaken me?"*

The fifth was a very human word or phrase, *"I am thirsty"* To their credit, the soldiers dipped a sponge in wine vinegar and moistened His lips.

The sixth phrase is also found in John's Gospel. After receiving the vinegar, Jesus cried out, *"It is finished,"* a cry of sublime victory, bringing to mind the prayer that Jesus had prayed in the Garden of Gethsemane when He told His Father that He had finished the work He was given by His Father to do.

The final phrase, found in the twenty-third chapter of Luke, is one of peace and restored calmness of mind and soul when Jesus said before his final breath: *"Father, into your hands I commit my spirit."*

Yet, of course, His life did not end there. The Son of God rose from the tomb on the Sunday we call Easter to defeat death not only for Himself, but also for everyone who will follow Him. We too may have the assurance of eternal life because Jesus died and rose again.

The Light Is on Again
April 01

A chaplain in the Royal Canadian Air Force was returning home on a troopship at the end of WWII. They were passing Britain's Land's End in the mist, and he was out on deck, walking by himself, at the stern of the ship. Spotting a squadron leader leaning over the rail, he walked over to him. Looking towards Land's End, the squadron leader spoke, "My brother is over there. He was last seen there."

The padre responded, "I'm sorry, I didn't mean to break your meditations."

"It's all right," the officer commented. "It's all right," he repeated and, pointing to the light of the lighthouse visible through the mist, added, "The light is on again."

That was the feeling of the disciples of Jesus after the desperate and grueling days leading up to the crucifixion. It was and is the message of the first Easter and every succeeding celebration of Easter.

Evil men had done their very worst. They had sent Jesus to His death by the most fiendishly designed cruelty ever imagined—crucifixion. They had succeeded in scattering His followers, clearing them off the streets into hideaways. Make no mistake about it, Jesus was dead that first Good Friday, and so were his follower's hopes.

Then, as someone has said, "Evil can go a long, long way. It can gloat the first day; it can swagger the second day, but the third day God speaks."

His was the voice of the risen Savior who was walking in the Garden near His tomb. An utterly distraught Mary Magdalene had backed off from the empty sepulcher to which she had returned after racing to inform Peter and John of what had happened. Still thinking that her Master was dead and that His body had been spirited away, she turned at a sound behind her and saw, through her tears, a man she took to be the gardener.

"'Woman,' he said, 'why are you crying? Who is it you are looking for?' Thinking he was the gardener, she said, 'Sir, if you have carried him away, tell me where you have put him, and I will get him'" (John 20:15).

Jesus' response was one word: *"Mary"*—and "the light went on again."

Missing the Master?
April 02

The day of the Resurrection, two of Jesus' followers were walking the dusty road from Jerusalem to Emmaus, a village about 11 kilometers from Jerusalem. They were discussing, of course, the events of the past week, including the terrible death of their Master on Friday. They had heard rumors about an empty tomb . . . rumors they could not or would not credit. Thus desperately downcast, they were just trudging along when a stranger caught up with them.

Noticing their downcast looks, He asked them, "What are you discussing?" They told Him about Jesus, His death, the empty tomb, and rumors that some had seen Him. The stranger then began to talk of the Old Testament prophecies concerning the Messiah, gripping their interest. Then as He was about to leave them (by that time they had entered the village and the two had reached their destination), they hospitably asked the stranger to stay the night with them.

When they sat down for the evening meal, they suddenly recognized that the stranger was Jesus.

For many years, the two who walked the Emmaus road that day—man and wife perhaps— undoubtedly told many, many times of their glorious experience when the risen Jesus walked with them. I'm sure they would add, "And to think, we almost missed Him."

Could that, perhaps, be a possibility this Easter?

A Foolish Cross
April 03

There was a man who captured headlines by allowing his beard to grow full, putting on a long flowing robe, and over several days, carrying a large wooden cross along the one hundred eighty-five mile stretch of freeway between Edmonton and Calgary. Conveniently, at Ponoka, which is about sixty-five miles along the highway from Edmonton and where there was a mental hospital, the authorities took the cross-carrier in for a check-up. They decided to allow him to continue on to Calgary.

I happened to be in a hotel room in Brandon, Manitoba, when a documentary of the event was showing, so I watched it. The next morning, at breakfast, I overheard some men who were talking quite loudly, discussing the incident. Quite a bit was said until one man concluded: "You know the thing that bothered me about that TV presentation: never once was the purpose stated for that trek."

For there was none, of course, unless you accept notoriety on the part of the cross-bearer or filling in an hour on the national television network as purposeful.

Some in our world would put the cross that Jesus bore in the same category as the Canadian cross-bearer—foolishness. Strangely, perhaps, that is the very word used by the apostle Paul. *"Jews demand miraculous signs and Greeks look for wisdom, but we preach Christ crucified: a stumbling block to Jews and foolishness to Gentiles"* (1 Corinthians 1:22-23).

At one point, in the mockery of the trial of Jesus, Pontius Pilate actually said to the accusing Jewish leaders, *"Take him yourselves and judge him by your own law"* (John 18:31a). They sanctimoniously replied that their law would not permit them to put a man to death by crucifixion, the Roman manner. Why did they want crucifixion? Because it was the most terrible death ever conceived and because Jewish law brought the curse of damnation upon anyone hung on a tree. *"Anyone who is hung on a tree is under God's curse"* (Deuteronomy 21:23b). They wanted Jesus cursed.

So it still remains . . . that cross, a stumbling block to many of Jesus' own people and foolishness or wasted effort to many in the rest of the world.

Paul continues on from that verse in which he suggests that the Cross is a stumbling block or foolishness. He says, *"But to those whom God has called* [that cross shows] . . . *Christ the power of God and the wisdom of God"* (1 Corinthians 1:24).

In short—God's purpose.

Greater Love
April 04

Peter Miller was a Baptist preacher in the United States at the time of its revolution and birth. Where Peter Miller served, there also lived a fellow by the name of Michael Wittman, a man of some prominence. Wittman despised Peter Miller and did all he could to oppose and humiliate him. Wittman's evil deeds eventually caught up to him, and he was arrested on a charge of treason and sentenced to die.

Peter Miller traveled seventy miles on foot to Philadelphia, the American capital during those war years, to try to save Wittman's life. Miller requested and received an audience with George Washington, where he pleaded for Wittman's life. Washington said he could not spare the life of Miller's "friend." Miller went on to explain that Wittman was his worst enemy, but he had forgiven him and would like to save his life. "What?" cried Washington. "You've walked seventy miles to save the life of an enemy?" Washington was so moved that he granted the pardon, and Wittman lived.

There are two precepts of Peter Miller's Master that immediately come to mind. The Master says in Matthew 5, *"If someone forces you to go one mile, go with him two miles."* The background of this goes back to the Roman custom of cheaply staffing the postal system by compelling civilians to carry the mail a fixed distance. "Go the second mile," said Jesus. In other words, don't do just what duty demands. Show the grace that your God has shown to you. Do it for someone else.

The second precept of Jesus that is brought to mind was spoken to His disciples while they were on their way to the Garden of Gethsemane just prior to Jesus' Crucifixion. *"Greater love has no one than this,"* Jesus said, *"that he lay down his life for his friends"* (John 15:13). Yet Jesus Himself did more . . . far more. He laid down His life for His enemies. Peter Miller didn't go nearly that far, but he did trudge one hundred forty miles there and back both to forgive and to plead for the life of an enemy.

I wonder how far you and I would walk down either of these roads. I'm not sure . . . or at least not as sure as I should be.

Remember to Forget
April 05

The older we get in this life, it seems, the more forgetful we become. However, there are things in our lives that we should intentionally forget.

The apostle Paul has particularly meaningful advice on that score in Philippians 3:13–14. Noting that his life is not complete or perfect, he writes: "*Brothers, I do not consider myself yet to have hold of it* [i.e. perfection]. *But one thing I do: Forgetting what is behind and straining toward what is ahead, I press on toward the goal to win the prize for which God has called me heavenward in Christ Jesus.*" Lest we feel that we have more to forget than most and find it impossible to push out of our memories some unwanted material, may I suggest that it was the same apostle Paul who wrote: "*For I am the least of the apostles and do not even deserve to be called an apostle, because I persecuted the church of God. But by the grace of God I am what I am, and his grace to me was not without effect*" (1Corinthians 15:9–10a).

The grace of God in his life had not only produced newness, but God's forgiveness had banished an undesirable past. Paul was able to forget the past and have a clear, unhindered view of the goal ahead. So may we.

The Psalmist, David, writes: "*He* [the Lord] *does not treat us as our sins deserve or repay us according to our iniquities*" Psalm (103:10). If God forgives and forgets our past, why shouldn't we? And shouldn't we also let go of a grudge or two toward another for something done in the past?

We have a superb goal ahead!

Remember to forget.

Broken Crystal
April 06

Crystal is very delicate and very beautiful. Someone has mentioned that if we hold it to the light, it will "paint rainbows on the wall." Of course if we drop it—perish the thought—it shatters with pieces flying all over the place.

Unfortunately, some of us can have feelings as delicate as crystal. Those feelings may sometimes be so delicate that if dropped, they lie shattered like colorless pieces of broken crystal.

From time to time, we observe someone whose marvelous way of life seems to reflect all the colors of the rainbow ... whose daily living is marked by "the music of the spheres," as it were. Then suddenly the gorgeous colors seem to fade, the music stills, and we wonder what has happened. Has someone been treading on that person's dreams?

You might think King David of Israel, a mighty warrior and fine musician, the Psalmist, would be the last person on earth to be hurt, to be shattered. In one of the Psalms credited to him, he writes: "*Scorn has broken my heart and has left me helpless; I looked for sympathy, but there was none, for comforters, but I found none. They put gall in my food and gave me vinegar for my thirst*" (Psalm 69:20–21). Here is a man who was bitterly hurt. We do not know how or why. Perhaps it was just a careless word or two.

Moses, while still in Egypt, came upon two Israelites who were fighting. He tried to reconcile them by saying, "Men, you are brothers; why do you want to hurt each other?" Why? A very good question. Why do we wish to hurt one another physically or, what is just as cruel, with our cutting words? And especially we who are brothers and sisters in the Christ—why would we want to hurt one another?

"*A word aptly spoken is like apples of gold in settings of silver,*" so writes the author of Proverbs in chapter 25, verse 11. On the other hand, writes Frederika Bremer, "There are sharp words which sever hearts more than sharp swords; there are words, the point of which sting the heart through the course of a whole life."

May our words be apples of gold and not ones that shatter crystal.

Heart Music
April 07

Years ago, phrenologists claimed that they could tell a great deal about you by feeling the position and size of various bumps on your head. Phrenology was trendy for a while but was eventually discredited by scientific research.

Gypsy Smith, the well-known evangelist of a past generation, was once approached by someone who began to run his fingers through Gypsy Smith's thick hair and to feel about for bumps. "Are you a phrenologist?" asked Smith.

"No, not quite," came the reply. "I am trying to find the secret of your success."

Then Gypsy Smith placed his own hand on his heart and said, "Well, sir, you are feeling too high. You must come down here."[1]

How true! The secret lies not in the head, but in the heart. You could . . . I could . . . spend a whole lifetime with our head knowledge, proving the existence of our God. Some would still respond, when face to face with the evidence, "So what" or "I couldn't care less." We need to speak of a God who cares for you and for me so passionately that He sent His Son to die the cruelest death ever devised by evil minds and then rose again from the tomb so that we could have eternal life. Jesus put it this way: *"Because I live, you also will live."* That's heart music!

The way of Jesus is reasonable and academically acceptable. But far more important, it reaches your heart and mine, and in turn, our caring hearts reach out to others.

Foolish Man
April 08

A parable that comes to mind when one thinks of "the things of this world" could be named "The Foolish Man of Wealth." A man in the crowd, where the Master was, called out: "Teacher, tell my brother to divide the inheritance with me." We are not told how much the inheritance was, who left it, or why one brother seemingly received it all.

Before telling the parable, Jesus indicated to the complaining brother that He, Jesus, was not interested in being an arbiter over secular money matters. He warned the crowd and the man against greed, noting that one's life does not consist in the abundance of one's possessions.

Then He told of a wealthy farmer whose crop that year was splendid. The farmer's barns were already full from previous crops, and there was just no room to store any more. The farmer thought, "What shall I do?" Suddenly he came up with the answer: "I know; I'll tear down my present barns and build bigger. Then I'll have room for everything." Then he added, "After that, I'll be able to say to myself, 'You have everything you need for many, many years. Take it easy and live it up.'"

"But God said to him, 'You fool! This very night your life will be demanded from you. Then who will get what you have prepared for yourself?'" (Luke 12:20).

The farmer, you see, had no thought for anyone or anything but himself.

There is a powerful lesson here about the frailty of life and the ultimate unimportance of the "things" of this world. I think many seniors would recognize that truth. As we get older, the value of most of the articles around us simply lessens. The important aspects of life are things like the God we worship, the friends we enjoy, and the clear conscience we possess.

The Lord Is My Shepherd
April 09

There are quite a few advantages in growing older. One of the greatest, I think, is that our needs—and especially our wants—become less and less. As we reflect upon it, many of the "things" of our life, so cherished by younger people and perhaps by most of us too when we were younger, don't really matter very much after all. We don't need them for health, for making friends, nor for any of the many blessings that abound in a meaningful life. In any event, as William Gilbert put it, "Things are seldom what they seem. Skim milk masquerades as cream."

Sir George Savile, Marquess of Halifax, gave some rather good advice to a daughter about things. "Children and fools want everything because they want [or lack] wit to distinguish, and there is no stronger evidence of a crazy understanding than the making too large a catalogue of things necessary, when in truth there so very few things that have a right to be placed in it."[2]

Well, having disposed of the "things unnecessary," we still have basic needs: food, some clothes, shelter, etc. However, there are some deeper needs of the soul, and these the writer of the Shepherd Psalm (Psalm 23) addresses. The Psalmist offers, through our Heavenly Shepherd, green pastures and still waters—these do restore the tired and fractured soul. God prepares a veritable banquet table for our spiritual and physical enjoyment. He accompanies us in every storm of life . . . even the valley of the shadow. We are assured that goodness and mercy will be our partners through a long and fruitful life, for our dwelling is the house of the Lord—now and eternally.

"The Lord is my shepherd. I shall not want." KJV

"Sympathy's Sustaining Bread"
April 10

Louisa May Alcott is probably best known for her book *Little Women*, one of the most popular books for girls ever written, not only cherished by little women or girls, but by many older women as well. Louisa May Alcott was also an author of many inspirational poems. Among them was one she called "My Prayer," in which she asked for the following ability:

> To smooth the rough and thorny way
>
> Where other feet begin to tread;
>
> To feed some hungry soul each day
>
> With sympathy's sustaining bread.[3]

To a cowed and stumbling Peter, early one morning on the shore of the Sea of Galilee soon after the resurrection (as recorded in the Gospel of John, chapter 21), Jesus pointedly said to Peter, *"Do you truly love me?"*

Peter replied, *"Lord, you know that I love you."* Three times Jesus asked the same question. Three times Peter gave the same answer—equal to the three times Peter had denied His Master before the Crucifixion. Then three times the same directive was given to Peter from the Master he had defamed, "Feed my sheep."

Our response to God's love and salvation is directed to us in that day's directive to Peter. "Feed my sheep," or to love and care for others, should be our response to His love for us.

The apostle John writes the following in his first epistle: *"This is the message you heard from the beginning: We should love one another"* (1 John 3:11). He adds in verse 16: *"This is how we know what love is: Jesus Christ laid down his life for us. And we ought to lay down our lives for our brothers."*

At the very least, we should share our love and concern, "sympathy's sustaining bread," as Louisa May Alcott put it.

Faith Plus
April 11

Albert Schweitzer was truly a great man. He was a philosopher, theologian, musician, and medical doctor. He was awarded the Nobel Peace Prize in 1952.

Revealing the kind of man Albert Schweitzer was, someone has told of a reception's being held for him at a Chicago railway terminal where he was arriving from Africa for a furlough. Speeches were given in three languages—English, French, and German—to honor him.

In the middle of it all, he spied an elderly woman in the distance on one of the platforms, struggling with heavy bags. With an apology to those closest to him, Schweitzer hurried to her side, picked up her luggage, helped her on board, and wished her a good journey. He then returned to the crowd and said simply, "Excuse me, but I was just having a bit of my daily fun." A newsman was heard to remark, "It was the first time I ever saw a sermon walking."

The writer of the epistle of James had something like this in mind as he wrote:

> *What good is it, my brothers, if a man claims to have faith but has no deeds? Can such faith save him? Suppose a brother or sister is without clothes and daily food. If one of you says to him, "Go, I wish you well; keep warm and well fed," but does nothing about his physical needs, what good is it? In the same way, faith by itself, if it is not accompanied by action, is dead* (James 2:14–17).

That's how sermons go walking—in darkest Africa and right here at home.

Taxes

April 12

One of the most popular topics of conversation in our society and especially around this time of year is taxes. The topic seems to be a subject for grumbling. We have the impression, in fact, that a government's chief objective is to impose taxes, while the aim of most of the rest of us is to avoid them.

When Michael Faraday first produced a continuous electric current through a moving conductor in a magnetic field (essentially the first dynamo), Britain's Prime Minister Peel asked Faraday of what use it was. Faraday replied, "I don't know, but I wager some day you will tax it." And, of course, he was right. Electricity for light, heat, and power is quite a source of taxation for governments.

Jesus Himself was asked about taxes. A group of Pharisees and Herodians was sent to try to trap Him. They asked if they should pay taxes to Caesar or not. In reply, Jesus asked for one of the coins in circulation at the time. Looking at it, He asked his questioners, *"Whose likeness and title are these?"*

"Caesar's," they responded.

Then Jesus left them speechless as He said, *"Pay therefore to Caesar the things that are due to Caesar, and pay to God the things that are due to God."* In short, the Christian should be a good Christian citizen—a better citizen, in fact, just because he/she is a Christian. God cares for us as we are bound together in the bundle of life.

Aim High
April 13

As part of a course of studies I was taking, a lecturer told a humorous, yet pointed story concerning the old Wild West: "It seems a stranger came into town and noticed targets strung up all over town with each and every one of them having a bullet hole right in the bull's-eye. After locating the man who had done the shooting, the stranger asked him what his secret was. "It's easy," explained the shooter. "You shoot first and then you draw your target."

Unfortunately, there are folks even today who spend most of their waking hours firing around in all directions. Aiming at nothing, they always hit it, life becoming less and less meaningful with every passing day and every random shot.

The apostle Peter, in his first epistle, writes as a pastor deeply concerned for his suffering people. They were not suffering because of something they had done or had not done, but simply because of evil persecution. Peter writes to his people, encouraging them. Peter says: *"You are receiving the goal [or target] of your faith, the salvation of your souls"* (1 Peter 1:9). God's greatest gift to anyone is personal salvation, which of course changes aimlessness to purpose.

I had an aunt who loved maxims or mottoes. One of them had to do with aim.

> Aim high
> The trying will suffice
> The goal, if reached or not,
> Makes great the life.

Great counsel in these words. The apostle Paul also had great counsel at the end of his second letter to the Corinthians, where he similarly writes, "Aim for perfection."

One of the great advantages of the senior years is the opportunity to reflect. Sober reflection would seem to indicate the very careful choice of both a target and an accurate aim—which may be achieved by the grace of God.

I Tell You the Truth
April 14

I remember a time when a couple of us were tramping through the thick forest of Mt. Douglas Park in Victoria, British Columbia enjoying God's nature thoroughly—the wild blooms, the thickly carpeted forest floor. Walking along a path, we noticed, just off the trail, three blooms on one of the bushes. They were pure white, as large as good-sized roses. They seemed strangely out of place in those forested surroundings. And they were very much out of place. They were, in fact, paper blossoms—imitations. Someone had placed them in a fork between two branches on one of the bushes. Artificial flowers may not look out of place in a living room, but in a forest they just do not belong.

Falseness does not really belong in the kind of world God planned for mankind. Yet God's history of humankind, the Bible, has stories of human falseness on page after page. We read of false hopes and false dreams and false prophets who peddle them. There are false witnesses, false charges, false oaths, and even false brothers, false Christs, and false gods.

It is little wonder that when He was before Pontius Pilate, Jesus responded to a question and said that He had come into the world to testify to the Truth. The Roman governor cynically asked: "What is truth?"

Our Master was and is strongly opposed to every form of untruth. Probably the most common expression on his lips was *"verily, verily"* or, as the modern translations have it, "I tell you the truth." He used the comment literally dozens and dozens of times. John the Baptist said of Him: *"For the law was given through Moses; grace and truth came through Jesus Christ"* (John 1:17).

A world longing for Truth rather than falsehood and the real rather than the artificial will find just that in Him. That is His promise. One that He never fails to keep.

The Unspoken Word
April 15

Many years ago, I was pastor of a church in Gaspereau, Nova Scotia. Those of you who know the Maritimes may recognize Gaspereau as the middle of a delightful little valley of the same name . . . just off the larger and more well-known Annapolis Valley of apple blossom fame. Gaspereau is, in fact, just over the ridge from Wolfville—a mile or so away. Wolfville is the seat of Acadia University, where I was also taking classes at the time.

The Gaspereau church has a long history. I have seen original records of the church with the financial figures in pounds, shillings and pence. Other records of those ancient times are most interesting. One item, in the church minute book, told of the church's dealing with two men who, they had discovered, were quarrelling over an ox. At a church meeting called for the purpose of settling the matter, the good brethren and sisters made their decision and added this pearl of wisdom: both men thereafter were required to keep silent about the matter . . . and the first one speaking about it would be deemed the guilty party and would be dealt with accordingly.

Who was it who said, "The unspoken word never does harm?"

The New Testament writer, James, in a much more ancient record, has some pointed things to say about silence and speech . . . so pointed in fact that they bother me. And perhaps they should. James suggests that our bodies are like a sail ship, and the part we call our tongue is like the ship's rudder. *"Take ships for example. Although they are so large and are driven by strong winds, they are steered by a very small rudder wherever the pilot wants to go. Likewise the tongue is a small part of the body, but it makes great boasts."* (James 3:4–5a)

He adds how difficult it is to tame this tiny tongue of ours, which may praise God at one moment and denounce men or women at another. *This should not be*, He writes.

Upon reflection, I think that the Gaspereau church decision was like the wisdom of Solomon.

A Homing Experience
April 16

My wife's father, Fred Parfitt, was a builder in Victoria, B.C., for many years. One of his firm's undertakings was the still imposing Christ Church Cathedral. While construction was well underway, with the massive pillars in place but as yet no roof, one of the workmen noticed a robin making trip after trip to the top of one of the pillars. There, with the only protection being some of the framing that still remained in place, the robin was bringing bits of straw and twigs, making a nest. The workmen called Mr. Parfitt over, and the two of them watched as the robin continued her task. Orders were given to leave the bird undisturbed as long as possible, and for some time they literally built around her . . . indeed until she laid her eggs, hatched them, and left at the end of the season. Because of the connection between the experience in God's house and a favorite Psalm, the builders arranged for a permanent sculpture to be placed at the top of the pillar.

If you happen to go to Victoria, visit Christ Church Cathedral and ask to see the robin pillar, not far from the altar, where at the top of the great column sits a sculpted robin on her nest.

The Psalm that provided the inspiration was the eighty—fourth from the King James Version.

> *"How amiable are thy tabernacles, O LORD of hosts! My soul longeth, yea, even fainteth for the courts of the LORD: my heart and my flesh crieth out for the living God. Yea, the sparrow hath found an house, and the swallow a nest for herself, where she may lay her young, even thine altars, O LORD of hosts, my King, and my God."*

This is a very happy Psalm, the praise of a pilgrim telling the whole world, as it were, what it means to him (or her) to attend services of worship—in this instance the autumn festival—at God's temple in Jerusalem. The pilgrim feels a strangely emotional kinship with the birds—the sparrows, the swallows . . . yes and the robins—who find refuge, rest, and peace at the altar. For him or her, as for them, it is a homing experience.

Like the robin, we may find permanent peace and rest by God's altar, for time and eternity.

Signs

April 17

Allan G. Odell was a man who created some signs that were the talk of North America in the 1920s and 1930s. Just out of college, Allan Odell joined his father's company, Burman Vita Inc. The company had developed a brushless shaving cream called Burma Shave that young Allan wanted to advertise in a creative manner. Allan persuaded his father to spend two hundred dollars to give his advertising campaign a try.

Allan's idea was to have sets of small wooden signs spaced one hundred feet apart along the highway, each sign carrying one line of a rhyme with the clincher on the last sign—the product, "Burma Shave." In the fall of 1925, the first signs were erected. The idea quickly became a success. At one time, there were seven thousand sets planted along the highways of North America. The signs were gradually removed with the coming of high speed travel and billboard bans.

Signs not only are a means of advertising, but also are used as guideposts to guide us along life's way. "Your word," writes the Psalmist of God's Word, the Bible, "is a lamp to my feet and a light to my path." Christians have valuable signs both for witness and guidance. They have nothing to sell, but they do have the good news, the water of life to offer freely to all. Those signs should never be removed.

Signs 2
April 18

Continuing with yesterday's topic of signs, sometimes it is difficult for us to carry our Christian signs. Once while doing a little therapeutic walking in Calgary, Alberta, a sudden change in the weather occurred. It had been a reasonably good day at the start. I was about a mile or so from home when one of those sudden prairie windstorms sprang up. Building paper was soon flying across the road from a nearby building site. Signs were blowing down; garbage cans were blowing over with refuse strewn all over. The wind was so violent at times that I had trouble keeping my feet on the ground. And dust was flying everywhere.

In the midst of all this, I passed two boys endeavoring to carry a large sign up the street between them. By holding it edgeways to the wind, they were just making it, but it was tough.

In the center of all that confused buffeting, you could sense somehow a parable of life. It has become very difficult in our world, with all its carnage, for Christians to carry their signs—to let others know what they believe and try to practice.

In this vein, the apostle Peter has some excellent advice for us: *"In your hearts set apart Christ as Lord. Always be prepared to give an answer to everyone who asks you to give the reason for the hope that you have. But do this with gentleness and respect"* (1 Peter 3:15).

Paul puts it this way: *"Make the most of every opportunity. Let your conversation be always full of grace, seasoned with salt, so that you may know how to answer everyone"* (Colossians 4:5b-6).

That's the message we can put on our signs as we carry them even in the buffeting winds of this world's carnage.

Well Done
April 19

"Well done thou good and faithful servant: thou hast been faithful over a few things, I will make thee ruler over many things: enter thou into the joy of thy Lord." KJV

This well-known verse is a central part of a parable called the Parable of the Talents.

In the story, an obviously wealthy man was going on a journey, called in three of his servants, and entrusted his property to them. One was given five talents, the second was given two talents, and the third was given one talent (a talent was a weight measure of silver, between sixty and eighty pounds). Each was expected to put the talents to work according to his ability.

After being gone for a while, the businessman returned and asked his servants for an accounting. The man with the five talents had earned five more, the man with the two, two more. The man with one talent had buried his because he was afraid of what his master would do to him in the event that he lost it. The first two were commended: "Well done, good and faithful servant." The third one was banished for wasting his talent by burying it.

A parable is a story with a deeper spiritual meaning. Jesus stated plainly that he was talking about the Kingdom of Heaven . . . His own journey to that far country and His return at an unstated time to ask an accounting of His own servants. In other words, what have we done with the talents God has given us, whether they are five, two, or only one?

Will His response be, "Well done, good and faithful servant"?

About Greatness
April 20

Have you ever really thought about greatness—what makes a man or a woman great? The financial empires they build? The wars they win? The money they make? The pinnacle in government they reach? The number of followers they have? The number of sporting events they win?

Jesus' disciples decided one day to be a little loftier in their thinking about the greatest . . . going beyond the greatest in the world. So they came to their Master posing this question: "*Who is the greatest in the kingdom of heaven?*" I wonder what sort of answer they expected. They were dumbfounded when Jesus, seeing a little child in the crowd, called the youngster over to Him and had him or her stand among the disciples. Then He said to His followers: "*I tell you the truth, unless you change and become like little children, you will never enter the kingdom of heaven. Therefore, whoever humbles himself like this child is the greatest in the kingdom of heaven*" (Matthew 18:3, 4).

Greatness is not found in the questions I asked at the onset about the world's famous, but it is found in loving service to others. As Jesus Himself said on another occasion: "*The greatest among you will be your servant.*"

"Just Not My Day"
April 21

Have you ever had "one of those days"—one of those days when everything seems to go wrong? I'm sure you've had them. We all do. To help us through those days, we need to look to a well-known verse that has also become a well-known chorus sung in Christian circles—Psalm 118:24: *"This is the day that the LORD has made; let us rejoice and be glad in it."*

Every day we live is a gift from God, a very special gift for seniors and even for senior seniors. Sometimes we wonder about the value of the gift when our bones ache and our bodies are tired and weary. We may feel low and remark, "It's just not my day." We need to think of each day as God's day—His very special gift to us, and then we will likely have a totally different attitude.

First, our grumbling turns to gratitude just for the rich privilege of being alive. *"The heavens declare the glory of God,"* the Psalmist sings in Psalm 19. *"The skies proclaim the work of his hands. Day after day they pour forth speech; night after night they display knowledge."* Then there comes the knowledge of God's promised and continuous care. Again the Psalmist in Psalm 27:5 says, *"In the day of trouble he will keep me safe in his dwelling; he will hide me in the shelter of his tabernacle and set me high upon a rock."*

What about the future? Just a few verses later in Psalm 27 is this assurance: *"I am still confident of this: I will see the goodness of the LORD in the land of the living. Wait for the LORD; be strong and take heart and wait for the LORD."*

Every day is God's day, a day in which to be thankful, a day when we sense His love and care, a day of confidence as we look ahead.

Mary Magdalene
April 22

Piecing the various accounts of the resurrection of Jesus together, it seems almost certain that Mary Magdalene was the very first person to see the risen Savior. Mary had come out very early in the morning, along with some other women, to anoint Jesus' body with spices. She saw as she entered the tomb that the body was gone. She no doubt was overcome with fear and confusion, as looking into the empty tomb there were now two angelic figures seated where the body of Jesus had been. When they asked her why she was crying, she replied, "They have taken my Lord away, and I don't know where they have put him."

Turning around, she saw through her tears the figure of a man she took to be the gardener. When he too asked why she was weeping and who she was looking for, Mary simply asked , *"Sir, if you have carried him away, tell me where you have put him, and I will get him"* (John 20:15b).

The man she thought was the gardener said one word, *"Mary,"* and her whole world was changed completely. Her Lord and Master was alive, and she fell at His feet in humble adoration.

What a difference a day makes . . . or two! Two days before, she, two other Marys, and the apostle John had been at the foot of the cross watching Jesus dying. His body had been placed in a newly-hewn tomb and a massive stone rolled in front of the opening; on it was the seal of Rome—not to be broken. A guard was set to watch. Now the seal was broken, the stone was rolled away, and the guard was gone. Here He was . . . alive! And Mary too came alive. All the Scriptures tell us about Mary is that Magdala was her hometown and that Jesus had performed a miracle in her life earlier in His ministry, casting out seven devils. What those devils were—some mental condition perhaps—is not known, but Mary had become a new person and a close follower of Jesus.

Now here He was, having defeated death and the grave, paving the way for all to be redeemed and gain eternal life. To Mary Magdalene that first Easter morning, the resurrection was a glorious reality, and she too was alive in Christ. May it be so to us this very day.

Pass It
April 23

Wayne Gretzky is, arguably, the best player to ever lace up a pair of hockey skates. He holds many NHL records, some of which will likely never be broken. He is quoted as saying, "You'll never catch me bragging about goals, but I'll talk all you want about my assists."[4]

Gretzky, you see, is a team player, not really concerned about personal glory.

In the "game" of life, team playing is of vital importance. That was God's original purpose for humankind. A long time ago, the Psalmist put it this way in the *"God sets the solitary in families."* KJV It is the will of God that the family (the team) be the basis of society. That is why the breakdown of that essential unit, the family, is so hazardous in our time. That is why the motto of so many individuals, "Do your own thing," has become so tragic. Rather, writes Paul in Philippians 2:3, *"Do nothing out of selfish ambition or vain conceit, but in humility consider others better than yourselves."* And Peter adds: *"Show proper respect to everyone: Love the brotherhood of believers"* (1 Peter 2:17a,b).

When Jesus began His ministry, He chose a team of twelve who were with Him almost constantly. When that group dared to ask who was the greatest in the Kingdom of Heaven, Jesus brought them to task with a jolt by calling a little child into their midst and chiding them: *"And he said: 'I tell you the truth, unless you change and become like little children, you will never enter the kingdom of heaven.'"* Be humble team players.

A four-person team is more than 1+1+1+1. That's the mathematical total. The human total is far greater, for not only do you have the total of four individual strengths, but each member of the team picks up extra strengths from the others, and good teamwork results.

It doesn't really matter who scores the goal. All achieve it.

False Hopes
April 24

Sometimes when we try some new gadget or buy some replacement product, we find that it doesn't do the job it was supposed to do or not nearly as well as we were led to expect.

Some young people and some not so young are enticed by the promise of a new high if they try some exotic substance or other, only to be disappointed or worse—"hooked"—in the process.

Helmut Thielicke, the well-known German Theologian, tells of how as a boy he was on a cycling tour of southern Germany. One morning he had started out without breakfast and about mid-morning was delighted when he came upon a shop that had a sign reading "Hot Rolls." He entered the shop with his mouth watering, only to find out the shop sold no rolls but was a print shop. The sign was an example of the lettering they could do.

False hopes. The prophet Jeremiah had something to say about that. Jeremiah lived during the subjection of Jerusalem in 609 BC, its capture in 598 BC, and its destruction eleven years later. Jeremiah's nation of Judah based their foreign policy on the expediency of the moment rather than on the will of God and paid a terrible price. First, they paid tribute to Egypt, but when Nebuchadnezzar defeated that country, Palestine fell to the Babylonians. In chapter 23 of the book that bears his name, Jeremiah, writing with a truly prophetic voice (not long before his people became subject to Babylon), warned his nation of their danger. He was particularly incensed that certain false prophets had surfaced, telling the people that everything was going to be okay. Not so, he said, and then wrote: *"This is what the LORD Almighty says: 'Do not listen to what the prophets* [the false prophets] *are prophesying to you; they fill you with false hopes.'"* (Jeremiah 23:16a).

Some in our world would say that the prospects for peace among nations were never better. One hopes they are right. False hopes? We don't know. Voices are heard, saying that we in the Western world can work our way out of our terrible indebtedness and that all our problems are solvable. Again, we truly hope so. We trust that, when looking for hot rolls, we find a bakery and not a sign shop. God's Word offers that hope through the bread of life.

Where Is God?
April 25

The cathedral in the German city of Cologne is a very impressive structure. During the rule of Adolph Hitler, the cathedral became secretly known among Jewish fugitives as a place of refuge. Someone tells of a message that was left etched in the wall by a hunted Jewish refugee. It read: "I believe in the dawn, even though it be dark. I believe in God, even though He be silent."

Ask the man or woman on the street if they would have God take an interest in their activities, and the answer would likely be a resounding "No." The only time most want any interference from the Almighty in human activities is when they run into trouble. Then they may ask, "Where is God?"

We sometimes wonder where God is when there are wars, insurrections, kidnappings, or violent crimes taking place in our area of the world. Some say, "Why does God allow these things to happen?" It's strange, but the ones who ask the question "Where is God?" are usually the ones who have little to do with Him at any other time. God doesn't just jump into our world at every foolish misstep we humans make. He's given us a beautiful world, and He has given us both the brains and the free will to choose. Then He has laid down the rules and the means that make for abundant living. Unfortunately, ever since our first parents broke those rules and rebelled against their Creator, most who have followed in the human race have been similar rebels; their rebellion results in harmful consequences for themselves and in many cases for innocent bystanders.

Sometimes it seems that God has been silent . . . but He has not. He has spoken in history through His prophets and again most forcefully at Calvary and the empty tomb. The apostle Peter had both the teaching of the Old Testament prophets and the salvation offered to us today—both personally and corporately—when he wrote in his second epistle, verse 19: *"We have the word of the prophets made more certain, and you will do well to pay attention to it, as to a light shining in a dark place, until the day dawns and the morning star rises in your hearts."*

Our Legacy
April 26

Have you ever thought about what kind of legacy or inheritance you will leave at the end of a long and meaningful life? I'm not talking about the dollars we leave—that may or may not be essential to those who receive it, but I mean the real legacy of our lives. I mean the things we have accomplished and even more important—the loving, the caring, and the memories that follow us.

The famous Dutch painter Rembrandt in his early life had some great successes. Like many artists, Rembrandt didn't manage his money very wisely. Following a slump in the art market, he had to declare bankruptcy. His personal life continued to be marked with misfortune and sorrow. Many felt that Rembrandt was a failure. Hardly. His legacy, appreciated by the whole world, was a rich one—priceless paintings spread throughout the globe. You never know what a remarkable legacy you may be leaving.

Elijah was one of the greatest prophets of the Old Testament. A bulwark against foreign idols in his own land of Israel, he was pitted against four hundred prophets of the false gods. In a test between the two sides, Elijah, with God's help, triumphed. For this endeavor, Elijah had to flee for his life from a vengeful Queen Jezebel but was soon back performing a number of remarkable miracles.

Coming toward the latter years of his life, Elijah was guided by God's spirit to select a young man, Elisha, to succeed him. On the day when God was to take Elijah to his heavenly home in a direct manner, differing from the way most of us go into eternity, Elijah said to the young Elisha, *"Tell me, what can I do for you?"*

Elisha asked for a remarkable legacy. *"Let me inherit a double portion of your spirit"* (2 Kings 2:9b). That legacy was his, and Elisha became about as great as his mentor.

I wonder what sort of legacy we are leaving. Would even a double portion of my spirit be of much worth?

Changing the Course of History
April 27

Early in the fifth century, in the Coliseum of Rome, seventy-five thousand people were assembled with their Emperor to watch the gore and violence of fighting gladiators. As the gladiators took their places that day, suddenly a man jumped into the center of the ring and cried, "In the name of Christ, forbear!" There was a growl from the crowd, then a roar—"Strike him down." There was a flash of a Roman sword, and the man, named Telemachus, lay bleeding on the ground.

Slowly, one by one, then ten by ten, then by hundreds, then by thousands, they filed silently from the arena. History records that as the last time the gladiator contests were held in Rome. One man had changed the course of history. Today on the spot where Telamachus died, there is a simple wooden cross bearing these words: "In the spirit of this Cross lies the hope of the world."

The cross changed world history forever. Even the secular world recognizes that fact as evidenced in the designation of the millennia as BC (before Christ) and those after as AD (Anno Domini - the Year of Our Lord). The cross on which Christ died, on "Good Friday" as we call it, is the watershed of history. Before Christ, a searching God sought the prophets, priests, and kings to reach His fallen people. When these failed, He sent His Son. He sent Him to die for you and for me.

The book of Hebrews, towards the end of the New Testament, has a verse that at first seems very strange. *"Let us fix our eyes on Jesus, the author and perfecter of our faith, who for the joy set before him endured the cross, scorning its shame"* (Hebrews 12:2).

Joy? One senses anything but joy in contemplating that excruciating experience—condemned as a common criminal to die probably the most terrible death devised by the fiendish mind of mankind and, far beyond that, to bear your sins and mine. To the mind and compassionate heart of the Son of God, that last pain—bearing our sins and guilt—was the cause for His deep joy. That's why the emblem marking the spot of the martyrdom of Telemachus is so eternally true. "In the spirit of this Cross lies the hope of the world."

Seniors with Experience
April 28

Edward Gibbon, the famous British historian, is well-known for his work, *The Decline and Fall of the Roman Empire*. Appearing in six large volumes over the years 1776 to 1783, Gibson's massive record of the fading years of the Roman Empire was widely acclaimed immediately and retains its popularity even today. Here are his five main reasons for Rome's collapse.

1. The rapid increase of divorce; the undermining of the dignity and sanctity of the home, which is the basis of human society.

2. Higher and higher taxes and the spending of public monies for free bread and circuses for the populace.

3. The mad craze for pleasure; sports becoming every year more exciting and more brutal.

4. The building of gigantic armaments when the real enemy was within, the decadence of the people.

5. The decay of religion—faith fading into mere form, losing touch with life and becoming impotent to warn and guide the people."[5]

In view of the well-known adage that "History repeats itself," do you recognize any dangers?

My favorite definition of senior citizens is "travelers who have been a little longer on the road." In most areas of life, experience is considered to be of exceptional value. That's why we seniors cannot really claim, as so many do, that we don't have much to offer at this stage of life. As a matter of fact, we all have—a great deal. If a young person wants to go fishing, he/she would be wise to look for an experienced fishing partner. If a young person wants to know about cooking, he/she would be wise to locate an experienced cook.

We've lived in a time when the unbroken home was central to society, a time when government debt was non existent or modest, a time when free anything to our citizenry was very limited, a time when at least one day a week was free from mad craziness, a time when religion was considered a clear guide for morality and life in general. Those days are gone. Is Western civilization fading?

At a dangerous time in the nation of Israel's history, recorded in the Old Testament, God called an experienced man, Ezekiel, to be His spokesman, His prophet. This was a major part of that call: *"Son of man, I have made you a watchman . . . so hear the word I speak and give them warning from me"* (Ezekiel 3:17). A watchman is simply a person who sounds a warning. With our background and experience, quite a few perceptive seniors could perform that role.

Naomi
April 29

The story of Naomi is captivating. The time is about 1000 BC. There was a serious famine in the land of Israel. Naomi, along with her husband and sons, was forced to move into the nearby land of Moab to secure food. While there, Naomi's two sons married Moabite girls, Ruth and Orpah. Seemingly, tragedy dogged Naomi's footsteps. Early in their sojourn in Moab, Elimelech, Naomi's husband, died and she was left a widow. After they had been in Moab for some ten years, both sons died.

Naomi, with her two daughters-in-law as her only connection in Moab, decided she must return to her home in Bethlehem, where the famine was now over. Both daughters-in-law said they would go with her, and they started out. Soon, however, Naomi realized that while she would be returning home, Ruth and Orpah would be strangers in a foreign land, and she strongly urged them to go back to their homes in Moab. Finally and reluctantly, Orpah agreed and prepared to go back to Moab, but Ruth insisted on going on with Naomi. Her words have become famous in literature:

> *Where you go I will go, and where you stay I will stay. Your people will be my people and your God my God. Where you die I will die, and there will I be buried. May the LORD deal with me, be it ever so severely, if anything but death separates you and me*

(Ruth 1:16b–17).

So Naomi, the woman who inspired such devotion, took Ruth back with her to Bethlehem and a new beginning. The full story goes on at length in the book of Ruth. Naomi had an influence in Ruth's remarriage to a splendid, Godly man. As the book closes, Naomi is seen satisfied and comfortable, holding and cuddling little Obed, Ruth's firstborn son, in her lap.

You may feel a special sense of kinship with Naomi, for some of the aspects of your life may seem to parallel some of hers. However, my prayer would be that the difficulties in your life will also fade into the background as you think of the many ways God has blessed and the many times His hand has been upon your life. May those blessings continue as you too mark these later years.

Ruth
April 30

Complementing the story of Naomi expressed in yesterday's devotion is the story of Ruth. Soon after arriving in Bethlehem, Ruth secured what many would deem a menial position, that of gleaner. It was a dirty, backbreaking job, picking up the leftover grain after the harvesters had scoured the fields. However, Naomi's God was in it. The field where Ruth gleaned belonged to Boaz, a wealthy relative of Naomi's deceased husband. Boaz learned of Ruth's situation and invited her to have lunch with his harvesters. Later, he told those same harvesters to drop some stalks of grain purposely along the rows where Ruth was gleaning.

Eventually, Boaz learned that according to Hebrew law, he, as a relative of Naomi's, had a responsibility to the younger woman. To shorten the story, he married the girl. Thus, Boaz was the father of Obed, the little boy Naomi was cuddling as the book of Ruth ends. Obed became the father of Jessie, and Jessie the father of Israel's great King David.

Now fast forward to the birth of Jesus. Matthew chapter one begins with a very long genealogy. Most genealogies don't make very interesting reading, and we skip them. But listen to the very first verse of the chapter: "*A record of the genealogy of Jesus Christ the son of David, the son of Abraham.*" And further on in verse five, we read this: "*Salmon the father of Boaz, whose mother was Rahab, Boaz the father of Obed, whose mother was Ruth, Obed the father of Jesse, and Jesse the father of King David.*" And far down at the end of the long list, we find these words: "*And Jacob the father of Joseph, the husband of Mary, of whom was born Jesus, who was called Christ.*"

Humanly speaking, Boaz and Ruth were a part of the long line God used to usher His Son into the world a thousand years later.

God blessed Naomi, Ruth, Boaz, and a baby boy . . . and through them to Jesus . . . and rich blessings to us this very day.

A Fine Honor
May 01

I happened to be watching TV when Billy Graham was presented the Congressional Gold Medal (the United States' highest civilian decoration) for leadership in the areas of faith, morality, and clarity. During a life in the ministry that has spanned many decades, Dr. Graham has spoken to millions of people around the globe. Speaking of his life, a news commentator used two very special words: integrity and humility. These are the marks of a great man, one honored for character traits the world seldom regards: integrity and humility.

A person of integrity is one of whole, unbroken character—completely upright, completely honest, and completely sound.

The author of Proverbs has quite a bit to say about integrity in various chapters: *"The integrity of the upright guides them; Righteousness guards the man of integrity; The man of integrity walks securely."* The suffering Job said to his doubting friends: *"Till I die, I will not deny my integrity"* (Job 27:5b).

Humility. I think humility is especially difficult these days as the whole mythology of the times points to the macho man and the overpowering woman. Pride is the order of the day . . . not humility. Peter had this to say: *"Clothe yourselves with humility toward one another, because,* [and Peter quotes one of the Proverbs] *God opposes the proud but gives grace to the humble"*

(1 Peter 5:5). Jesus Himself said, *"Take my yoke upon you and learn from me, for I am gentle and humble in heart, and you will find rest for your souls"* (Matthew 11:29).

Integrity and humility—two of life's finest qualities, whether exhibited by Godly people of the Bible, by our Lord and Savior, or by those of us who try to live by His message.

Growing, Though Weary
May 02

How should we measure our spiritual growth? Sometimes we may feel that we are not growing fast enough spiritually, especially new adult Christians. Spiritual growth is best measured not by a great jump and then a lull of years, but by slower, steadier growth and maturity. William James Linton has a little poem he calls "Patience" that concerns growth. Here is the first verse:

> Be patient, O be patient! Put your ear against the earth;
>
> Listen there how noiselessly the germ o' the seed has birth;
>
> How noiselessly and gently it upheaves its little way
>
> Till it parts the scarcely-broken ground, and the blade stands up in the day.[1]

The apostle Paul begins his second letter to the Christians at Thessalonica in this vein: "*We ought to thank God for you brothers, and rightly so, because your faith is growing more and more, and the love every one of you has for each other is increasing*" (2 Thessalonians 1:3).

One of the problems of growth, both natural and spiritual, is a lack of sustaining food and moisture, without which any growth withers. The book of Job in the Old Testament refers to that very situation in chapter 8, verses 11-13. "*Can papyrus grow tall where there is no marsh? Can reeds thrive without water? While still growing and uncut, they wither more quickly than grass. Such is the destiny of all who forget God; so perishes the hope of the godless.*"

We all want to grow spiritually, whether we are young or old. The secret of that progressive growth is not in fits and starts, but it is to keep close to God through regular prayer and Bible reading.

However, as seniors we may feel weary, even in well doing. What then is the answer for us? Isaiah 40:29 answers that question, "*He* [God] *gives strength to the weary and increases the power of the weak.*" We will continue to grow—until one day we shall be like Him.

How are we measuring up?

"Songs of Praise"
May 03

Concerning the book of Psalms—perhaps the most loved book of the Old Testament— someone has said, "Every Psalm (is) a draft from the very fountain of life." The Hebrew meaning of the word Psalms is "Songs of Praise," and the beautiful and meaningful poetry, set to music, was an essential part of ancient worship. Indeed, the first hymns in our own language were selected Psalms set to music.

The preeminent Psalm writer, of course, was the nation of Israel's greatest king—David. David did not come to the throne by the usual route of succession. He was not from a royal family; he was the youngest of the eight sons of Jesse. He was a simple shepherd boy, tending his father's flock on Bethlehem's hills, when God's prophet anointed him in God's name for a future task entirely unknown to him or his family. His life thereafter was a series of ups and downs . . . from his slaying of the giant Goliath to many flights for his very life, until finally he was crowned. Even then, serious sin entered his life, but he found forgiveness. One of his beloved sons raised a rebellion against him, but it sputtered out.

Out of these up and down experiences of life and guided by the eternal hand, David wrote many Psalms. The Psalms speak to us in many life situations . . . even today.

> *O Lord, for I call to you all day long. Bring joy to your servant,*
> *for to you, O Lord, I lift up my soul. You are forgiving and good,*
> *O Lord, abounding in love to all who call to you. Hear my prayer,*
> *O LORD; listen to my cry for mercy. In the day of trouble I*
> *will call to you, for you will answer me*

(Psalm 86: 3b–7).

Obstacles
May 04

You may have had the sometimes—discomforting experience of driving through the forest on a rough rural road, only to be stopped—completely stopped—by a large tree fallen across the road. American poet Robert Frost even wrote a whole poem about it called "On a Tree Fallen Across the Road." The experience Frost writes about took place in the winter—not in a warm car, but with a horse and sleigh. The poem is not really about a tree, but about overcoming life's obstacles.

Seniors know a great deal about obstacles. As we get older, we are not so inclined as the rest of society to barrel along life's highways. We do, or should, take time "to stop and smell the roses" and reflect on the whole of life's journey, not just to focus on the obstacles in our way.

The good news from God is that you don't have to face those obstacles alone. In one of David's greatest Psalms, the Psalmist is very sure of that . . . God is with him at all times, especially when there are obstacles, difficulties along the way. In Psalm 27:5, David says this:

"*For in the time of trouble he shall hide me in his pavilion: in the secret of his tabernacle shall he hide me; he shall set me up upon a rock.*" And the following well-known assurance comes from Psalm 46: "*God is our refuge and strength, a very present help in trouble.*"

Memories
May 05

According to an ancient Greek legend, a woman came down to the River Styx to be ferried across to the place of departed spirits. The ferryman, Charon, reminded her that it was her privilege to drink of the waters of Lethe to allow her to forget the life she was leaving. Eagerly she said, "I will forget how I have suffered."

"And," added Charon, "remember too that you will forget how you have rejoiced."

"Well, I also shall forget my failures," the woman said.

"And your victories," Charon added.

She continued, "I will forget how I have been hated."

"And how you have been loved," replied Charon.[2]

The woman then paused to reconsider the whole matter. She decided not to drink the water, preferring to retain even memories of sorrow and failure, rather than give up memories of life's loves and joys.

Those who have placed their faith in Jesus have already made that choice. Proverbs 10:7 in the King James Version of the Bible tells us: *"The memory of the just is blessed."* This is true both for the memories held by the just one (himself or herself) and the memories left behind. Failures are canceled. Successes become living memories. God forgives His children. As for sins of the just (and we are all sinners ... some saved by God's grace), the Psalmist writes: *"As far as the east is from the west, so far has he removed our transgressions from us"* (Psalm 103:12).

Paul quotes the Psalmist, David, in Romans 4:7a: *"Blessed are they whose transgressions are forgiven."*

Their lives are crammed with gratifying memories.

New Opportunities
May 06

Those of you who have been business secretaries or stenographers during your vocational careers may be familiar with the Pitman system of shorthand. With the later invention of the Dictaphone and more recently the use of various devices with the computer, the Pitman system of shorthand has faded from view.

Isaac Pitman, just twenty-four at the time, invented the Pitman shorthand system in 1837. He had already been fired from one teaching position. Undeterred, he went on to open a private school, where, among other subjects, he taught a system of shorthand invented by Samuel Taylor. Later on of course, he developed his own system of shorthand. He became so successful at what he was doing that Queen Victoria knighted him in 1894 for his contributions to education and business. If Isaac Pitman had not been fired from that teaching position, the world might never have learned of Pitman shorthand.

Losing your means of livelihood can be a devastating experience. Sometimes God speaks to us through the closing (and opening) of doors. The obstacles that appear along life's roadway may become either stumbling blocks or stepping stones.

In his marvelous Sermon on the Mount in the book of Matthew, Jesus indicated that we should not sit idly by, expecting God to open a door of opportunity for us.

"'Ask,' Jesus said, 'and it will be given to you; seek and you will find; knock and the door will be opened to you. For everyone who asks receives; he who seeks finds; and to him who knocks, the door will be opened'" (Matthew 7:7-8).

God expects us to ask. New opportunities are not only for the young. God can open new opportunities for those of us who are older. He can open new opportunities for older folks to serve one another. Life continues to be worthwhile, and our lives can be a real blessing.

True Freedom
May 07

Throughout the years, the Christian church has been a stalwart defender of spiritual truth and moral freedom. The Christian church cherishes and strives for, even suffers for, the freedom that her Master proclaimed and died for.

The significant basis for freedom of all humankind is the fact that we are all created in the image of God as thinking, feeling, and willing parts of His creation. No one has the right to enslave any fellow member of that creation.

When Moses, called to be the deliverer after his people had suffered centuries of enslavement in Egypt, appeared before Pharaoh, his call to that ruler was crystal clear, "God says, 'Let my people go.'" That call for freedom echoes down the long avenue of the ages. "Let my people go! Let them be free!"

Looking forward to the coming of freedom through the Messiah, the prophet Isaiah penned these words many centuries before His coming.

"The Spirit of the Sovereign LORD is on me, because the LORD has anointed me to preach good news to the poor. He has sent me to bind up the broken-hearted, to proclaim freedom for the captives and release from darkness for the prisoners" (Isaiah 61:1).

Jesus quoted those words in the synagogue at Nazareth at the very first of His ministry, adding, *"Today this scripture is fulfilled in your hearing"* (Luke 4:21).

His message even today is one of freedom—freedom of spirit, freedom from sin and guilt, freedom of conscience. *"You will know the truth, and the truth will set you free"* (John 8:32).

Later Jesus added, *"If the Son sets you free, you will be free indeed"* (John 8:36).

Free to live life to the full.

That's the freedom Christ's church seeks for all men and women everywhere. And freedom to make that choice.

Just Ask
May 08

Much of children's learning comes from their inquiring minds: they ask a lot of questions.

With at least some of us, as we get older our inquisitive streak becomes a little more "streaky" and less focused. Yet there is an area of life in which our asking should grow.

"Ask and it will be given to you," Jesus said pointedly. To His followers, Jesus also said, *"If you remain in me and my words remain in you, ask whatever you wish, and it will be given you"* (John 15:7).

Solomon, King David's son, had succeeded his father when God appeared to him in a dream and told him to, *"Ask for whatever you want me to give you"* (1 Kings 3:5b). Solomon could have asked for the wealth of the world, but he did not; he requested wisdom and discernment.

The New Testament author James says this: *"If any of you lacks wisdom, he should ask God, who gives generously to all without finding fault, and it will be given to him. But when he asks,* [James continues], *he must believe and not doubt, because he who doubts is like a wave of the sea, blown and tossed by the wind"* (James 1:5–6).

The apostle John writes this: *"Dear friends, if our hearts do not condemn us, we have confidence before God and receive from him anything we ask"* (1 John 3:21–22a). Then notice this final word from Jesus: *"Which of you, if his son asks for bread, will give him a stone? Or if he asks for fish, will give him a snake? If you, then, though you are evil, know how to give good gifts to your children, how much more will your Father in heaven give good gifts to those who ask him!"* (Matthew 7:9–11).

Perhaps we should always be like children in our inquisitiveness—to ask God what good things He has for us. Of course, make sure your heart is right.

God's Laugh
May 09

Looking at our world, particularly our Western world, one sometimes wonders what it would take to impress us. We've become rather blasé in our day. We can travel around our world very quickly in modern jets. We have computers that can store and reissue almost uncountable masses of information. We can beam TV broadcasts now to people in the billions. And we've even put a man on the moon.

One who is a little cynical might just ask the question, "So what?" I think such a thought was in the Psalmist's mind when he wrote the second Psalm. Whenever I read the fourth verse, it hits me right between the eyes. "*The One enthroned in heaven laughs . . .*" and I believe I know why. God is not laughing because the situation the Psalmist is describing is funny. On the contrary, it is tragic—the nations of the world gathering together against God. God's laugh is derisive, and He is showing us how absurd the hostility of the enemies of God is.

The wonders of God have become so commonplace, the visions of God so blurred, the call of God so indistinct, and the trappings of our world so compelling that we hardly look or listen for God any more.

The refrain of our God to Solomon after he had completed the building of the Temple goes this way:

> *If my people, who are called by my name, will humble themselves and pray and seek my face and turn from their wicked ways, then will I hear from heaven and will forgive their sin and will heal their land* (2 Chronicles 7:14).

May we and our world hear this loving invitation. God will not be ignored forever.

"Plumb Line over the City"
May 10

My wife and I traveled a small part of the cathedral circuit in the United Kingdom. One part of that trip that particularly stands out was the Cathedral at Coventry. Badly bombed in World War II, the Cathedral arouses in the visitor many emotions. A modern structure has been erected right alongside the starkly suggestive ruins. Thus, there is the artistic mingling of the old and new . . . a bold, bold wall hanging . . . a twisted iron cross among the still standing ruins . . . and a two word plea: "Father, Forgive." All of this was very poignant.

For me, however, the most impressive object was a sculptured micro-city, set up in a corner of the Cathedral, the gift of an American church. Over the perfectly formed city core, with its skyscrapers and a multitude of other buildings, hangs a carpenter's plumb, an instrument used to judge perpendiculars. Above it all is the inscription: "Plumb Line over the City."

The notion of using a plumb line as a measuring instrument of the judgment of peoples comes from the book of the prophet Amos. He was God's prophet to the Northern Kingdom of Israel, the last of their prophets, in fact, until that kingdom fell prey to Assyria, its people scattered everywhere. Just before this happened, Amos saw a vision in which God was holding a plumb line. Amos continued: "*This is what he [God] showed me: The Lord was standing by a wall that had been built true to plumb, with a plumb line in his hand. And the LORD asked me,*

'What do you see, Amos?' 'A plumb line,' I [Amos] replied. Then the Lord said, 'Look, I am setting a plumb line among my people Israel; I will spare them no longer'" (Amos 7:7–8). And God continues, telling of the destruction about to occur . . . because the Kingdom of Israel simply did not measure up to God's plumb line.

I wonder sometimes how God is judging our nation . . . our city or town. That is really the meaning of the micro–city in Coventry Cathedral with the plumb line hanging over it—our city.

How straight are we?

Ethics
May 11

Some years ago a cartoon appeared in the Regina Leader Post; the cartoonist was Gable. There was no title; the cartoon pictured an aging professor, complete with gown and mortarboard, seated in his university office poring over a book where the title was simply marked by one word: Ethics. The professor was alone, the door was closed. Lettered on the outside of the glass panel of the door were the words: "Department of Quaint, Fading Notions and Pre–20th Century Studies."[3] There was no one, not a soul, at the door....

The message was simple. Few were interested in ethics at the time of the printing of that cartoon. And it continues to be the case. Probably the simplest definition of ethics is "the basic principles of right action."

I can't remember ever reading the precise word ethics in any translation of the Bible, but God's Word has a great deal to say about ethical living, ethical conduct: what is right and what is wrong. The whole Bible is a volume concerning not only the way to salvation and eternal life, but also the way to live a right or righteous life in this world. The words right and righteous appear many hundreds of times throughout the Bible.

"Blessed are they who maintain justice," says the Psalmist in Psalms 106:3, *"who constantly do what is right."* Good ethics or right living should start early. *"Even a child is known by his actions,"* writes the author of Proverbs, adding, *"by whether his conduct is pure and right"* (Proverbs 20:11).

The prophets of the Old Testament often thunder their call for righteousness. Says Amos in Amos 5:24: *"Let justice roll on like a river, righteousness like a never-failing stream!"*

May our prayer be today that the world will turn once more in thought and action to ethical living and turn to the One who makes it possible.

Reading the Manual
May 12

How often in life we try to do things without reading the manual. We expect to understand things without reading the manual—whether it's trying to figure out how something works in our car or the function of some dial on the latest technological gadget.

The same is true of Christianity. We often try to understand it and apply it without reading the manual. If we expect to have a meaningful and fulfilling relationship with God, then we need to read from His Word.

After the nation of Israel had been freed from four hundred years of slavery in Egypt and had traveled in the wilderness for forty years and just before moving into their Promised Land, we find this incisive statement by Moses found in Deuteronomy 8:3b. It is important to all of us. *"Man does not live on bread alone but on every word that comes from the mouth of the LORD."* Complete fulfillment in life (and for eternity) truly comes when we recognize that we have spiritual as well as physical yearnings—and the former are greater.

The great Augustine stated it plainly— "Our hearts are restless until they find their rest in God."

One of the great thinkers of the twentieth century, Karl Barth, a great Swiss philosopher and theologian, was once asked by a student during a discussion period following a lecture: "Dr. Barth, what is the greatest theological thought that has ever crossed your mind?"

Karl Barth quietly responded: "Jesus loves me, this I know, for the Bible tells me so." The Bible is the manual for life and eternal life. Fulfilling life.

The Prodigal Son
May 13

One of the best-known parables of Jesus was that of the prodigal son. It is the story of a father and his two sons. The father was "comfortably fixed," as we would say. The younger son was a restless type who wanted everything now and not as an inheritance. He was brash enough to ask for his share of the inheritance, and the father gave it to him. You likely know the rest. The son blew the inheritance on "wild living." That was not the last time a prodigal son or daughter ended up broke.

At the same time, a severe famine had hit his new country, and the prodigal son was needy— even hungry. He secured a job, of sorts, with a local farmer who put him to work feeding pigs.

At this crisis point in his life, the young man finally came to his senses. Realizing he had made an utter failure of his life, he decided to eat some "humble pie." Not demanding or even expecting anything, he decided to return home as a very needy man and seek work as one of his father's servants.

He went home, and while he was still a long way off, the Scriptures tell us, his father spotted him. Compassionately, the father ran to his penitent son and threw his arms around him to welcome him back. The father told his servants to bring a fattened calf and kill it. *"Let's have a feast and celebrate. For this son of mine was dead and is alive again; he was lost and is found"* (Luke 15: 23–24).

The point of this parable is obvious . . . lovingly obvious. Jesus was teaching us about our Heavenly Father. Though we stray in headlong fashion and often come to a crisis as serious as did the prodigal son, our Heavenly Father waits with open arms to receive us, His penitent children. That's what repentance means, very simply.

"I tell you," said Jesus, *"there is rejoicing in the presence of the angels of God over one sinner who repents"* (Luke 15:10). The book of Hebrews adds in the fourth chapter, verse 16: *"Let us then approach the throne of grace* [i.e. an awaiting Heavenly Father] *with confidence, so that we may receive mercy and find grace to help us in our time of need."*

The Proper Son
May 14

As was pointed out in yesterday's devotion, the younger son took his inheritance, blew it, realized his failures, and humbly returned to the welcoming hands of his father. The father threw a party celebrating the young man's return. Everyone was celebrating—except one.

That would be the elder brother. We might call him "the proper son." He was out in the fields working hard, as always, when he found out his brother had returned and that his father was celebrating his safe return. Angry, the elder son refused to join the celebration. He vented to his father that for many years he had slaved for his father, yet his father hadn't even given him a goat. The elder son continued and declared that the younger son had squandered the father's property with prostitutes. He complained that despite this, the father had killed the fattened calf (i.e. the very best) in honor of the younger son's return.

We have to admit, in fairness, that the proper son had a point.

The father's reply was this: *"My son you are always with me, and everything I have is yours. But we had to celebrate and be glad, because this brother of yours was dead and is alive again; he was lost and is found"* (Luke 15:31–32).

Most of us are looking at the situation from a very human and even selfish point of view, while the father is looking at it through God's eyes.

There is a vast difference between justice and mercy.

If our Heavenly Father treated us from a justice point of view, every single soul would be lost. As God's Word says: *"For all have sinned and fall short of the glory of God."* In Peter's second epistle, chapter three and verse nine, the apostle writes: *"He [God] is patient with you, not wanting anyone to perish, but everyone to come to repentance."* James writes: *"Judgment without mercy will be shown to anyone who has not been merciful. Mercy triumphs over judgment!"* (James 2:13).

Mercy triumphs over judgment—as it does for all prodigal sons . . . and prodigal daughters.

When We Suffer

May 15

Suffering and sacrifice. Seniors know a lot about these two loaded words. We have experienced both, and some have experienced both to a great degree.

In the devotional book *Unto the Hills*, Billy Graham writes: "At the heart of our universe is a God who suffers in redemptive love. We experience more of His love when we suffer within an evil world. Someone has said that if one suffers without succeeding, he can be sure that the success will come in someone else's life. If he succeeds without suffering, he can be equally sure that someone has already suffered for him."[4]

In the twenty-second Psalm, verse 24, the Psalmist has a rather special word for those who suffer: "*For he [The Lord] has not despised or disdained the suffering of the afflicted one; he has not hidden his face from him but has listened to his cry for help.*" Then in Psalm 119:49–50 we find these words: "*Remember your word to your servant, for you have given me hope. My comfort in my suffering is this: Your promise preserves my life.*" Paul, in Romans 5, indicates that suffering is a valuable attribute of life. "*We also rejoice in our sufferings, because we know that suffering produces perseverance; perseverance, character; and character hope*" (Romans 5:3–4).

O.P. Clifford has written, "The altar of sacrifice is the touchstone of character."

I am sure that you have made sacrifices for your family, your loved ones, and your friends. If you and I have succeeded, we can be sure that someone else has made a sacrifice.

This brings us to the greatest sacrifice and the greatest suffering of all—that of our Savior, Jesus Christ, who came to this earth to give us a powerful demonstration as to how to live, who died on a cruel cross to make it possible, and who rose again to give us eternal life.

In Hebrews 9:27–28a, we have these words: "*Just as man is destined to die once, and after that to face judgment, so Christ was sacrificed once to take away the sins of many people.*"

His sacrifice means life to all who call upon Him—life eternal.

Life's Most Important Lesson
May 16

Author Dennis DeHaan once asked a centenarian he knew, "After living more than 100 years, what is the most important lesson you've learned in life?"

The lady paused, then answered with certainty, "Everything is from the Lord. 'Nothing in my hand I bring, simply to Thy cross I cling.' "[5]

Do you remember King David's testimony in the thirty-seventh Psalm? *"I was young,"* he writes, *"and now I am old, yet I have never seen the righteous forsaken or their children begging bread."* That's not the so-called "prosperity gospel" that we sometimes hear about, that goes something like this: "If you follow God, you are promised a comfortable future with very few risks." As the old, familiar song puts it, "God has not promised skies ever blue, flower-strewn pathways all the way through." But, as the Psalmist stated, *"I have never seen the righteous forsaken"* . . . and that is a reliable promise.

As the centenarian expressed it, "Everything is from the Lord." Agreeing with these words by the centenarian, the great apostle Paul makes this marvelous affirmation in Romans 8:28: *"We know that in all things [everything] God works for the good of those who love him, who have been called according to his purpose."*

The centenarian's second word is even more affirming. It's from an old, familiar hymn. The words "Nothing in my hand I bring, Simply to Thy cross I cling" are from the third verse of the beloved "Rock of Ages."

Suppose we were asked the same question as the centenarian: "What is the most important lesson you have learned in life?" I have a feeling there would be some marvelous answers.

A Consuming Passion
May 17

Many people in our modern world, especially in the Western hemisphere, greatly admire wealth and pleasure and ardently pursue one or both of them. Lao Tzu, the Chinese philosopher of the fifth century BC, has left a pearl of wisdom that touches on one very prevalent aspect of modern life. Twenty-five centuries ago he wrote, "It is wealth to be content."

The writer of Proverbs actually puts it this way. *"He who loves pleasure will become poor."*

There are two serious disappointments in life: never to get what you yearn for or to get it and find that it was empty and meaningless.

Jesus in the Sermon on the Mount stated it like this: *"Seek first his [God's] kingdom and his righteousness, and all these things will be given to you as well"* (Matthew 6:33). *"These things"* are the items of life which Jesus has been exploring—food, drink, and clothing—and I believe that in our day Jesus would add cars, houses, computers, vacations to exotic places, etc.

I think, somehow, that we appreciate these finer aspects of life in proportion to their importance in our lives. The pursuit of things can become such a consuming passion that even the wonders of God's world—the beauty of the rose or the beauty of a sunset—are waved into the background of our being.

The book of Ecclesiastes has a marvelous little word in the second chapter. *"To the man who pleases him, God gives wisdom, knowledge and happiness, but to the sinner he gives the task of gathering and storing up wealth to hand it over to the one who pleases God"* (Ecclesiastes 2:26).

An Encouraging Word
May 18

American artist Benjamin West is well-known by Canadians and others for his famous painting "The Death of Wolfe." One time in his boyhood, he decided he would paint his sister Sally and, using colored ink, made a huge mess. His mother picked up the sheet of paper with the crude strokes. "Why," she said, "It's Sally!" and stooped down and kissed the boy on the cheek. Thereafter, West would say, "My mother's kiss made me a painter."

We all appreciate encouragement, whether we are ten or many times that number. In the New Testament church described in the book of Acts, there is one man who seems to stand above all the others in this regard. His name was Barnabas. Even his name fits. Acts 4:36 points out that Barnabas means "son of encouragement," a name given him by the Apostles. Barnabas first appears on the New Testament pages as selling a field he owned and then giving all the proceeds into the common pot for mutual support. Next, he appears as an encourager of Saul of Tarsus who, after being the chief persecutor of Christians, became one of them when he met the risen Christ face to face on the Damascus Road. Later Saul returned to Jerusalem and tried to join the Christians there, but all were afraid of him until Barnabas took Saul to the apostles, telling them of Saul's transforming experience.

A good deal of the Barnabas philosophy of encouragement must have rubbed off on the great apostle, for in Romans 15 Paul writes: "*We who are strong ought to bear with the failings of the weak and not to please ourselves. Each of us should please* [or encourage] *his neighbor for his good, to build him up.*"

Your encouraging word will make someone's day—today, tomorrow and every tomorrow we have.

Walking the Right Way
May 19

There is a very beautiful walk along the edge of the cliffs at the oceanfront by Beacon Hill Park, in Victoria, B.C. I was striding along one day, alone, watching the ever-changing sea but not much else. A little man, traveling the other way, came up to me and excitedly mumbled something I had to ask him to repeat—I didn't get it. "Don't you see the rainbow?" he then spoke more loudly and clearly, and I had to confess I had not seen it. Then I added rather lamely, "I guess I was walking the wrong way." For meanwhile, I had looked around and there it was, God's gloriously multicolored promise to humankind, and I almost missed it.

Often we miss a lot in life, walking the wrong way or failing to look around us.

The Old Testament prophets, particularly Isaiah, often look on life as a pathway and upon us as travelers walking that path. Very frequently, the travelers are walking the wrong way. In chapter 65 of the book that bears his name, Isaiah writes of his own nation—speaking in God's name: "*I revealed myself to those who did not ask for me; I was found by those who did not seek me. To a nation that did not call on my name, I said, 'Here am I, here am I.' All day long I have held out my hands to an obstinate people, who walk in ways not good, pursuing their own imaginations*" (Isaiah 65:1-2).

Millions upon millions in our world are trudging upon life's way, similarly bound up in their own imaginings, their own agenda, so much so that they cannot even hear the voice of a loving Heavenly Father who offers forgiveness for sin, peace for warfare, and new life for old.

A Knock on the Door
May 20

I once read a very intriguing quotation attributed to Charles Lamb, the English author, poet, essayist, and critic. Said he, "Not many sounds in life, and I include all urban and rural sounds, exceed in interest a knock at the door."

Doesn't the thought pique your interest . . . tease your imagination? Our immediate response, of course, spoken or unspoken is, "Who's there?" In our mind there flashes a whole range of possibilities. We wonder if it is a neighbor, friend, relative, political campaigner, delivery person, total stranger, even a police officer, and many more possibilities. Then after that, "I wonder what he or she wants?" Many thoughts rush to your mind before you open the door.

Perhaps you know Holman Hunt's famous painting of Jesus standing alone before a closed door. Some might wonder why He just keeps standing there knocking—waiting. Why doesn't the artist show Jesus going in instead of waiting outside? Look closely at the painting, and you will discover that the artist hasn't painted a latch on the outside of the door. It's on the inside . . . and the door can only be opened from the inside. The painting was inspired, of course, by the well-known verse in Revelation 3, where Jesus issues this invitation: *"Here I am! I stand at the door and knock: If anyone hears my voice and opens the door, I will come in"* (Revelation 3:20).

As Charles Lamb put it, "Not many sounds in life exceed in interest a knock at the door"—especially the knock I just mentioned.

A Suffering, Singing Heart
May 21

What a thrill passed through the Western world when the Berlin wall was toppled and freedom came to East Berlin and East Germany—freedom from the debilitating grip of Communism.

At that time, National Geographic had a moving article on the almost immediate changes that were happening in both West and East Berlin. The article concluded with the story of a grandmother, Gertrude Scholze, who, with husband Johannes, lived in East Berlin.

She told the compelling story of how, only a few weeks before, she had been caught with 30 West German marks as she tried to cross the border to get some fresh fruit for her hospitalized husband. She was put in a room and questioned, later reporting: "After an hour I fainted, and they let me out. But other people have had bigger problems."

"Then," wrote the author of the article, "she pulled herself erect, eyes shining, and said, 'Remember, a heart that has never suffered is a heart that will never sing.'"[6]

I don't have any pat answer for the very evident problem of suffering and pain, nor do I know anyone who does. But I do know that out of the crucible of suffering have come some of humankind's most sublime benefits and many of the world's finest men, women, and children. I also know that a loving Heavenly Father does give healing, not always physical healing but, if we ask, healing of mind and soul—peace. I do know too that God Himself suffers and that Calvary was the pinnacle of that suffering. It was for you and for me.

As the apostle writes in 2 Corinthians 1: 3–5, *"Praise be to the God and Father of our Lord Jesus Christ, the Father of compassion and the God of all comfort, who comforts us in all our troubles . . . For just as the sufferings of Christ flow over into our lives, so also through Christ our comfort overflows."*

That's why through suffering, we can sing.

Blowing the Future
May 22

One afternoon while walking alone in a residential area, I happened to pass two young men who were chatting. As I came alongside, I couldn't help but overhear the young fellow in the car say loudly to his companion leaning against the car door on the outside, "I only live once. I'm going to blow it all now."

That young man had a philosophy of life that is very prevalent in our times. The young man's expressed philosophy, of course, revolved around the search for novelty, some new immediate thrill. But it's an old, frustrating search.

I am reminded of a Scripture in the seventeenth chapter of Acts, in which the Biblical record says of the Athenians of Paul's day: "*All the Athenians and the foreigners who lived there spent their time doing nothing but talking about and listening to the latest ideas*" (Acts 17:21). The old search for novelty.

Paul had arrived in Athens alone, having to flee for his life from Berea, leaving his co-workers behind. While he waited for them to catch up, he was not idle. He addressed the Jews of the city in their synagogue and the Greeks in the marketplace and Areopagus. Apparently, he did a little sightseeing around the beautiful city too . . . for he noticed around Athens a large number of inscriptions "to an unknown God," and taking that as his starting point, Paul told them of the loving God he did know—personally.

Somehow that's the message we have to share in our present world too. Many see nothing worthwhile ahead. The future is bleak.

Paul's word to the Athenians is just as relevant today, both for the young and old. After speaking of God's purposeful creation, both of the world and the men and women who inhabit it, the apostle concludes: "*God did this so that men would seek him and perhaps reach out for him and find him, though he is not far from each one of us. 'For in him we live and move and have our being'*" (Acts 17: 27–28a).

That's how you live, really live—not once, but eternally.

The Christian Citizen
May 23

I once heard a story about a couple that went to great lengths to exercise their citizenship. Great Britain was voting as to whether or not the nation should fully enter the partnership of the European Common Market, and a plebiscite was held in which voters had a very simple choice—to vote "yes" or "no." The couple had lived in London but, just before the plebiscite, moved. In order to vote, they had to return to their former home polling station, a long and costly trip. But return they did. One voted "yes," and the other "no."

Depending upon your point of view, that was either a demonstration of extraordinary civil responsibility or a singular exercise in futility. I suppose there's a third option—that despite many years of marriage, each didn't know the other's mind.

However, when you come right down to the bottom line, there was something just right about their demonstration of good citizenship.

Several New Testament references indicate that the Christian should be a good citizen and take his or her responsibility very seriously. "*It is necessary,*" writes the apostle Paul in Romans, "*to submit to the authorities . . . for the authorities are God's servants, who give their full time to governing. Give everyone what you owe him: If you owe taxes, pay taxes; if revenue, then revenue; if respect, then respect; if honor, then honor*" (Romans 13:5–7). The apostle Peter in his first epistle writes: "*Live as free men, but do not use your freedom as a cover-up for evil; live as servants of God. Show proper respect to everyone: Love the brotherhood of believers, fear God, honor the king*" (1 Peter 2:16–17).

A Roman garrison commander in Jerusalem saved Paul's life when a Jewish mob tried to lynch him. Later, standing before the commander, Paul was asked (as recorded in the twenty-second chapter of Acts), *"Are you a Roman citizen?"*

"Yes I am," Paul replied.

At his words, the commander wistfully commented, *"I had to pay a big price for my citizenship."*

"But I was born a citizen," Paul replied proudly.

You see, whether one votes "yes" or "no," being a Christian should make one a good Christian citizen.

The Dark Before the Dawn
May 24

You have heard it said that the older one gets, the quicker time flies or at least seems to fly. I believe that is true, but at times the opposite can happen, particularly when one is in pain or having some difficulties. We end up going through all the hours, minute by minute, and we wonder if "the dawn" will ever come. Life for some has gone this way. Some of you have gone through all those hours, minute by minute, second by second, and many have been long, aching hours. The extended hours of many dark nights have been particularly difficult.

David, the Psalmist, often had such dark nights of the soul. It was out of one of those dark experiences that he wrote Psalm 139. Here is part of it:

> *If I say, "Surely the darkness will hide me*
> *and the light become night around me,"*
> *even the darkness will not be dark to you;*
> *the night will shine like the day,*
> *for the darkness is as light to you*
>
> (*Psalm* 139:11–12).

Time does not stand still. We sometimes pass through the dark nights of the soul. Yet we are reminded that it was at dawn on the first day of the week that the resurrection occurred.

"*The path of the righteous,*" writes the author of Proverbs, "*is like the first gleam of dawn, shining ever brighter till the full light of day*" (Proverbs 4:18).

Dawn comes, and with it light, to shatter the darkness. God's clock keeps moving on inexorably, through each hour, each minute, and each second. With the break of each new dawn, He offers new hope, new vision, and new promise to all who will travel His way.

God's Handiwork
May 25

Perhaps the best-known Canadian poet of his generation, Bliss Carman passionately loved God's nature. This is particularly evident in his poem called "Vestigia." The first two verses are these.

> I took a day to search for God,
> And found Him not. But as I trod
> By rocky ledge, through woods untamed,
> Just where one scarlet lily flamed,
> I saw His footprint in the sod.

> Then suddenly, all unaware,
> Far off in the deep shadows, where
> A solitary Hermit Thrush
> Sang through the holy twilight hush—
> I heard His voice upon the air.[7]

The apostle Paul also uses the thought of man's recognition of God's handiwork in nature to prove that all people everywhere have that privilege. "*Since what may be known about God is plain to them [people], because God has made it plain to them [people]. For since the creation of the world God's invisible qualities—his eternal power and divine nature—have been clearly seen, being understood from what has been made so that men are without excuse*" (Romans 1:19–20).

In his famous address to the philosophers, the Stoics, the Epicureans, and others of the Greek Areopagus, the apostle added this thought: "*God did this so that men would seek him and perhaps reach out for him and find him, though he is not far from each one of us. For in him we live and move and have our being*" (Acts 17:27–28a).

So as with Bliss Carmen, we may find God through His handiwork in nature, but clearest of all through the Son He sent to show the Father's love. "*I have come*," said Jesus, "*that they may have life, and have it to the full*" (John 10:10b).

Twisting the Truth
May 26

Many of us are disturbed about the deteriorating attitude toward truth. Quite obviously, we live in a world that plays fast and loose with truth.

Looking down the avenue of the ages, the apostle Paul anticipated this when writing to his young co-worker Timothy. Paul says:

> *For the time will come when men will not put up with sound doctrine. Instead, to suit their own desires, they will gather around them a great number of teachers to say what their itching ears want to hear. They will turn their ears away from the truth and turn aside to myths* (2 Timothy 4:3–4).

It is tragic that some in our times, who presume to speak for God, twist the Truth in order to fit in with the world's agenda. According to their assumptions, wrong becomes right and right becomes wrong. All actions are relative . . . according to human standards, not God's. There are no absolutes. Myths have replaced the truth of God. Jesus Himself describes this dangerous situation very specifically. *"Whoever lives by the truth,"* He said, *"comes into the light, so that it may be seen plainly that what he has done has been done through God"* (John 3:21). The "light," of course, is the Word of God. That essentially is the litmus test of truth. Does what is being said or being done measure up to that standard . . . or is someone trying to appeal to the "itching ears" around him or her?

If we would really let the truth of God, uncensored and unchanged, live in us and through us out into the world, evil would soon be in retreat.

Dreams Die . . . Hope Brightens
May 27

One time while taking a bus to Vancouver, a young man, probably in his late twenties, was seated next to me. Very outgoing, he began to tell about his life in an open way. He said he was an unemployed carpenter but was preparing himself for the future, having come to Vancouver to take a course. He mentioned too that his wife was from the Vancouver area and said they were no longer living together; his wife had left him and had taken their two small children. And he missed them. I expressed my sympathy, remarking that such a situation, although common in our day, is never easy. "No," he said, "but I think I can handle almost anything." Then his voice softened, and he added wistfully, "I think facing death is easier." Dreams die hard.

Numbers of people, many of them young, have begun to realize that accumulation of all the items in the nearby mall complex will not bring satisfaction. Nor can they find it within. They are beginning to look outward, and out there one might find both hope and despair.

There is despair when you find out (and soon) that the world doesn't have many answers to your problems, and generally speaking, few are interested. "Doing your own thing" desensitizes you.

What about hope? The New Testament book of Hebrews gives us this assurance: "*We have this hope* [therefore in God] *as an anchor for the soul, firm and secure*" (Hebrews 6:19a)

The poet, Oliver Goldsmith, sees hope this way:

> Hope, like the gleaming taper's light
>
> Adorns and cheers our way;
>
> And still, as darker grows the night
>
> Emits a brighter ray.[8]

Hope in God is like that . . . a light in a dark place. You see, we can't handle most things alone.

On the Rails
May 28

Remember the classic children's story "The Little Red Engine"? The train is blissfully chugging along until it suddenly thinks it would be great to be free of the confining tracks. That craving for freedom became so great that the little engine left the tracks and headed for the wide blue yonder. However, as the little engine discovered things weren't what it had expected, it was soon bogged down with all its wheels churning. It realized that indeed, it was not free, and so by a Herculean effort, it managed somehow to get back on the tracks where, in real freedom, it cruised on and on as far as the tracks were laid.[9]

Human freedom is much like that. When we drop all restraints and claim the liberty to do as we please, we have accepted a recipe for disaster. An unknown sage has described this danger aptly. He writes: "There is no liberty in wrong-doing. It chains and fetters its victims as surely as effect and cause." Says the book of Romans, "*When you were slaves to sin, you were free from the control of righteousness*" (Romans 6:20). Or put another way, you were "off the rails." Romans continues: "*What benefit did you reap at that time from the things that you are now ashamed of? Those things result in death! But now that you have been set free from sin and have become slaves to God, the benefit you reap leads to holiness, and the result is eternal life*" (Romans 6: 21–22).

Then we find these words in Galatians 5:1: "*It is for freedom that Christ has set us free. Stand firm, then, and do not let yourselves be burdened again by a yoke of slavery.*"

There is freedom riding on God's rails.

For Others
May 29

One of the greatest attributes of the Christian faith is a concern for others. To a Jewish teacher who asked what the most important commandments were, the master responded: *"'Love the Lord your God with all your heart and with all your soul and with all your mind and with all your strength.' The second is this: 'Love your neighbor as yourself'. There is no commandment greater than these."* (Mark 12:30–31). When his questioner said further to Jesus that he agreed wholeheartedly with that assessment, Jesus replied to him in appreciation. *"You are not far from the Kingdom of God"* (Mark 12:34). Love your God and love your neighbor. Right next to our love for the Heavenly Father is our deep concern for others.

On the day our Lord was crucified, the passing mob hounded Him to come down from the cross. The hateful leaders mockingly said among themselves: "He saved others, but he can't save Himself." Had He saved Himself that day, others—you and I—would have been lost eternally.

That is why Paul was able to write the Christians at Philippi: *"Each of you should look not only to your own interests, but also to the interests of others. Your attitude should be the same as that of Christ Jesus"* (Philippians 2:4–5).

A Strong Tower
May 30

Hear my cry, O God;
listen to my prayer
From the ends of the earth I call to you,
I call as my heart grows faint;
Lead me to the rock that is higher than I.
For you have been my refuge,
a strong tower (Psalm 61:1–3).

The sixty-first Psalm is one of the many Psalms of David that reflect the dual feeling of changing from a mood, almost of despair, to one of supreme assurance. The background story of this Psalm gives sufficient cause for such despair. It was a very difficult time in the kingdom of Israel and Judah. Indeed rebellion had broken out against the king who had made the nation great—David. What made the rebellion so personally tragic for David was that none other than his beloved son, Absalom, led the revolt. David's faith was fully justified as the rebellion soon sputtered out.

David had some dark times along the way. So do we. Despite this season of growth and all the wondrous signs of nature, there are times when we feel down. Perhaps the past night has been not only dark, but dismal, and we have not slept. But through it all, we have One who is higher than us, who can be our refuge and strength.

Ambassadors for Christ
May 31

The name David Livingstone has been a household word in Christian circles for many, many years. Born in Scotland in 1840, he sailed for Africa as a missionary doctor. He soon became interested in exploration and explored large parts of Africa. Many feel that his activities and writings were largely responsible for the abolition of the slave traffic and for the opening of Africa to the rest of the world. Above all, he regarded himself as a missionary of Jesus Christ. He died while on his knees by the side of his African bed, at the age of sixty.

What would motivate a man like that? What would motivate a man to leave the security of his home to go into the far reaches of Africa? We can find the answer in God's word. When Jesus said: *"If anyone would come after me, he [she] must deny himself [herself] take up his [her] cross and follow me"* (Matthew 16:24). Livingstone took Him seriously, as have a host of men and women down through the ages.

The Great Commission is still the directive of our Master to every follower: *"Therefore go and make disciples of all nations, baptizing them in the name of the Father and of the Son and of the Holy Spirit and teaching them to obey everything I have commanded you. And surely I am with you always, to the very end of the age"* (Matthew 28:19–20).

Just as Jesus left them, He indicated the way to carry out this commission found in Acts 1:8b, " . . . *You will be my witnesses in Jerusalem, and in all Judaea and Samaria, and to the ends of the earth."*—first in your hometown, then in your home country, then in the neighboring countries, and finally throughout the whole wide world.

Adds the apostle Paul: *"We are therefore Christ's ambassadors"* (2 Corinthians 5:20a). That, in fact, means right where we are.

As an ambassador for the Master, yours is the world's highest calling.

A Scarecrow in a Melon Patch
June 01

It's hard to imagine a world without computers. The world's first general-purpose electronic computer, called ENIAC, was developed in 1946. The beast weighed thirty tons, contained eighteen thousand vacuum tubes, occupied a room thirty by fifty feet, and cost a fortune.

There are computers today with many thousand times more computing power than ENIAC, built at a fraction of the cost, and they can be held in one hand. There have been many wonderful scientific achievements in our lifetime, such as the development of the computer. Certainly there have been greater human attainments in our lifetime than in any other comparable period in history, and creature comforts are at their peak. I can remember my grandmother using a scrub-board, and dishwashers were a pair of hands. In every area of life, except one, our human advance has been breathtaking.

That one area is the spiritual. One senses that in this area we have not progressed, but we've lost ground. There has been a general discovery that all of the gadgets, all of the creature comforts, all of the fine inventions have not really increased our happiness.

Jeremiah, the very dynamic prophet, has said something that our modern world should note. He speaks to his people about the idol-worshipping peoples in the nations surrounding Israel. He warns of the utter uselessness of the gods they worship, fashioned out of a piece of wood, adorned with gold and silver. *"Like a scarecrow in a melon patch, their idols cannot speak; they must be carried because they cannot walk. Do not fear them; they can do no harm nor can they do any good"* (Jeremiah 10:5).

Occasionally, one gets the impression that some of the good things—the mechanical wonders of our day—are almost worshipped and have become the gods of our day. A scarecrow in the melon patch perhaps?

Love in Action
June 02

Kip Keino was one of Kenya's greatest Olympic athletes. He won Olympic gold twice, once in spectacular fashion. The bus transporting him to the fifteen hundred meter event at the 1968 Olympics in Mexico City was stuck in traffic. Kip jogged a mile to get to the stadium for his race. Kip won the race in Olympic record time. He won a second Olympic gold in the three thousand meter steeplechase at the 1972 Olympics in Munich, West Germany.

After he retired from track, Kip and his wife Phyllis purchased a farm that they converted into an orphanage. The Keinos have provided a home for many, many children. They come from all over Kenya and Uganda, from many different tribes. In 1996 in recognition of his efforts in helping people, Kip Keino was inducted into the World Sports Humanitarian Hall of Fame.

Kip and Phyllis have made a significant difference in the lives of others. That's love in action— the Golden Rule.

"*Religion that God our Father accepts as pure and faultless is this,*" writes James, "*to look after orphans and widows in their distress and to keep oneself from being polluted by the world.*"

The Master had this to say: "*Inasmuch as you have done it unto one of the least of these my brethren, you have done it unto me.*" And setting a child in the midst of His hearers, Jesus said: "*Whosoever shall receive one of such children in my name, receives me.*"

Bits of Time and Opportunity
June 03

Centuries ago lived a great mosaic artist who did outstanding work with pieces of glass and stone. He had in his employ a young lad whose main job was to clean up the floor and tidy the room. The quiet boy one day timidly asked his employer if he could have the bits of discarded glass. His employer consented, and slowly but surely over the course of years, the lad took the discarded pieces and compiled them into his own marvelous piece of art. His own master, on seeing the work, was taken aback and thought a fellow great artist had created the work.

There's a lesson in there for all of us. The bits of glass and stone were really bits of time and opportunity that the lad carefully selected and early in life turned into a mosaic masterpiece. Similarly, during a long lifetime, we have been gathering many, many of these bits and pieces. Some we have discarded for various reasons, but others will be the means of our fashioning a wonderful mosaic of life. Even now in the senior years, one has the opportunity to form such a mosaic of glorious colors. Jesus put it this way: *"As long as it is day, we must do the work of him who sent me. Night is coming, when no one can work"* (John 9:4).

"I have no talents," you say. To which the old New England minister, Cotton Mather, would reply, "Our opportunities to do good are our talents."

Let us make the most of our opportunities today.

Savior
June 04

If you and I were to use one word to sum up the life and service of Jesus, that word would be "Savior." He was described in many ways in the New Testament: Lord, Master, Son of God, Son of Man, Messiah, the Christ, and others. It was the name "Savior" by which He was and is best-known and for which he is best-loved by multi-millions past and present. Those who call Him Savior know that He has saved us—rescued us if you like—many, many times, not only once for all eternally, but on many, many occasions when we have slipped into difficulty . . . whether those difficulties were large or small.

Looking down the long avenue of the ages, many centuries before the coming of the Savior, the prophet Isaiah wrote: *"The LORD has made proclamation to the ends of the earth: 'Say to the Daughter of Zion, "See, your Savior comes! See, his reward is with him, and his recompense accompanies him."' They will be called The Holy People, the Redeemed of the LORD"* (Isaiah 62:11–12a). Then He was introduced to the world that first Christmas through the angelic message to a group of simple shepherds: *"The angel said to them, 'Do not be afraid. I bring you good news of great joy that we be for all the people. Today in the town of David a Savior has been born to you'"* (Luke 2:10–11a).

"I have come into the world as a light," Jesus said, *"so that no one who believes in me should stay in darkness"* (John 12:46). He also said: *"I have come that they [you] may have life, and have it to the full"* (John 10:10b).

That's rescue . . . by the Savior Himself.

For Ballplayers and Others
June 05

You baseball fans have likely heard of the famed Satchel Page. He was the fabulous black pitcher, with the smoking fastball, who didn't make it into the majors until he was in his fifties because of an earlier discriminatory rule barring black players. He was still smoking his high hard one when he was fifty-six. Something of a unique character, Satchel Page expressed an intriguing philosophy of life. Some of his advice was particularly pertinent for seniors:

> If your stomach disputes you, lie down and pacify it
> with cool thoughts.
>
> Keep the juices flowing by jangling around gently as you move.
>
> Don't look back. Something may be gaining on you.[1]

Despite the humorous presentation, the aged ballplayer has offered some points of excellent counsel. The notions of "cool thoughts" and moving "around gently" are particularly helpful—whether the problem is a stirred up tummy or some other disturbing pressures of daily living. We don't simply grow out of the worries of life as we get older. Indeed, unless we are careful, the worries seem to increase.

Jesus addressed the subject very directly: *"So do not worry, saying, 'What shall we eat?' or 'What shall we drink?' or 'What shall we wear?' For the pagans run after all these things, and your heavenly Father knows that you need them. But seek first his kingdom and his righteousness and all these things will be given to you as well"* (Matthew 6:31–33).

As to the advice to not look back, the apostle Paul had some reflections as he grew older when he said: *"Forgetting what is behind and straining toward what is ahead, I press on toward the goal to win the prize for which God has called me heavenward in Christ Jesus"* (Philippians 3:13b–14). Then he adds, *"And if on some point you think differently, that too God will make clear to you. Only let us live up to what we have already attained"* (Philippians 3:15b–16).

These are good points of view for older baseball players and for those simply on the course of life.

Noble Character
June 06

The book of Proverbs in the Old Testament is filled, as its name suggests, with brief Proverbs: short, concise gems of wisdom for daily living. The last 22 verses of chapter 31, the epilogue of the book, contain one of the finest tributes to women in literature. It specifically points to the wife of noble character:

> *She is worth far more than rubies. Her husband has full confidence in her and lacks nothing of value. She brings him good, not harm, all the days of her life. She selects wool and flax and works with eager hands . . . She is clothed with strength and dignity; she can laugh at the days to come.*

So continues the description. I would like to highlight and quote one other characteristic: *"She opens her arms to the poor and extends her hands to the needy."*

"Inasmuch," said Jesus to those who had given food to the hungry, drink to the thirsty, a home to the stranger, and love to the sick and imprisoned—*"Inasmuch as ye have done it unto one of the least of these my brethren, ye have done it unto me"* (Matthew 25:40 KJV).

Good counsel to noble women and men alike is given in these words. We can be God's answer to someone's prayer. And they to ours.

The Supreme Pearl
June 07

June is a fitting month to be talking about pearls. Those of you who were born in June would likely know why—because the pearl is the official birthstone of June.

The pearl has been a long-treasured gemstone. Pearls (real pearls) are expensive. The reason, of course, is that real pearls that develop naturally in oysters are rare. Cultured or imitation pearls are a much less expensive alternative.

Jesus, in one of the briefest of His parables, talked of one supremely valuable pearl—the most real of the real, of course, not just the cultured variety that would satisfy most of us. In fact, Jesus likened the Kingdom of Heaven to that exquisite pearl. He said: *"The kingdom of heaven is like a merchant looking for fine pearls. When he found one of great value, he went away and sold everything he had and bought it"* (Matthew 13:45-46).

For many years, commentators have called this little parable "the pearl of great price." In the ancient world, a pearl was considered one of the most precious of all possessions—not only for its value in terms of money but also for its rare beauty. Thus, merchants would search the earth for a pearl of surpassing beauty.

God's Kingdom has that sort of surpassing value; the wise person would willingly give up all that he or she has in order to possess it—to be part of that Kingdom. And that pearl is the most real of the real, not imitation.

The Eternal Dimension
June 08

Many neglect the eternal dimension of life. I say "neglect" because so many push the idea into the back of their minds. They go about the daily routine of their lives, paying little attention to their own mortality. However, you will notice the thought quickly becomes vitally important in times of great danger.

I was struck, for example, at the number of D-Day veterans who, when reminiscing, said openly that they prayed when the Allied forces invaded Normandy in World War II.

When one is thrown from a canoe into raging water and lives to tell about it or is surrounded by flame in a fire with seemingly no way out and lives to tell of the experience, inevitably the person involved will confess, "I prayed."

In the final year, the third year of Jesus' ministry, the vast throngs of people who followed Him everywhere began to thin out. They (many of them) had discovered that His Way included, besides healing and other miraculous benefits, a rigorous decision to follow all the way—even to a cross. As a good number began to disappear from the scene, the Master turned almost wistfully to His little band of twelve apostles, asking, "*'You do not want to leave too, do you?' Simon Peter answered him, 'Lord, to whom shall we go? You have the words of eternal life'*" (John 6:67–68).

That, you see, was the ultimate consideration. Immortality, eternal life, is not any man's to give . . . only God's.

Needed Pardon

June 09

From time to time, we hear of a head of state granting pardon to someone. Pardon is often associated with those who have committed some sort of crime. However, all of us are in need of forgiveness and pardon. That's a thought that falls on many unwilling ears in our times. Even the idea of sin and wrongdoing is not well received by many, though we increasingly read of evil and wrongdoing daily in our newspaper, or we see it daily on the news we watch on TV. Sin, we are told, is simply social maladjustment, and our environment is responsible. If what one does is not sin, then why worry about forgiveness?

God's Word sets the issue in proper perspective: *"For all have sinned and fall short of the glory of God"* (Romans 3:23). And in Romans, it is also written: *"There is no one righteous, not even one"* (Romans 3:10). Yet if God insists on calling the wrong that we do "sin" and holds us responsible for it, He also provides the answer: *"If we confess our sins, he [God] is faithful and just and will forgive us our sins and purify us from all unrighteousness. If we claim we have not sinned, we make him out to be a liar and his word has no place in our lives"* (1 John 1:9–10).

The Psalmist adds: *"As far as the east is from the west, so far has he [God] removed our transgressions from us"* (Psalm 103:12).

That's true pardon for sinners like you and like me.

We Matter

June 10

Sometimes when we think of the wonderful world around us, the glories of nature and the billions of people, not counting the untold billions of the past, we wonder where our value in God's scheme of things is.

David, the Psalmist, pondering this question, wrote in the eighth Psalm these now familiar words:

> *When I consider your heavens, the work of your fingers, the moon and the stars, which you have set in place, what is man that you are mindful of him, the son of man that you care for him? You made him a little lower than the heavenly beings and crowned him with glory and honor. You made him ruler over the work of your hands* (Psalm 8:3–6a).

Every one of us is of utmost importance in the eyes of our Heavenly Father. We are so important that He sent His Son to die on the cross to make forgiveness and new life open to us. Perhaps the little sparrow is the commonest of birds worldwide. Jesus said this about sparrows. *"Are not two sparrows sold for a penny?"* He asked. *"Yet not one of them will fall to the ground apart from the will of your Father . . . So don't be afraid; you are worth more than many sparrows"* (Matthew 10:29, 31).

The sparrows are all-important in God's scheme of things. However, they pale into insignificance as God looks at you, me, and every one of the men, women, boys, and girls He has made.

You and I really matter! We matter to God.

Reaching Out
June 11

Henri Dunant, Swiss businessman and humanitarian, was born into a wealthy family. He also achieved early success in business. During one of his attempts to further his business interests, he witnessed a bloody battle in Northern Italy and was shocked at the inhumane treatment wounded soldiers were receiving. He organized a band of helpers to attend to the wounded. He wrote of his thoughts and experiences in a book that became the inspiration for the creation of the International Committee of the Red Cross.

In his pursuit of humanitarian causes, Dunant neglected his own personal affairs and went bankrupt. He moved around to various locations and eventually settled in an Alpine village. When he became ill, he was moved to a hospice. The world ultimately rediscovered him and heaped prizes on him, including the Nobel Peace Prize in 1901. However, Dunant continued to live in his little room at the hospice and refused to spend the prize money he received, instead bequeathing it to help others.

"Freely you have received, freely give" was Jesus' principle of reaching out. *"Give,"* the Master also said, *"Give, and it will be given to you. A good measure, pressed down, shaken together and running over, will be poured into your lap"* (Luke 6:38a). Not literally, but you will receive the return gift of an immeasurable feeling of well-being and satisfaction.

The apostle Paul in the epistle to the Romans lists a number of the endowments God gives his children. One of them is the talent of giving to others. Writes the apostle, *"If it is contributing to the needs of others, let him* [her] *give generously"* (Romans 12:8b).

It is significant that the emblem of the work Henri Dunant founded is a cross—a red cross. For it was on a cross our Savior died—giving His life for ours.

Like Jesus
June 12

One year at the annual National Prayer Breakfast held in Washington, D.C., the story was told about a businessman who was trying to catch his commuter train. In trying to catch his train, he jostled and knocked over a crippled boy who was selling apples. He paused, looked at the boy, and then ran to catch his train. Another businessman, following closely behind, paused but then came back and assisted the boy in picking up his apples, also giving him five dollars. As he turned to leave, the boy grabbed him by the coat and asked, "Mister, are you Jesus?"

The crippled apple seller had obviously heard about the concern Jesus showed for folks like him, and so have we. The picture we have of Jesus is one of a man who was always reaching out to someone in need. A paralyzed man was lying on a mat when Jesus told him to take up his mat and go home, and he did. A boy undergoing regular, terrible seizures had one just before Jesus arrived, and he was lying on a roadway. Jesus lifted him up . . . healed. A woman was desperately ill with fever—again Jesus reached out to heal. A foreign mother, deeply disturbed at her daughter's mental condition, cried out to Jesus for help. The Scriptures tell us that the daughter was *"healed from that very hour."*

But the little apple-seller's question to his benefactor has a very disturbing element about it. Is there the possibility that some of the kinder things that you and I do just might remind someone of our Savior? Or do I rush on to catch the train?

"I am among you as one who serves," Jesus said. That too is our privilege.

Humble Men and Women
June 13

Strange as it may seem, many of the truly great men and women of the world have also been most humble. I don't mean by humble, a cowering, hesitating, overly bashful sort of a person. Humble means "modest, unassuming," and as such, it is a mark of the Christian.

Large manufacturers in the United States and in Europe, in deciding to locate their plants or mills in a certain area, have sometimes attracted workers to those areas by building model towns to provide accommodation and other facilities. One such model town was built in Yorkshire, England, in mid–nineteenth century and was named Saltaire.

Its builder was Sir Titus Salt, a worsted manufacturer whose family name the town bore. Salt had stone houses built for his workers. He built a hospital, school, library, etc. And the most impressive of all—a church.

The Salts had a family pew in a gallery at the church entrance. However, it is said that Titus Salt seldom used it, preferring to sit among the people.

"*I urge you to live a life worthy of the calling you have received,*" writes Paul to the Ephesian Christians, and he added, "*Be completely humble and gentle; be patient bearing with one another in love.*

In the following magnificent paragraph in the second chapter of Philippians, Paul describes the utter humility, the humbleness, of our Savior:

> *Who being in very nature God, did not consider equality with God something to be grasped, but made himself nothing, taking the very nature of a servant, being made in human likeness. And being found in appearance as a man, he humbled himself and became obedient to death—even death on a cross!*

May our prayer be "Lord, give me a servant heart . . . like my Master."

The Quality of Love
June 14

I had a very rewarding experience of studying, for a short time, under Dr. George A. Buttrick, one of the great preachers of North America. For twenty-eight years, Dr. Buttrick was minister of the famed Madison Avenue Presbyterian Church of New York.

On one occasion, he told of a lad who was caught stealing from cars parked outside Madison Avenue Church. A lady coming up Madison Avenue saw the boy caught between two police officers, trying to talk his way out of his predicament. Brandishing her umbrella, the good lady scolded the boy, pointing to the church and saying, "Why don't you come inside and learn what's right."

"Lady," the lad responded, "I know what's right."

Dr. Buttrick added, "He did know what was right, but he did not know love."

In one of the Bible's greatest chapters, the point is clearly made.

> *If I speak in the tongues of men and angels, but have not love, I am only a resounding gong or a clanging cymbal. If I have the gift of prophecy and can fathom all mysteries and all knowledge, and if I have a faith that can move mountains, but have not love, I am nothing. If I give all I possess to the poor and surrender my body to the flames, but have not love, I gain nothing* (1 Corinthians 13: 1–3).

Love, then, is that eternal quality of tender concern that regards and treats others (all men and women, boys and girls) as of supreme value in the eyes and heart of the Creator God, so valuable that His divine Son, Jesus, loved so deeply that He gave His life that they might live and live abundantly.

"*Dear friends,*" writes the Apostle John, "*let us love one another, for love comes from God.*"

An outreaching love goes beyond what is merely right, to reach and touch the soul.

Good News
June 15

We are all familiar with the saying, "I've got good news and bad news. Which would you like first?" It's too bad we can't just take the good news.

Why can't there be news that is only good? So much of that which passes for news is dismally and depressingly negative. Open a newspaper looking for good news? You'll most likely not find much, and you'll feel like folding the paper up. Well, there is always the television newscast— there must be some good news there. Turn to a TV newscast looking for good news, and you'll likely end up wondering why you turned it on in the first place.

The word translated gospel, in the New Testament means literally "good news." We can find specific references to good news in a number of different passages. Luke 8:1 tells us: *"Jesus traveled about from one town and village to another, proclaiming the good news of the kingdom of God."* This good news was for all mankind as Jesus Himself said, *"Go into all the world and preach the good news to all creation"* (Mark 16:15). The Bible tells of man's importance in the eyes of the Creator, of God's love for every one of us. It tells of His concern for each person's welfare here and now—as well as for eternity—and of God's free offer of pardon for all our misdeeds.

This, I submit, is good news with no bad.

A Happy Face
June 16

Some people in our world claim that there is no God or that God is dead. Even some religious people, although not making those claims, live and act as if God were dead.

To have even a few of the followers of God looking sad rather than glad, haunted rather than happy, is a serious reflection upon their particular brand of Christianity. The Christian can never really be a pessimist. The Psalms are packed with songs of joy, the Gospels with expressions of hope. Every Christmas the carol rings out: "Joy to the world, the Lord is come!"

True, the modern world is hardly a joy-full habitation. There is so much hurt and agony, so much of man's hatred of his fellow man. But there is hope.

Quite a few years ago, while traveling, I saw an excellent advertisement—one of those few ads that rivet your attention and pique your imagination. It was promoting, of all things, a breakfast food. Superimposed on a lovely, verdant scene with the sun just beginning to break over the early-morning horizon were the simple words, "Today is the first day of the rest of your life . . . start it right."

I have seen the proverb a number of times since, as no doubt have you, but it has not lost, for all its repetition, the effectiveness of its message of joyful anticipation.

For today offers opportunity rather than obstruction, opening rather than closing, beginning rather than ending—excellent reasons for a happy rather than a sad face. God is still on the throne.

Be Perfect
June 17

Sir Frederick Royce was co-founder, along with Charles Rolls, of the Rolls Royce Company. Their company manufactures arguably the world's finest automobile. Royce, who was a mechanical genius, once said (and this could be a fine motto for any of us), "Strive for perfection in everything you do. Take the best that exists and make it better. When it does not exist, design it. Accept nothing nearly right or good enough."

God knows that we, his children, will never quite reach that absolute perfection in ourselves or in the tasks we attempt for God in this life. In almost the last word in his second letter to the Corinthians, Paul wrote, "*Finally, brothers, good-bye. Aim for perfection.*"

Paul has a marvelous word of impetus toward this perfection of character and purpose in Philippians 3, a comfort to all who are trying and a spur to keep on trying. He writes:

> *Not that I have already obtained all this* [the gifts of character from God], *or have already been made perfect, but I press on to take hold of that for which Christ Jesus took hold of me. . . . I do not consider myself yet to have taken hold of it. But one thing I do: Forgetting what is behind and straining toward what is ahead, I press on toward the goal to win the prize for which God has called me heavenward in Christ Jesus* (Philippians 3:12-14).

The advice on life given by Sir Frederick Royce may enable you to build the world's best automobile . . . or a life with the apostle's splendid goal, surging beyond to the glory of God.

You see nearly right or good enough are not sufficient for God either.

Closed Doors, Open Doors
June 18

The name Helen Keller I'm sure most of you know. She was born with the ability to see and hear, but at nineteen months of age, she contracted an illness that left her blind and deaf, and thus unable to talk. She eventually was able to overcome her disabilities and lead a full life. With reference to our feelings of disappointment when someone else has grasped the opportunity we wanted, Helen wrote, "When one door of happiness closes, another opens; but often we look so long at the closed door that we do not see the one which has been opened for us."[2]

I don't know about you, but God has not given me guidance in my lifetime through unusual or dramatic means but usually through the opening and closing of doors. A door would appear to be open, but suddenly it closed. Then another one would open.

The book of Hosea has a remarkable promise to God's people in the second chapter. God is speaking: "[I] *will make the Valley of Achor a door of hope. There she will sing as in the days of her youth.*" The reference of the prophet to the Valley of Achor has to do with a serious incident in the history of Israel, back in the days of Joshua. Achor literally means "trouble"—closed doors, if you like. Here in Hosea, God is promising His people that the valley of trouble will become a door of hope, and they would sing as when they were young.

Sometimes as we get older, we feel that the door of opportunity is closing for good. Not so. Each day brings new occasions for the happiness Helen Keller talks about, opportunities for enjoyment and service to one another and to our Heavenly Father.

The Sun Has Come Out Again
June 19

Children can be very spontaneous. One time when I was listening to the children's story time in church, this became especially evident. The church's youth pastor sat on the edge of the platform surrounded by youngsters, speaking to them about participation. He referred to people taking part in that very service. He spoke of the participation of the seniors' choir, the hand-bell players, and the youth worship team. Then he moved on to another thought, only to have the cutest little girl you ever saw put up her hand. The youth pastor stopped and asked the girl what she wanted. The small youngster replied, "My daddy played."

He had, and the storyteller had not mentioned him. He had played a fine clarinet solo accompanied by the bell choir. I don't think the omission bothered the young father a bit, and the speaker hadn't time to refer to everyone, but it did concern the young daughter, and she wanted to correct the omission.

When you come right down to it, none of us likes to be missed. We sometimes feel like David the Psalmist in the thirteenth Psalm, where he cries out: *"How long, O LORD? Will you forget me forever? How long will you hide your face from me? How long must I wrestle with my thoughts and every day have sorrow in my heart?"* (Psalm 13:1–2).

Sometimes when the floods of life pour over us, when dark clouds of despair blot out the sun, we do cry out to God like that. The two verses from Psalm 13 were just a third of a very short Psalm. The concluding two verses say this: *"But I trust in your unfailing love; my heart rejoices in your salvation. I will sing to the LORD, for he has been good to me."*

The sun has come out again. And it always does. It may seem at times that the world has forgotten us. God never does.

Worthy of Our Calling
June 20

Christians need to be reminded that the world around us is watching whether we live like Christians or not, and strangely enough, most of the world knows how Christians should act and how they should live.

Simon Peter gave the following advice in his first epistle, chapter three and verse fifteen: "*Always be prepared to give an answer to everyone who asks you to give the reason for the hope that you have. But do this with gentleness and respect.*"

Our Christian way of life should be a witness to those around us. Paul gives similar advice in a well-known chapter in his letter to the Ephesians. He writes, "*I urge you to live a life worthy of the calling you have received*"—the highest call in the world . . . God's call. Paul continues, "*Be completely humble and gentle; be patient, bearing with one another in love. Make every effort to keep the unity of the Spirit through the bond of peace*" (Ephesians 4:1–3).

The late Mahatma Gandhi of India, after observing the way some Christians live—or fail to live—reportedly expressed great admiration for Jesus Christ, saying, "I think I would have become a Christian, [adding sadly] except for the Christians."

Is this a rebuke? Well, yes, it is. Ghandi must have encountered Christians, or so-called Christians, who hadn't been a positive influence on him.

It is up to each of us to ask the penetrating question suggested by the apostle Paul's letter: "Am I walking and living the life worthy of my high calling?"

The Lawnmower Has Been Eaten
June 21

My wife and I once had an opportunity to visit Africa and participate in what was called a "flying seminar." We stayed in various places in Kenya and Zaire. On a Sunday, our party was divided into very small groups to go out and conduct services in rural churches. After we had conducted the service at our appointment, we had lunch and were about to leave when our rural hosts presented us with a gift.

From their point of view and out of their poverty, this was a very costly gift—a live goat. We had been forewarned that this might happen and told not to refuse the gift; that would have been unforgivable. So we tied up the goat in the back of the land rover and drove back to our missionary hosts' home in the city. They understood the situation, of course, and tied up the goat in their back yard. Some time later, happily relieved of our goat, we flew back to our home in Calgary.

It so happened that the husband of the host missionary couple had a sister who attended our same church. One Sunday shortly after our return, the missionary's sister came to me with a message from her brother. She said, "I have a strange message from my brother. I don't know what it means." Then she gave me this five-word message: "The lawnmower has been eaten." The goat, of course, had graced her brother's dinner table.

That goat represented a very valuable possession and a very costly gift, in appreciation of simple Christian service. It was a gift of love.

Jesus Himself illustrated a marvelous example of the gift of love. He was sitting one day in the courts of the Temple in Jerusalem, opposite the place where offerings were being given, and was watching the crowd place money into the temple treasury. Many rich people gave large amounts. A poor widow came and put in two small copper coins, worth only a fraction of a penny. Jesus called his disciples over to Himself and said: "*I tell you the truth, this poor widow has put more into the treasury than all the others. They all gave out of their wealth; but she, out of her poverty, put in everything—all she had to live on*" (Mark 12:43–44).

Coolness & Balm
June 22

One of the hymns written by master poet John Greenleaf Whittier, "Dear Lord and Father of Mankind," speaks in a very real way, I think, to the depth of one's soul. The final verse is this:

> Breathe thru the heats of our desire
>
> Thy coolness and thy balm;
>
> Let sense be dumb, let flesh retire,
>
> Speak thru the earthquake, wind, and fire,
>
> O still, small voice of calm![3]

Whittier's allusion to earthquake, wind, and fire, and the still, small voice of calm is directly biblical of course, referring to the experience of the prophet Elijah in the first book of Kings, chapter 19. Elijah had sorely annoyed both King Ahab and particularly his venomous wife, Jezebel, and the prophet had to flee for his life into the desert. Alone and desperately forlorn, Elijah prayed that God would take his life. Finally, he reached Mt. Horeb and spent the night in a cave. Then in the morning, a heaven-sent message reached him: "Go out and stand in the mouth of the cave." There he met God in a rather unexpected way. First, a violent wind seemed to tear the very mountain apart. But God was not in the wind. Then an earthquake, but God was not in the earthquake. Then a fire, but God was not in the fire. After the fire, there came a still, small voice, and that was the voice of the Lord God.

And we have to be quiet and still to hear it.

The voice of God is the coolness and balm that He brings to the strains and stresses of life and that of which Whittier wrote.

God, Are You Listening?
June 23

Have you ever felt that God wasn't listening to you—listening to your prayers? Have you ever felt that He was far away?

Jeremiah, one of the Old Testament's greatest prophets, is often called the "weeping prophet" because his task was to speak out for God at a time of his people's most flagrant transgression. Jeremiah was not included in Israel's wrong doing, but he felt deeply for them and cried many tears on their behalf. *"Since my people are crushed, I am crushed; I mourn and horror grips me. Is there no balm in Gilead? Is there no physician there?"* (Jeremiah 8:21–22a). Jeremiah's reference to the "balm of Gilead" was to a healing potion for wounds produced by trees in Gilead east of Jordan. Jeremiah's God was silent for a time. There didn't seem to be any balm in Gilead.

God hears. God always hears. There are many reasons why he postpones His answer. Perhaps one is not ready for it—time is needed in preparation. Perhaps we should not receive what we are asking for, because the implications might be damaging to us. Sometimes we are holding grudges, bad feelings in our heart. There may be unconfessed wrong doing in our lives. But as the Psalmist has written, God does answer even if sometimes we have to wait awhile. The majestic ninety-first Psalm concludes with these words:

> *"Because he loves me," says the LORD, "I will rescue him; I will protect him, for he acknowledges my name. He will call upon me, and I will answer him; I will be with him in trouble. I will deliver him and honor him. With long life will I satisfy him and show him my salvation."*

And the sun comes out. And the love of a God, who is nearer than hands or feet, is spread in your heart and life.

Removing Rocks
June 24

There's an ancient legend about bad luck that goes something like this. A certain king often heard his subjects complaining about "bad luck"—about all the bad things that had happened to them. Believing that "bad luck" generally comes to the lazy and careless, the king decided to try an experiment. He had his servants place a large rock in the center of a road where he could view the reaction of his subjects to this obstacle.

He first saw a farmer approach with his ox-cart, then veer to the side—losing some of his corn and muttering as he passed by. Next came a soldier, swaggering along as he fell over the rock, grumbling about the "stupid drones" that would leave a rock in the middle of the road. Finally, merchants came with their goods on packhorses with barely room to get by. They too moaned about the lazy people who had left the rock there.

The next day the king summoned his subjects to the spot where the rock remained and easily rolled it away. It was a specially crafted hollow rock, prepared for the purpose. Underneath the spot where the rock had been half-buried was a small iron box. The king held up the box and had someone read aloud the inscription: "For him who lifts the stone." The king opened the box, and therein were 20 bright and shining gold pieces.

Not many actual gold pieces are under the stones on the road of life, but there are a host of blessings for those who remove the stones. There is a verse in Isaiah where the prophet writes: *"Build up, build up, prepare the road! Remove the obstacles out of the way of my people"* (Isaiah 57:14). Isaiah's people were heading into disaster. The prophet knew that. Looking much farther ahead, he knew that God would forgive, as He so often had, and his nation would be able to return from exile. Hence, we recognize the call to prepare the way, to remove the obstacles from the road—the rocks, if you will.

So may we assist in removing those rocks, the obstacles that, along life's way, keep men and women from God. We see them before us from time to time. To remove them brings its own rich reward.

The Race of Life
June 25

Many of us are sports fans. We may have been fans for many years and continue to be in our senior years. Most likely, the participation in sports has waned, but the enthusiasm of being a fan has likely remained.

I think that the apostle Paul was a sports buff, judging by the occasions when he used a sporting metaphor in his writings. Actually, the ancient Olympic Games were being held during Paul's time, as were another set of Games called the Isthmian Games, held in between the Olympic dates.

Paul writes in the ninth chapter of his first letter to the Corinthians, giving advice not only to runners running a race, but more importantly to those running in the race of life.

> *Do you not know that in a race all the runners run, but only one gets the prize? Run in such a way as to get the prize. Everyone who competes in the games goes into strict training. They do it to get a crown that will not last; but we do it to get a crown that will last forever* (1 Corinthians 9:24–25).

Paul is likening the race of life to a race on the track, speaking of the training one must undergo and the goal of a crown (the Greeks had used a garland of leaves, but ours is an eternal crown of God's glory). We are to race persistently, not aimlessly, but of course loyally to those around us and to God.

Losing Our Freedom
June 26

The price of freedom has always been high. Despite the massive advances and advantages of our Western world, the cause of freedom is eroding. I was talking with another senior about these very things. This lady, who had been raised in a city in British Columbia, made these poignant remarks: "I never had a key to our house as a youngster. The door was never locked during the daytime." Then she mentioned about walking alone through a local park and there being no danger. Then after pausing, she said, "Do you know what we have lost? Freedom. Freedom to move about singly and freely, freedom to trust the folks you meet."

Instead of moving forward to greater freedom, we are moving back to less. Emancipation is going to be very, very difficult—perhaps nearly impossible. You can only do so much to protect yourself and your property.

However, there is a way you can be certain of your freedom of conscience and your freedom of soul. In a day when the Empire of Rome ruled the world with an iron fist and freedom could only be imagined, Jesus came, offering absolute freedom of heart, soul, and mind. Sending out His twelve apostles, He gave them this confident word, after telling of the dangers they would face. *"Do not be afraid of those who kill the body but cannot kill the soul. Rather, be afraid of the One who can destroy both soul and body in hell"* (Matthew 10:28).

The answer to spiritual freedom lies right at the door of our soul. If you haven't already, won't you let Him, our Savior, come in today?

In the Hands of the Master
June 27

Niccolo Paganini, famous violin virtuoso of the nineteenth century, had what could have been a completely devastating experience happen to him at a concert. While performing a stirring concerto, suddenly a string on his violin snapped and hung limply. Paganini, improvising, continued to play when, lo and behold, a second string broke. He continued to improvise on his two remaining strings when, a moment later, a third broke. Paganini finished the piece, drawing magnificent music from that one remaining string.

The violin was only an impaired instrument, but in the hands of a master, it made superb music.

"What is that in your hand?" God asked, as recorded in chapter four of Exodus, to a very reluctant Moses who was squirming every way he could to avoid the call of God to return to Egypt and lead his enslaved people to freedom. Moses finally replied that he had a staff. God continued, *"Throw it on the ground."* As Moses did so, the staff turned into a snake, and Moses ran from it. God called him back by saying: *"Reach out your hand and take it by the tail."* Very gingerly, Moses did, and the snake turned back into his shepherd's staff. God was showing Moses that with God he would be a powerful leader, quite able to free his people.

Like Moses, we often protest that we are unable to do the tasks—some smaller, some bigger—that God asks us to do. Often we indicate that we are just too old. Moses was a man eighty years of age when God called him that day in the wilderness to return to Egypt and face Egypt's Pharaoh, demanding that Pharaoh let Gods people go free.

Yes, though we sometimes feel very inadequate, God can and does use us day by day to reach out to others . . . someone disturbed . . . someone hurting . . . another puzzled. Like an impaired violin, we feel inept, unable to be of much use. But in hands of the Master, the Master of life, we can make glorious music.

Sowing Seed
June 28

The parable of the sower and the seed found in each of the synoptic Gospels—Matthew, Mark, and Luke—happens this way. A farmer went out one morning with his special bag of seed and from this bag began to sow the seed by hand. As the farmer sowed, some seed fell on the path, and the birds had easy picking. That seed vanished. Some seed fell on rocky ground at the edge of the field, where there was very little soil. The seed sprouted quickly on that surface, but the hot, brilliant sun quickly scorched the tiny plants, and they perished. They had no root. Other seeds fell among thorns, which choked the plants as they grew toward maturity. Then a good deal of the sown seed fell on good ground and brought forth the harvest desired. It produced a crop that multiplied the seed thirty, sixty, even one hundred times.

This parable, as Jesus later pointed out to His apostles, is a story about life and the sowing of the seed of the Word of God in human hearts. The hard-hearted religious leaders of the day inevitably opposed Jesus, His teaching, and His words, and the seed to them was valueless, stolen away by the birds of evil. Other hearers listened attentively, agreed with His message, and accepted His way, but through the cares of the world around them, soon fell away, having lost interest. Still others were attracted by His Word but became caught up and choked by other worldly interests, riches, or pleasures and never matured. A final group, the good soil, gave a warm and hospitable welcome to His Gospel. Their lives produced rich fruit, some more than others.

It is obvious that Jesus knew His hearers then as He knows his hearers now. Each had an opportunity to hear, and the response was up to them—a personal decision. It remains a personal decision for each of us.

What sort of soil are we providing for the Sower of Life and the Good Seed He is spreading abroad in our midst?

Integrity
June 29

A person of integrity is one we know we can depend on when others might fail. A person of integrity is faithful and true.

In the seventh Psalm, David was willing to allow his life to be judged on that basis. In fact, he called on God to do just that. In verse eight of that Psalm, he calls to God, *"Judge me, O LORD, according to my righteousness, according to my integrity, O Most High"* (Psalm 7:8b).

Most of us believe that the quality of character most lacking in people in high places in our times is that same integrity or trust. A man or woman of integrity does not involve himself/herself in activities that result in scandal. People with integrity can't be bought. A lack of integrity is not only found among the power brokers of this world, but also found in great abundance right down where we are—in our homes, our schools, in business and everyday dealings of life. That's tragic. Lack of integrity has simply come to mean that we don't trust one another.

The book of Job in the Old Testament is the life story of a man of integrity. Some say that Job suffered and lost more terribly than any man except our Savior, yet he kept his integrity. His so-called "friends," who had come around to visit Job, gave the opinion that the cause of all his problems was his own life and attitude. That was not the case, of course, and one of Job's replies rings as true today as it did then: *"Till I die, I will not deny my integrity. I will maintain my righteousness and never let go of it; my conscience will not reproach me as long as I live"* (Job 27: 5b–6).

God vindicated Job as a person of integrity, a person of honesty and trust. So God does with those of us who follow His way.

Bread on the Waters
June 30

When Herbert Hoover, later to be US President, was a college student, he supported himself by arranging concerts for his fellow students. On one occasion, with another student, he arranged for the well-known Polish pianist Jan Paderewski to give a recital. Because of scheduling and publicity problems, the turnout was very small. It was so small that Hoover was compelled to explain to the pianist that only part of his fee could be paid. He promised in good faith that the rest would be sent to Paderewski later. Paderewski graciously told Hoover to take from the proceeds whatever Hoover's expenses were and to give him the rest, which he would accept as full payment.

Shortly after World War I, each had changed his role—Paderewski was prime minister of Poland and Hoover was overseas aid representative of the US. Millions of people in Poland were starving from the ravages of war. Desperate to help his people, Paderewski turned to the agency Hoover headed. Hoover's response was to coordinate the shipment of tons of food to Poland. On his next trip to the States, Paderewski sought out Hoover to express his personal gratitude and that of his nation. As Paderewski was thanking him, Hoover interjected saying: "You may not remember this, but several years ago, you helped two young students go through college. I was one of them."[4]

I don't know whether Paderewski knew the maxim in Ecclesiastes 11:1 or not, but the principle involved is clear: *"Cast your bread upon the waters, for after many days you will find it again."* The pianist's generosity to a struggling university student paid rich dividends for his country many years later, although such a thought did not enter his head at the time, I am sure.

Paul in his first letter to Timothy urged Timothy to tell his Christian hearers to *"Do good, to be rich in good deeds, and to be generous and willing to share. In this way they will lay up treasure for themselves as a firm foundation for the coming age, so that they may take hold of the life that is truly life"* (1 Timothy 6:18–19).

Prayer for the Nation
July 01

When he was leaving for his first inaugural as President, Abraham Lincoln said to his friends who were seeing him off, "I now leave . . . with a task before me greater than that which rested upon [George] Washington. Without the assistance of the Divine Being, who ever attended him, I cannot succeed. With that assistance I cannot fail."[1] It is well documented that often during a crisis, Lincoln would send for his pastor, and the two of them would spend much time in prayer, seeking the Lord's guidance.

Today Canada is celebrating its national holiday, and the United States a few days hence. It is a good time to be reminded that our countries' leaders surely need our prayers, that they may govern wisely and well in difficult times.

"*Righteousness exalts a nation,*" writes the author of Proverbs, to which the Psalmist adds, "*Blessed is the nation whose God is the LORD.*" Speaking of good citizenship, Jesus said: "*Give to Caesar what is Caesar's, and to God what is God's*" (Matthew 22:21).

The apostle Paul called on his young co-worker Timothy: "*I urge, then, first of all, that requests, prayers, intercession and thanksgiving be made for everyone—for kings and all those in authority, that we may live peaceful and quiet lives in all godliness and holiness*" (1 Timothy 2:1–2).

The apostle Peter's plea was this: "*Submit yourselves for the Lord's sake to every authority instituted among men*" (1 Peter 2:13a). And later on in the same chapter, in verse 17, we read: "*Show proper respect for everyone: Love the brotherhood of believers, fear God, honor the king.*" Let us offer prayers for our national and world leaders.

Where We Live
July 02

Many seniors have lived in quite a few places over the course of their lives. It seems to be a fact of life that we live in a very mobile society. No matter where you live, what is important is not so much the place, but your attitude that you bring toward the people who live in the places where you live. We need to ask the question: what sort of a difference do we make where we live?

In the fourteenth chapter of Romans, the apostle Paul has left us these words in verse seven: *"For none of us lives to himself alone and none of us dies to himself alone."* What Paul is saying is that our lives have a strong influence on others, for good or for ill. Even in a quarrelsome environment, we can stand out, showing love and concern . . . and making a difference.

William Channing saw your influence and mine as flowing out in ever broadening circles. "Others are affected by what I am, and say, and do," he wrote. "And these others have also their spheres of influence. So that a single act of mine may spread and spread in widening circles through a nation or humanity."[2]

No matter where we go, we take our attitude with us. We can make it a good experience or a bad experience. The choice is ours.

A Perspective on Living
July 03

Rudyard Kipling, famed British author of an earlier era, once addressed an assembly of the students at McGill University, Montreal. Speaking of the relative importance and unimportance of material possessions, Kipling said to the crowd of young people: "One day you will meet someone who cares for none of these things, and you will realize how poor you have become."

What then are life's priorities, life's most important qualities?

The Master of life had something rather potent to say concerning this matter. He was talking to His followers about anxiety, food, clothing and the necessities of life. Then he startled them with these words: *"But seek first his* [i.e. God's] *kingdom and his righteousness, and all these things will be given to you as well"* (Matthew 6:33).

These words set things in perspective. Jesus did not say that food, clothing, making a living, even enjoying some of the luxuries of life were not important. He simply said that meaningful life must have spiritual values as its number one focus, the surrender of life to something and Someone beyond itself.

As to anxiety about the lesser priorities, Jesus had this observation:

> *"Therefore I tell you, do not worry about your life, what you will eat or drink; or about your body, what you will wear. Is not life more important than food, and the body more important than clothes? Look at the birds of the air; they do not sow or reap or store away in barns, and yet your heavenly Father feeds them. Are you not much more valuable than they?"* (Matthew 6:25–26).

Thus, God promises to care for His own.

Certainly, as we get a little older, the material possessions of life drop in importance. To paraphrase Kipling, someday you will meet other men and women who, like you, care for none of these things, and you will realize again not how poor, but how rich you are; for yours is the Kingdom of heaven.

Permanent Treasures
July 04

The Mentholatum Company was founded by A. A. Hyde of Kansas. Early in his life, Mr. Hyde had made a fine success in banking and real estate, until a drought hit that part of the country in the early 1880s and he found himself deeply in debt. He had to mortgage his home to meet some of his obligations. Later he confided that this whole humbling experience was the best thing that had ever happened to him. Always prominent in his church, but never really committed, he was driven to an intensive study of the Bible in order to find the real meaning of life. A verse that hit him between the eyes contained the words of Jesus from the Sermon on the Mount: "Do not store up for yourselves treasures on earth."

After A. A. Hyde began to manufacture Mentholatum ointment, his financial picture brightened, and after years of struggle, all his debts were cleared. A. A. Hyde then began to give his money away . . . and very generously. He came to believe that all he had belonged to God, to be given to worthy causes.

The section of the Sermon on the Mount that caught Mr. Hyde's eye was Matthew 6: 19–21 where the Master said:

> *"Do not store up for yourselves treasures on earth, where moth and rust destroy, and where thieves break in and steal. But store up for yourselves treasures in heaven, where moth and rust do not destroy and where thieves do not break in And steal. For where your treasure is, there your heart will be also."*

Jesus is contrasting here, the temporary and the passing with the permanent. He indicates that your heart, your deepest feelings and longings, will be focused on either one or the other. That's a choice each one of us has to make.

Changed Lives
July 05

The English scientist, Charles Darwin, could not be described, by any stretch of the imagination, as a religious man. Indeed, many of his theories were in direct conflict with the cherished beliefs of many Christians. As part of his scientific investigations, Darwin visited Tierra del Fuego (east of the Southern tip of the United States) in 1833. Back in those days, he found its people brutal and crude beyond description. Thirty-six years later, he revisited the island to discover these same people with an entirely new culture—gentle, literate, and hospitable. Darwin, in some amazement, sent a twenty-five pound note to the London Missionary Society and asked if he might be enrolled as a member. Jesus Christ and Christian missions had made the difference.

One day at the beginning of His ministry, Jesus was walking along the shore of the Sea of Galilee. Two brothers, Peter and Andrew, were fishermen who were casting their nets into the lake. "Come follow me," said Jesus, "and I will make you fishers of men." They followed, and their lives were changed, as well as the lives of countless others. They had met Jesus a short time before. In fact, Andrew had met Him first and introduced his brother. The call at the lake that day made the difference.

Andrew served effectively during Jesus' ministry as a strong and steady member of Jesus' band of apostles and then as a continuing leader in the heady, yet stressful days of the New Testament church as described in the book of Acts. His brother, Simon Peter, became the charismatic spokesman for the group. Peter was an impulsive, endearing man who fell from time to time, only to pick himself up, go on, and finally become a solid rock for Christ. Under Peter's ministry and effective preaching, literally thousands of people found new life through the way of the cross.

Jesus continues to make a difference in countless lives today through Christian missions abroad and right here at home.

Faith in Action
July 06

Near the end of His ministry, Jesus entered the courts of the Temple in Jerusalem one day and began to teach the crowd that gathered around Him. The Jewish religious authorities were soon there too, asking Him by what authority He dared to teach the people.

"Who gave you this authority?" they demanded.

Jesus responded, "I'd like to ask you one question. If you answer me, I'll tell you about my authority. The baptism of John the Baptist, where did it come from? From God? Or did it have a human origin?"

Jesus' opponents then faced a problem. If they answered "of human origin," the leaders knew that the people around them would be furious, for they all held that John was a prophet. If they answered "from God," they knew that Jesus would respond, "Then why did you not believe in him?" So on the horns of a dilemma, they replied to Jesus, "We don't know."

Then Jesus said, "Neither will I tell you of my authority."

Jesus proceeded to tell the parable of the two sons. To the first son, the father said one morning, "Go and work today in the vineyard."

"No," said that son, "I won't," but a little later he thought better of his decision and went to work.

Similarly, the father approached the second son and asked Him to go to work. "Yes, sir," he said immediately, "I'll go," but he didn't.

"Which of the two did what his father wanted?" said Jesus to the religious leaders.

"The first," they had to admit.

Then powerfully, Jesus indicated that some of the people that the religious authorities disdained as "sinners" would enter the Kingdom of God before them, Jesus' tormentors. They were self-righteous, feeling that they were special favorites of God, but they were only "talking their religion, not doing."

The epistle of James puts it this way *"Faith by itself, if it is not accompanied by action, is dead"* (James 2:17).

Life's Struggles
July 07

Alfred Russell Wallace, a well-known naturalist of yesteryear, once tried to assist a struggling moth. He discovered the moth fighting wildly to break out of the cocoon that covered it. Wallace split the cocoon and released the moth from further struggle. That day, Wallace learned a lesson about nature he never forgot, for as we now know, that moth never developed into a beautiful butterfly. It died undeveloped, stunted, and ruined. The hard struggle with the cocoon was Nature's way of developing its splendid wings, of bringing out the glory of the emperor butterfly. The moth was saved from struggle, but man's ill-considered assistance doomed it.

Most of us would admit that many aspects of life are a struggle, and it is often of no benefit to us to remove all of that struggle. For example, many who went through the struggles of the "hungry thirties"—the Great Depression—must have looked back on it with mixed feelings. Although there was much deprivation, through it all there was much character building as well. Perhaps some of the succeeding generations having missed that struggle, have also missed a large slice of life. The results of too much ease are all around us.

Other than our Lord, no one exemplifies so intensely or majestically the struggles of life more than the apostle Paul. Beatings, stonings, a shipwreck, and imprisonment were just a few of the struggles Paul faced. In the book of Romans, chapter fifteen and verse thirty, Paul writes from Jerusalem to the Christians in that city: "*I urge you, brothers, by our Lord Jesus Christ and by the love of the Spirit, to join me in my struggle by praying to God for me.*" Paul did get to Rome as a prisoner and was able, through struggle, to minister there for a period until he was executed for his faith.

As the end of his struggle loomed, Paul wrote: *The time has come for my departure. I have fought the good fight, I have finished the race, I have kept the faith. Now there is in store for me a crown of righteousness*" (2 Timothy 4:6–8a).

Some of you who have faced such struggles, particularly physical, share a common feeling with the great apostle.

"*In this world,*" said Jesus, "*you will have trouble. But take heart! I have overcome the world.*"

Servant of the Lord
July 08

The prophet Isaiah, writing about 700 BC, tells about the coming "Servant of the Lord" (as he calls Him). In chapter 42, verse 6, Isaiah quotes that Servant: *"I, the LORD, have called you in righteousness; I will take hold of your hand. I will keep you and will make you to be a covenant for the people and a light for the Gentiles"*

In Isaiah 61:1, the prophet writes: *"The Spirit of the Sovereign LORD is on me, because the LORD has anointed me to preach good news to the poor. He has sent me to bind up the brokenhearted, to proclaim freedom for the captives and release from darkness for the prisoners."*

That was the precise passage from Isaiah that Jesus read in the synagogue in Nazareth at the beginning of his ministry. At the close of His ministry, Jesus gave a picture of the hereafter and the welcome awaiting those who had served in His name in this way: *"For I was hungry and you gave me something to eat, I was thirsty and you gave me something to drink, I was a stranger and you invited me in, I needed clothes and you clothed me, I was sick and you looked after me, I was in prison and you came to visit me"* (Matthew 25:35–36). Those to whom these words were addressed were surprised and asked Jesus where they had done such things for Him. He replied, *"I tell you the truth, whatever you did for one of the least of these brothers of mine, you did for me"* (Matthew 25:40).

Even the most callous can be touched by love, especially the love of Jesus through one of His followers. Be a servant of the Lord today.

Do You Want to Be Well?
July 09

Usually people want to be healed of their physical ailments, but some do not. There is a passage of Scripture from John 5: (1–3, 5–6), that raises the issue.

> *Sometime later, Jesus went up to Jerusalem for a feast of the Jews. Now there is in Jerusalem near the Sheep Gate a pool, which in Aramaic is called Bethesda and which is surrounded by five covered colonnades. Here a great number of disabled people used to lie—the blind, the lame, the paralyzed. One who was there had been an invalid for thirty-eight years. When Jesus saw him lying there and learned that he had been in this condition for a long time, he asked him, "Do you want to get well?"*

Do you ever wonder why Jesus asked that question—"Do you want to get well?" Could it be that Jesus had, those many, many years ago, come upon some who, for their own reasons, did not want to be cured?

This man did. Jesus told him to pick up his mat and walk. And—Glory to God—he did.

The man had been dealt a heavy blow by life, but he was made wonderfully whole. He could have preferred to remain in his sin and squalor . . . remaining as he was.

Is that not a parable of the human condition—two millennia ago and now. The Savior of the world offered then and offers now cleansing and healing of soul.

The choice must still be made by the individual—by you and by me.

What You Do; What You Are
July 10

Two little, two-letter verbs are among the most important words of the English language. One is "do" . . . to do. The other is "be" . . . to be. One is external action of all sorts. The other is internal—what goes on inside. One is what you accomplish; the other is what you are.

In the Christian's life, the verb "to be" comes first. You do because of what you are.

"*By the grace of God I am what I am,*" writes the apostle in his first letter to the Christians in Corinth. "*And whatever you do,*" he writes to the Colossians, "*whether in word or deed, do it all in the name of the Lord Jesus.*"

A fine and wealthy young man came to Jesus on one occasion, as recorded in Matthew chapter nineteen, and asked, "*Teacher, what good thing must I do to get eternal life?*" Jesus listed off a number of commandments. "*All these I have kept,*" the young man responded. Then this shocker: "*If you want to be perfect, go, sell your possessions, and give to the poor, and you will have treasure in heaven. Then come, follow me.*" But the young man couldn't. He turned away sadly, says the Scripture, "*because he had great wealth.*"

Jesus doesn't ask very many to make that sort of material sacrifice, unless a person's possessions are so important that they are blocking the way to God, preventing the development of both a being and a doing Christian. He expects us to be both.

Color Blue
July 11

Have you ever thought about the dual role the color blue plays in our culture? Sometimes it represents that which is dark and somber; on other occasions, that which is just the opposite— bright and cheerful. On one hand, we speak of blue Monday, blue laws (which are supposed to take the joy out of life), as well as "feeling blue." What a contrast when, enraptured, we talk of a bright blue sky or the beautiful blue waters of a lake or sometimes the ocean. These certainly don't give us a depressed, blue feeling.

Many of the Psalms pick up these contrasting moods of dark and light, providing us with a substantial, meaningful answer. The short thirteenth Psalm is typical as the Psalmist cries:

> *How long, O LORD? Will you forget me forever?*
> *How long will you hide your face from me?*
> *How long must I wrestle with my thoughts*
> *and every day have sorrow in my heart?*
> *How long will my enemy triumph over me?*
>
> *Look on me and answer, O LORD my God.*
> *Give light to my eyes, or I will sleep in death;*
> *my enemy will say, "I have overcome him,"*
> *and my foes will rejoice when I fall.*

Then the change:

> *But I trust in your unfailing love;*
> *my heart rejoices in your salvation.*
> *I will sing to the LORD,*
> *for he has been good to me.*

Let us count our blessings too on a bright blue day . . . as bright as the promises of God.

A Good Conscience
July 12

The story is told of President Lincoln who, while horseback riding, came across a couple of baby birds that had fallen from their nest. Mr. Lincoln spent considerable time hunting down the nest. His compatriots laughed at his undertaking this endeavor, to which Mr. Lincoln responded, "Gentleman, you may laugh, but I could not have slept well tonight if I had not saved those birds."

I have a feeling that a good, clear conscience is one of God's greatest gifts to His children. It certainly does help us sleep at night.

The apostle Paul refers on a number of occasions to the great benefits of a good, clear conscience, as in fact does Simon Peter. When the Jewish mob tried to murder Paul when he visited Jerusalem later in his ministry, he was saved by Roman troops under their commander, Claudius Lysias. Lysias sent him to Caesarea to appear before the Roman Governor Felix. On trial before Felix, Paul told the story of his conversion and subsequent life, making this very pertinent statement: "*I strive always to keep my conscience clear before God and man*" (Acts 24:16).

If we, for ourselves, cherish a superior character and desire to do what is right, our conscience must be sharp and, as Paul puts it, "*clear before God and man.*"

To his young co-worker, Timothy, Paul urges "*holding on to faith and a good conscience.*"

This is a marvelous recipe for living, for young and old alike.

Give Me This Mountain
July 13

Quite a few people attempt to climb Mount Everest and some die in their attempt. Many of us ask, "Why do men and women try such things?" That question was asked of British mountain climber George Mallory, who was to lose his life on his third attempt to climb Everest, "Why do you do it?"

Mallory's simple reply was, "Because it's there." That's the challenge of the human spirit.

There's a story in the Old Testament Book of Joshua about a very vigorous man of eighty-five who demonstrated that spirit exceptionally. That man was Caleb who, as a young man, was sent by Moses, along with young Joshua and ten other men, to check out the land God had promised them. Caleb and Joshua brought Moses their famous minority report—let's go in! The other ten were terrified by the obstacles, and the people didn't go in. For forty years, they simply wandered. Now a new generation has gone in, and Caleb (now eighty-five years old) has gone to Joshua, who is now the leader, and asked for his promised inheritance—the area around the community of Hebron. Caleb speaks to Joshua.

"*Here I am today, eighty-five years old! I am still as strong today as the day Moses sent me out; I'm just as vigorous to go out to battle now as I was then. Now give me this hill country that the LORD promised me that day*" (Joshua 14:10b–12a).

Caleb was given the mountain to conquer, and in God's strength, he made it—right to the top!

Age, you see, is no barrier to a conquest we attempt with God.

God's Assurances
July 14

In one of the *Peanuts* cartoon strips, by Charles Schulz, the cartoonist has two of his heroes staring out of a window. It is just a terrible day, the rain pouring down, and Charlie Brown and Linus are the wondering onlookers. As usual, the pessimistic Charlie Brown is very worried about the situation. In the next frame, Linus assures Charlie that everything is going to be okay because God promised Noah that He would never again destroy the world by a flood. Charlie Brown expresses relief. His anxiety has been allayed. On the final frame, Linus notes, "Good theology has a way of doing that."[3]

These words by Linus are another way of saying that the promises of God to His children are their dependable assurance. We are talking here about faith–faith as described in the very stimulating eleventh chapter of the New Testament book of Hebrews as *"being sure of what we hope for and certain of what we do not see."* The Hebrews writer then gives us examples, a series of nearly a dozen heroes of faith, all of whom trusted the promises of God implicitly and were not disappointed. One of those heroes of faith, cited by Charles Schulz through Linus, was Noah, who received God's promise that the world would never again be destroyed by a universal flood.

We all have anxiety from time to time and in various ways—fear, apprehension of the future. *"Do not be afraid, little flock,"* Jesus said, *"for your Father has been pleased to give you the kingdom"* (Luke 12:32). That's the eternal kingdom of peace, forgiveness, healing, and love. Freedom from all fear. To those burdened, worried, or care-worn, Jesus invites, *"Come to me, all you who are weary and burdened, and I will give you rest"* (Matthew 11:28).

These assurances of God, through Jesus, touch every aspect of living and make life meaningful and fulfilling for all who call on Him. That's not only good theology—it's the very heart of life.

"My Grace Is Sufficient"
July 15

Some of you may be disabled. Some of you may have been disabled for most, if not all, of your life. I was reading about a disabled person—Thomas Roberts, founder and headmaster of a famous boarding school in the United Kingdom—who was also a very skilled woodworker, his specialty being the carving of model ships. As well, he was an accomplished painter, an expert fisherman, and the inventor of one of the first calculators—a fine record of achievement for a man who had lost both hands as a young man in a military accident with an exploding grenade.

Jesus' answer to the problem of disability was to heal the disabled person. He healed a lame man waiting by the Pool of Bethesda. He cast out an evil spirit from a man in the synagogue at Capernaum. He brought a permanent cure to a man who was deaf, mute, and blind. Throughout His ministry, Jesus gave a new life to dozens of men and women.

Not everyone who was disabled in Jesus' day was able to reach Jesus. Yet they carried on. God still heals in our day. Miracles do occur, although not many, to be truthful. God does not promise that each one who calls on Him will receive that healing. Even the great apostle Paul suffered with infirmity. Some students of God's Word suggest that it was some form of eye trouble. Paul called it his "thorn in the flesh." "*Three times I pleaded with the Lord to take it away from me. But he said to me, 'My grace is sufficient for you, for my power is made perfect in weakness.'* Concludes the great apostle, "*Therefore I will boast all the more gladly about my weaknesses, so that Christ's power may rest on me*" (2 Corinthians 12:8–9). Paul suggests, indeed, that his weakness has become his strength.

Pray for healing, yes, and for relief from pain. If perchance God should say, "My grace is sufficient, for my power is made perfect in weakness," dare I suggest that we thank Him for putting His trust in us?

The Face of God
July 16

Some of you may have heard the story of the little girl who was being put to bed and asked her mother if she would leave the light on. "Why, dear?" the mother asked, and the youngster confessed she was afraid of the dark. Mother assured her that God would take care of her. "I know," was the little girl's response, "but I want someone with a face."

Not only little girls are afraid of the dark and want "someone with a face" to look to for protection and care. That's why so many people of the world have made idols for themselves out of wood, stone, or metal—a human-like figure, perhaps, or a grotesque animal to scare away the evil spirits. A god with a face—something that can be seen and felt. These false gods are hopeless, of course, for giving any real assistance or assurance, as so many idol worshippers—multimillions of them—have discovered.

Yet our Master, Jesus, is—and I say this reverently—"God with a face." That's the simple meaning to the imposing theological word "incarnation," we hear so often at Christmas. God in human form. *"For in Christ all the fullness of the Deity lives in bodily form,"* Paul writes in Colossians 2:9.

In the Old Testament, we have the story of God's seeking; He used His prophets, the priests, and sometimes kings to be his instruments in that quest. Then, in a final effort to redeem mankind, God sent His only Son. Christ came to live as we live, to be tempted as we are, and although perfect, to die the death of a sinner—for all sinners. Then of course, He arose from the grave that we might be forgiven and find a fullness in life of which we had never dreamed, now and eternally.

Jesus went about the world healing, loving, caring, forgiving, encouraging, even chiding where necessary, calming, comforting, protecting . . . and offering salvation and peace. He was and is the answer to a child's bedtime prayer . . . and yours and mine.

Growing and Running
July 17

As seniors, most of us don't expect to grow much more in stature, but we can grow in character, in appreciation, in caring. An unknown writer has left us with the following little gem about growing

"Growing," he says, "is like running in a twenty-six mile marathon. If we give up on the twenty-fourth mile, we will never know what it feels like to finish the race.

There will be times in our growth when we will want to give up. Sometimes our pain seems never ending. In a sense, we are like the runner in the twenty-fourth mile of the marathon, who feels such pain that he is in danger of quitting the race. He feels that he has nothing left to enable him to go on. He is in danger of losing his ability to see things as they really are with only a couple of miles to go.

If a runner in that situation can bring to mind previous successes, perhaps he can carry on or at least give it his best shot. It doesn't really matter how many runners come in before and after him. It only matters that he has not given up . . . and when he crosses the finish line, all his pain turns to joy.

When we refuse to give up, whatever the situation in life, we accomplish something we can rejoice in—the reward of knowledge that we have done our very best.

As seniors, we know all too well that life may be a bitter marathon at times. Quitting the race is hardly a possibility, however, and despite the pain, we need to carry on. One day we'll say with Paul, as he wrote to his younger co-worker Timothy:

> *The time has come for my departure. I have fought the good fight, I have finished the race, I have kept the faith. Now there is in store for me the crown of righteousness, which the Lord, the righteous Judge, will award to me on that day—and not only to me, but also to all who have longed for his appearing* (2 Timothy 4:6b–8).

The Quality of Giving
July 18

Sometimes in life, and more so it seems as we grow older, we press the review button of our thoughts and reflect on times and people in the past who have influenced our lives. There are likely many people in your life, as there have been in mine, who have given unstintingly throughout these many long years, and those giving people likely enjoyed doing the giving. Parents . . . brothers . . . sisters . . . good friends . . . a schoolteacher . . . a Sunday school teacher . . . a pastor . . . a mentor. We recall fondly the givers of this world.

If there is one quality of the God we worship that seems to stand out above all others, it is the quality of giving. Our God is a giving God. The Psalmist writes in Psalm 115: *"The highest heavens belong to the LORD, but the earth he has given to man."* The writer of Ecclesiastes speaks of the life God has given us, and the Bible's golden text, John 3:16, says: *"For God so loved the world that he gave his one and only Son, that whoever believes in him shall not perish but have eternal life."* First, life itself is a gift from God. So is the earth that we inhabit. So is the air that we breathe. We are able to receive new life through His Son. All of these things are wonderful gifts from a giving God.

The eternal God loves each one of us. May we thank Him and love and serve Him in return.

A New Religion
July 19

In France in the last years of the eighteenth century following the revolution, a Directory was formed as the executive branch of government. A member of that Directory and a philosopher, Lapaux by name, decided that he would add to the lustre of the revolution and, of course, his own name by inventing a new religion that he would call Theophilanthopy—obviously by its name a combination of some divine-like qualities, with human good works. Lepaux put a great deal of thought and study into the effort. However, he made no headway as people were simply not interested.

Lepaux complained one day to the renowned French statesman of wit, Charles Talleyrand, a fellow member of the ruling Directory. Lepaux said he was having a great deal of difficulty in introducing his new religion.

"I am not surprised," replied Talleyrand, "It is no easy matter to introduce a new religion. But there is one thing I would advise you to do, and then, perhaps, you might succeed . . . Go and be crucified, and then be buried, and then rise again on the third day, and then go on working miracles, raising the dead, and healing all manner of diseases and casting out devils; and then it is possible that you might accomplish your end!"[4] The philosopher, crestfallen and confounded, went away without a word.

Jesus, His cross, and His resurrection were, and are, the watershed of history. Even the world has recognized that for many centuries. We compute the millennia before He came by designating them "BC"—"Before Christ" and on our side of his life by "AD"— "Anno Domini," which means "the year of our Lord."

No one can duplicate His life, death, and resurrection, for he was and is the very Son of God. Jesus said, *"I am the way the truth and the life."* He added these vitally important words: "No one comes to the Father but by me."

As two of Jesus' apostles on trial for proclaiming salvation through that cross said long ago: "We must obey God rather than men," It may cost us.

Being Forgiven
July 20

David, the Psalmist, was one who recognized the power and privilege of forgiveness. He had committed a terrible sin, which the prophet Nathan pointed out to him in no uncertain terms. David paid a heavy price for that sin, but recognizing that he had sinned against God, David repented, and Nathan was able to assure him of God's forgiveness. Later David wrote these words in the thirty-second Psalm (verses 1–5). They fit everyone who knows the peace and assurance of forgiveness.

> *Blessed is he whose transgressions are forgiven, whose sins are covered. Blessed is the man whose sin the LORD does not count against him and in whose spirit is no deceit. When I kept silent, my bones wasted away through my groaning all day long. For day and night your hand was heavy upon me; my strength was sapped as in the heat of summer. Then I acknowledged my sin to you and did not cover up my iniquity. I said, "I will confess my transgressions to the LORD"—and you forgave the guilt of my sin.*

These are the words of a man at peace with God, himself, and the world—looking to a significant future.

One of life's greatest blessings is to be forgiven—first by God and then by others. It is very significant that the second petition in the Lord's Prayer, immediately following the petition for daily bread, is for forgiveness. "Forgive us our trespasses," we pray, "as we forgive those who trespass against us." We make the qualification, you see. This prayer recognizes that to be forgiven, we plan to be forgiving of others. *"Bear with each other,"* writes the Apostle, *"and forgive whatever grievances you may have against one another. Forgive as the Lord forgave you"* (Colossians 3:13).

Forgiveness gives each of us that new start that opens vast possibilities before us, whether we are a king or simply a person with a burden rolled away.

On the Sea of Life
July 21

The hymn "Eternal Father, Strong to Save" has been described as the most popular hymn for travelers in the English language. The hymn was written by an Englishman, William Whiting, in 1860. Whiting was a schoolmaster and clergyman who published a book of poems and several other hymns.

The music for the hymn was written by John B. Dyke. Called "Melita," the tune was named for the island of Malta—Melita being the ancient name for Malta, where the shipwrecked apostle Paul had landed.

It is believed that Whiting's hymn was inspired by the vivid description of the ocean's dangers and God's promised deliverance found in Psalm 107.

The hymn was played at President John F. Kennedy's funeral by the combined Navy and Marine bands. The first verse is this:

> Eternal Father, strong to save,
>
> Whose arm hath bound the restless wave,
>
> Who bidd'st the mighty ocean deep
>
> Its own appointed limits keep:
>
> O hear us when we cry to Thee
>
> For those in peril on the sea.[5]

Often life itself is described as the "sea of life" and individual lives as little boats tossed about on that sea. Sometimes we feel like that . . . as if massive waves are going to engulf us. The following verse from Psalm 107 comes to mind: "*Then they cried out to the LORD in their trouble, and he delivered them from their distress.*" or as the hymn writer has put it: "O hear us when we cry to Thee/ For those in peril on the sea"—both on the ocean and on the sea of life.

A Famine of Hearing
July 22

I once saw a memorable video, produced by the Canadian Bible Society, about the distribution of Bibles in Romania following the collapse of the Communist regime. There was a particularly poignant scene in the video that showed a person being handed a Bible at a bus stop. The bus happened to be there, just about to take off, but the people on board, hearing of Bibles, emptied the bus in a frantic rush to secure one.

If that happened here, no one would move from the seat, and someone, I'm sure, would shout at the driver: "Let's get going. Why are we wasting our time here?"

Oh, of course we have Bibles, lots of them. Our problem is that mostly, they are never read.

I am reminded of a forecast by the prophet Amos, who lived in the eighth century BC, concerning the situation we are now facing in North America and other parts of the world. He wrote: " *'The days are coming,' declares the Sovereign LORD, 'when I will send a famine through the land—not a famine of food or a thirst for water, but a famine of hearing the words of the LORD'*" (Amos 8:11). The verse does not say a famine of God's Word, but of the hearing of that word. Changing the figure from a hunger for food to illumination for life's pathway, the Psalmist writes, *"Your word is a lamp to my feet and a light for my path"* (Psalm 119:105). That light is flickering.

If your flame for God's Word is flickering, rekindle it today.

Unknown
July 23

I heard a story about Golda Meir with dubious authenticity as there are different versions. The story goes that back in the days when Golda Meir was Prime Minister of Israel, she hosted a delegation from Japan on one occasion. The Japanese, in turn, wished to show a sign of respect for their hosts by placing a wreath at the Tomb of the Unknown Soldier. The Tomb of the Unknown Soldier is a type of memorial that has been adopted by many countries to honor their war dead.

There was only one problem, however. At that time in Israel, there was no tomb so precisely inscribed, so Prime Minister Meir gave instructions that the wreath be placed on the most grand tomb they had—which happened to be that of composer Felix Mendelssohn. However, one of the members of the Japanese delegation, who was able to read the Hebrew inscription, pointed out that this was not the Tomb of the Unknown Soldier but that of the famous composer. This did not even faze the unflappable Mrs. Meir as she retorted, "Mendelssohn was a very great composer—but as a soldier he was completely unknown."

To be unknown—to die without a name as unknown soldiers do—is a human tragedy. Yet to live feeling unknown and unloved is even more tragic. Jeremiah, one of the Old Testament's great prophets, was called to warn his people of Judah of the nation's danger, soon to come from Babylon if they did not change their evil ways. For his pains, Jeremiah's people despised him, ignored him, and later persecuted him terribly. Facing all this, the prophet called out to his God: *"You know me, O LORD; you see me and test my thoughts about you"* (Jeremiah 12:3).

God knows you, and God knows me. Not a single, solitary soul is unknown to Him. He made us; He sustains us with the very air we breathe. Yet, He does not force Himself on us. As Jeremiah puts it, "He tests my thoughts about Him."

So this is our assurance. Whenever or wherever we feel downcast and alone, even unknown, we are certain that God knows us. God loves us and cares for us. We just need to respond to Him.

Good News
July 24

You may have heard of the famous violinist Pinchas Zukerman. There was an attractive little story in the *Vancouver Sun* about him that concerned a performance he put on in that city. The newspaper column in which the story was written was headed, "A small corner of relief from the issues of great significance covered elsewhere on these pages."

Zukerman, dressed in tails and carrying his violin, was walking to the Orpheum, where he was to play that evening, when an unkempt street person, carrying a plastic bag, approached him.

"What do you do?" the man asked Zukerman.

"I play the violin," came the reply.

"In the street?" the man said.

"No."

"Do you play jazz?" inquired the man.

"No, I play classical music like Brahms."[6]

With that, the homeless man announced that he knew the difference between Beethoven, Schubert, and Schumann. The violinist then invited him to a concert he was about to give with the Vancouver Symphony. After the concert, the man went to see Zukerman to thank him and offered Zukerman the plastic bag—with his chicken dinner. Zukerman admitted that it was not unusual for him to stop and chat with street people and invite them to his concerts.

I don't know about you, but I am beaten down by the barrage of crime, hatred, and bloodshed that compose our news today. The editors may feel that these are matters of "great significance," but I think they've got it twisted. The significant issues are really about the Pinchas Zukermans of the world. That's good news.

After the resurrection, Jesus told his followers to "Go into all the world and preach the good news to all creation." The good news of the gospel is that God loves and cares for all His creation; everyone from those down and out to those up and in. Surely this is good news for our needy world.

"Little Notes Which Like Each Other"
July 25

Wolgang Amadeus Mozart, one of the greatest composers of all time, established his musical genius early in his life. One day while he was tinkering at the piano, his father asked him what he was doing. "Looking for little notes which like each other," little Mozart replied.

"As good a definition of harmony as you could find," someone has commented.

"Looking for little notes which like each other"—a description not only of musical harmony, but also of harmony in living.

A major quality that is missing from much of life in the world is that of harmony—harmony simply being "accord or agreement in feeling, manner or action." The world community is constantly striving for harmony, but harmony never fully comes. There are always some "trouble spots" somewhere. Even in our own country, there are those who seek to destroy the many years of common interest. As well on the domestic front, thousands and thousands of family break-ups not only point to the disharmony, but also seem bent on proving A.P.Herbert's description of marriage as "holy deadlock."

In the book of Romans, the apostle Paul has some excellent guidelines for daily life. He writes: *"Be joyful in hope, patient in affliction, faithful in prayer. Share with God's people who are in need. Practice hospitality. Bless those who persecute you . . . Rejoice with those who rejoice; mourn with those who mourn. Live in harmony with one another"* (Romans 12:12–16a).

If someone is playing the piano well and suddenly sour notes begin to appear, and then more frequently, the harmony of the musical performance has been marred. So it is with life's musical score. Those "little notes which like each other," are vital to life's importance, too.

Prayer and the Call of God
July 26

You may know or remember from previous devotions about Hannah, that she prayed desperately for a son, promising God that if He ever were to give her a son, she would dedicate him completely to God.

So Samuel, as he was subsequently named, arrived. True to her word, Hannah took him to God's house as soon as he was old enough, where he was left in the charge of the priest Eli. As he grew, Samuel served God in many ways, helping Eli.

One night while Samuel was still very young, the boy heard a voice calling his name, "Samuel."

He responded, "Here I am." Thinking it was Eli, Samuel ran to him. Eli had not called, so he instructed Samuel to go back to bed. A second time the same thing happened. Still a third time a voice called to Samuel. By now, the priest realized it could be none other than God calling the boy. Eli instructed Samuel as to how to respond the next time the voice called. Samuel did as instructed, and it turns out that it was indeed God's voice.

God told Samuel of the evil that Eli's sons were doing, evil that their father was either unwilling or unable to stop, and that He (God) would judge the whole family because of their misdeeds. Samuel lay down until morning, but I hardly think he did much sleeping. He was afraid to face Eli and tell him what God had said.

Eli questioned Samuel in the morning concerning what had happened that night and instructed Samuel not to hide anything, but to tell him everything. So Samuel told him . . . everything. The family was punished—the sons for their evil and Eli for doing nothing to stop them.

God's call, made insistently to the boy Samuel that night, was not only to warn Eli, but also to call Samuel to become God's prophet in Israel. He did become one of the greatest prophets in the nation's history. All because of a mother's prayers.

How many of us became a blessing in life to many because of a mother's prayers . . . or a father's . . . or someone else's who loved us dearly? The New Testament writer James says that, *"the prayer of a righteous man is powerful and effective."* And also for a righteous woman, as Hannah proved.

Does God Answer Prayer?

(Part One)

July 27

Prayer is vital to our lives, particularly as we grow older.

John Randolph, an American statesman who lived during the years when the ideas generated by the French Revolution were sweeping the world, is quoted as saying, "I believe I should have been swept away by the flood of French infidelity, if it had not been for one thing: the remembrance of the time when my sainted mother used to make me kneel by her side, taking my little hand in hers, and caused me to repeat."[7]

Prayer is not always asking God for something, although it often is. God encourages us to ask. Prayer is sometimes just listening . . . listening for a word from God. Undoubtedly, those prayers are the most effective as we listen for God's voice and learn His will.

Does God answer prayer? The response to one aspect of that question was given by Jesus Himself in a famous chapter on comfort, that of John 14. Jesus was facing the cross, and He was trying to prepare His apostles for facing a world without Him, following His resurrection and return to the heavenlies. *"I tell you the truth,"* He said to them, *"anyone who has faith in me will do what I have been doing. He will do even greater things than these, because I am going to the Father."* Then he said this: *"And I will do whatever you ask in my name, so that the Son may bring glory to the Father. You may ask for anything in my name, and I will do it"* (John 14:12–14). Jesus here is talking to His very closest followers, to *"Anyone who has faith in me,"* he says. So faith is a prerequisite to answered prayer and to being a follower of Jesus. Then the prayer is to be in Jesus' name and to bring glory to the Heavenly Father.

Yes, inevitably God does answer prayer when these conditions are met. Sometimes He answers when they are not. He is a loving God.

Does God Answer Prayer?
(Part Two)
July 28

Today we continue from yesterday with the theme of prayer and some further thoughts on the following question: Does God answer prayer?

God actually answers prayer a number of ways. The answer may be "yes." The answer may be "no." The answer may also be "later," after the conditions are met. What about a "no" answer? As we look back on some of our requests to God, we quickly realize that a "yes" answer at that time might well have been very harmful to us. Jean Ingelow wrote perceptively, "I have lived to thank God that all of my prayers have not been answered." In other words, God knows far better than do we when He should say "no."

Toward the end of His ministry, Jesus said to His Apostles: *"Have faith in God . . . Therefore I tell you, whatever you ask in prayer, believe that you have received it, and it will be yours"* (Mark 11:22,24).

In Romans 8 the apostle Paul speaks about some prayer problems we all face. What should we pray for? How should we pray? Paul himself writes: *"We do not know what we ought to pray for, but the Spirit* [therefore the Spirit of God] *himself intercedes for us with groans that words cannot express"* (Romans 8:26b).

Finally, Paul leaves us with this word about life and prayer as he writes to the Thessalonians: *"Be joyful always; pray continually; give thanks in all circumstances, for this is God's will for you in Christ Jesus"* (1 Thessalonians 5:16–18).

I Believe
July 29

George Whitefield was one of the most powerful preachers of the eighteenth century. Everywhere he spoke, huge crowds attended.

During a visit to Scotland, a man met the famous Scottish philosopher David Hume on the street . . . on his way to the place where Whitefield was speaking. The man was astonished that Hume, an openly avowed agnostic and skeptic, would be doing this. "But surely you don't believe what Whitefield preaches, do you?" the man asked.

"I don't," replied Hume, "but he does!"

The honest person is always impressed when a man or woman is able to say with conviction, "I believe" and to back up that belief with a fine quality of life.

Hosts of ordinary people, not nearly as articulate as George Whitefield, are able to say humbly, "I believe."

Toward the end of the Gospel of John, in which the apostle relates many of the activities of his Master Jesus—including miracles, healings, and outreaching love and concern, John writes: *"These are written that you may believe that Jesus is the Christ, the Son of God, and that by believing you may have life in his name."* To which the apostle Paul added in 2 Timothy 1:12: *"I am not ashamed, because I know whom I have believed, and am convinced that he is able to guard what I have entrusted to him for that day"*— "that day" being the day of eternity.

Poet John Oxenham reflects that trust in a poem, which he entitles "Credo." An excerpt is given here.

> Not what, but WHOM, I do believe,
> That in my darkest hour of need,
> Hath comfort that no mortal creed
> To mortal man may give;
>
> Not what, but WHOM!
> For Christ is more than all the creeds,
> And his full life of gentle deeds
> Shall all the creeds outlive.[8]

I believe!

Role Models
July 30

Good, wholesome characters have, for some reason it seems, gone out of favor. Now the heroes and heroines are the multimillionaires who throw footballs, hit baseballs, or scream as the lead singer in a rock band, or act as a talk show host, asking mindless questions. There are many fine people among these, but they have one thing in common. They are paid monumental sums, not because of who they are, but because of what they do to keep people pleasurably entertained. In the final analysis, their character isn't of great importance to people.

In the Old Testament book of Daniel, the Babylonian emperor Nebuchadnezzar had a dream. In the dream, a massive statue or image appeared, with a head of gold, chest and arms of silver, stomach and thighs of bronze, legs of iron, and feet a mixture of clay and iron. In the king's dream, a rock appeared that smashed the image. Into our language has come from that biblical picture the saying "feet of clay"—suggesting some thing or some person who is brought down by a basic weakness, a character flaw perhaps. Quite a few of the modern heroes or idols are being shown to have feet of clay, and that's a tragedy, particularly for young people who desperately need good role models.

Seniors can be good role models. Paul, writing to Titus in the New Testament book of that name, pleads: *"Encourage the young men to be self-controlled. In everything set them an example by doing what is good"* (Titus 2:6–7a).

There's something heroic about that.

Try the Up-Look
July 31

Henry Drummond, who lived during the last half of the nineteenth century, was an evangelist, author, and lecturer on science at the Free Church College in Glasgow, Scotland. Among other things, he addressed religious meetings for university students. His messages were very straightforward, and he used a down–to-earth style. At one such meeting, Henry Drummond reportedly made a memorable remark that should be a truism for all of us: "When the outlook isn't good, try the up-look."

We all have days when we're down: a very rainy day, perhaps cold, and our spirits are lower than the temperature and as damp as the day outside. There may be some problem, some difficulty or other, and it doesn't have to be very big. Actually, it doesn't have to be a poor weather day—it could be warm and sunny outside, but what is going on inside ourselves could be anything but warm and sunny. For many situations in our lives, the outlook simply seems bad.

What about the upward look which Drummond suggests? There's a very significant verse in Mark 8, where Jesus Himself calls for the upward look. He and His disciples had come to the town of Bethsaida where a blind man was brought to him. Verse 25 of the chapter in the KJV reads: "*He [Jesus] put his hands again upon his eyes, and made him look up: and he was restored, and saw every man clearly.*"

Many have been restored, healed, comforted, simply by looking up rather than out on a troubled world or in on a troubled soul. For looking up is to reach out to God, and it is in Him we find the assurance of peace.

"When the outlook isn't good, try the up-look."

Putting Our Best Into Life
August 01

Generally speaking, one of life's principles is that the more you put into things, the more you will get out.

Similar sentiments are expressed in the Old Testament Book of Ecclesiastes, where this little gem of wisdom is found in chapter 9, verse 10a: "*Whatever your hand finds to do, do it with all your might.*"

The apostle Paul speaks often about putting our very best into life. In the twelfth chapter of Romans, he writes fervently about the marvelous spiritual gifts God has given to each of His followers. These gifts are not to be kept simply for our own use, but to be shared with others—and shared zealously . . . "*with all your might,*" as Ecclesiastes has it.

Paul writes:

> *We have different gifts . . . If a man's gift is prophesying, let him use it in proportion to his faith. If it is serving, let him serve; if it is teaching, let him teach; if it is encouraging* [and we all can be encouragers], *let him* [or her] *encourage; if it is contributing to the needs of others, let him give generously; if it is leadership, let him govern diligently; if it is showing mercy, let him do it cheerfully* (Romans 12: 6–8).

Or again, as Solomon put it in Ecclesiastes: "*Whatever your hand finds to do, do it with all your might.*"

In other words, no matter what we are doing, we should do it to the best of our abilities. That's very true of life, no matter what your age.

No Light at the End of the Tunnel
August 02

I noticed a rather intriguing poster on a wall one time. It read something like this: "Due to the current shortage, we are forced to turn out the light at the end of the tunnel."

The remark was meant to be funny, and it is, but it is a bit of humor that has a bite in it, particularly in times of industrial downsizing and/or the loss of jobs. For someone out of work or perhaps with a diminishing income, "the light at the end of the tunnel" was meant to be the glimmer of hope at the end of a period of dark despair. Take away that symbolic hope, and the future is totally black . . . and bleak.

That's how some good folks look at our world, for them the lights have gone out—even at the end of the tunnel.

Yet there is a Light to end all darkness, especially the darkness of the soul, the darkness of the mind—the very worst darkness. The apostle John speaks of it right at the very first of his Gospel. Referring to that Light, which was the very Son of God, John writes: "*In him* [that is, Jesus] *was life, and that life was the light of men.*" And John continues, "*The light shines in the darkness, but the darkness has not understood it*" (John 1:4–5).

Jesus Himself confirmed John's statement when, teaching the people, He said: "*I am the light of the world. Whoever follows me will never walk in darkness, but will have the light of life*" (John 8:12).

Paul buttresses the view later in his letter to the Colossians: "*For he has rescued us from the dominion of darkness.*"

To be plucked from the darkness of the soul and into wondrous light is one of the richest blessings of the Christian way. There is no need of the light at the end of the tunnel because there is no tunnel. Life is full of light; the future is certain.

Known to Him
August 03

Métis storyteller Ron Evans tells of a legend about an overzealous anthropologist who wanted to bring an isolated native village into more modern times by giving them a television set. As the legend goes, all activity stopped when the television was turned on. The amazed villagers sat for days in front of the TV, amazed at all the pictures and sounds coming from it.

When the anthropologist returned six months later, the villagers were sitting in a circle listening to their storyteller—their TV having been abandoned to the outskirts of the village. The anthropologist inquired about why the natives weren't watching their TV. "Oh, we watched your box for several weeks," replied the village chief. "Now we listen to our storyteller instead."

"But doesn't the TV know more stories than your storyteller?" cried the anthropologist. The chief thought for a moment. "It is true, the TV knows many stories," he said, "but our storyteller knows us."[1]

Legend as it is, this is quite a parable of life, one that is particularly penetrating when there is so much counterfeit—sham, if you like—around us. Even in our society, television is a mirror of the tasteless state of our culture. Unfortunately, it seems to pick up and glamorize the very worst in us. Perhaps, like the villagers, we should from time to time banish that particular medium to the outskirts of the community.

In the Gospel of John, in the last two verses of Chapter 2, is found a very pithy comment about Jesus. It reads, *"For he [Jesus] knew all men. He did not need man's testimony about man, for he knew what was in a man."*

He knew, and He knows, that in spite of the things that allure us, eternity is in the heart of humankind. *"What good is it for a man, to gain the whole world, yet forfeit his soul?"* He asked.

He knew, and He knows, that sinners need, above all else, forgiveness. For those who nailed him to the cross, He prayed, *"Father forgive them, for they do not know what they are doing."*

He knew, and He knows, that those pressed down by the cares of life need release, and He called, *"Come to me, all you who are weary and burdened, and I will give you rest."*

Yes indeed, our Savior knows us.

Doors

August 04

Charles Harvey and his wife, personal friends of mine, spent many, many years as missionaries in Angola and Zaire. Charlie, also a writer, wrote a delightful little book. Within that book are stories of his boyhood days, growing up on a St. John River Valley farm in New Brunswick. One such story is called "The Tooth Door," and the heroine of the story is a single lady neighbor called Allie.

"Allie," writes the author, "was every little person's private possession." Allie was full of stories and songs "that never grow old with retelling." Allie was especially adept at pulling small children's first teeth when they became loose. When local youngsters needed a loose tooth removed, they showed it to Allie. She would carefully and skillfully inspect the degree of looseness. When it was just right—and she might wait up to a couple of weeks just to make sure, Allie would prepare the "tooth door." A strong black thread was tied carefully to the doorknob. "We stood," said Charlie, "so that the thread was just snug." The door was open about a foot. "It was traumatic," Charlie writes. By then, Allie was on the other side of the door, and at an unpredictable moment, she would slam the door shut. Nine times out of ten, it worked perfectly, and the youngster went home proudly bearing his or her tooth, to be placed under the pillow that night with a nickel's replacing it next morning.[2]

Doors, you see, have good uses other than for opening or closing passageways. Slamming them shut has a better use than annoying other members of the family.

Doors are very significant in the Bible of course. There is no record of one's being used for pulling teeth. There are, however, prison doors and other locked doors. There is a door of judgment. There are doors like the open door and the door of faith. There is a door of opportunity—a narrow door to be sure. The most important door is your heart's door, before which Jesus is standing. In Revelation 3:20, the Master issues this invitation: *"Here I am! I stand at the door and knock. If anyone hears my voice and opens the door, I will go in and eat with him, and he* [or she] *with me."*

Making a Difference
August 05

What sort of a difference do I make? In the book of Numbers, there is the tragic story of the Israelites, the people of God, and their refusal to go over into the land God had promised them after they had escaped from Egypt. Coming up to the border of this new land of promise, they hesitated, then sent in twelve spies to check it out, one from every tribe. When these men returned, all twelve said that the new land was splendid, but ten of the twelve said they shouldn't try to go in because the dangers were too great and the enemies unbeatable. Two men, Joshua and Caleb, presented a minority report, admitting the dangers were great but acknowledging that under God, they could overcome them. Because of the reluctance of the Israelites to trust Him, God would not allow any of that generation to go in except Joshua and Caleb.

Each of us, by the way we live, can make a difference. In the book of Acts, there is an intriguing story of two men who also made a difference. Two of Jesus' apostles, going up to the Temple at 3:00 prayer time, came upon a crippled man begging at the gate called "Beautiful." Through the power of God, they healed the man, and Peter addressed the crowd that thronged around following the miracle. The Jewish leaders, noting the hubbub, seized the two apostles, jailed them, and brought them before the Jewish Council, the Sanhedrin, the next day. Peter addressed the Sanhedrin in the book of Acts in chapter 4 verse 13: *"When they saw the courage of Peter and John and realized that they were unschooled, ordinary men, they were astonished and they took note that these men had been with Jesus."*

That's the difference that makes a difference.

Walking to Emmaus
August 06

One of the most gripping of the resurrection stories of Jesus is one recorded in the Gospel of Luke, chapter 24. On resurrection day, two followers of the Master were walking to Emmaus, about seven miles from Jerusalem. In deep conversation about the events of the last two or three days, they did not recognize the stranger who caught up to them and asked the reason for their heavy conversation and downcast looks. "Are you only a visitor to Jerusalem and do not know the things that have happened there in these days?" they said.

"What things?" the stranger asked, and so they told him about the events surrounding Jesus' death.

By this time, they had reached their destination, and the stranger prepared to move on. But something about him caused them to invite him in. Over the evening meal, the risen Savior was revealed to them.

Malcolm Muggeridge, the famous British writer and editor, made the Emmaus walk with a friend some years ago, living through the experiences of the travelers after the crucifixion.

The walk made a deep impression on him.

"So much so," he wrote, "that thenceforth I have never doubted that, wherever the walk and whoever the wayfarers, there is always, as on that other occasion on the road to Emmaus, a third presence ready to emerge from the shadows and fall in step along the dusty, stoney way."[3]

It's a matter of great strength and comfort to know that we never need to walk alone, that the One who lived and died and rose again is prepared to be by our side . . . even if sometimes we don't recognize Him.

"*Surely I am with you always, to the very end of the age,*" He promised. Perhaps you can witness to that fact . . . that particularly in the rough times He is right there by your side. As the writer of Hebrews has put it, "*God has said, 'Never will I leave you; never will I forsake you.'*" Adds the Psalmist: "*Though my father and mother forsake me, the LORD will receive me.*"

The personal experience of the walk of the Emmaus Road is one to be constantly cherished.

God Lost?
August 07

One time while glancing through a collection of religious works, I caught a cryptic little sentence that caused me furiously to think. The item was apparently culled from the classified advertising section of a newspaper, and to me it simply spoke of tragedy personified. "Having lost God, two saddened searchers seek a substitute." After the message, a box number was given.

How do you lose God? You lose God, I believe, when other elements so build up in your life that God is squeezed out. There is simply no room for Him. It's often not by conscious choice that this happens. We just allow other things to mount up, and soon God is out.

Jesus put it another way: *"The man who loves his life will lose it, while the man who hates his life in this world will keep it for eternal life"* (John 12:25). The choice is ours. Then in addition, there are times in the life of each one of us when God seems to be miles and miles away. We have not shut Him out—consciously or unconsciously, but a wall seems to keep us apart. Job had that feeling in the midst of terrible troubles.

> *"If I only knew where to find him,"* he cries, *"if only I could go to his dwelling! But if I go to the east, he is not there; if I go to the west, I do not find him. When he is at work in the north, I do not see Him; when he turns to the south, I catch no glimpse of him."* Then Job adds: *But he knows the way that I take; when he has tested me, I will come forth as gold* (Job 23:3, 8–10).

That's the faith that trusts. But what of a substitute . . . a replacement for God? There is none. *"I am the way,"* said Jesus, *"and the truth and the life. No one comes to the Father except through me"* (John 14:6). Those who seek to find some other way will find nothing but emptiness. The world's gods are utterly false.

You've lost God, you say. *"Wait for the LORD,"* suggests the Psalmist. *"Be strong and take heart and wait for the LORD."*

God will not keep you waiting long.

Personal Witness
August 08

At a meeting of ministers I attended, I was listening to a well-known speaker from across the Atlantic when the speaker, at one point in his address, was quite critical of Dr. Billy Graham. The speaker, at the conclusion of his address, invited questions from the audience. One of the ministers present asked, "You were somewhat critical of Dr. Graham. Would you care to amplify?"

And the speaker added to his criticisms, finally ending, "Can you tell me of any real lasting good that has come out of any of Dr. Graham's crusades?"

From the rear of the room came an immediate response, "I am, sir!" One of the ministers, an Anglican, told of his conversion at one of Dr. Graham's crusades. The speaker had very little to say thereafter.

"I am, sir!"

There's nothing quite as powerful as a personal testimony . . . a word that something has happened to you. This is firsthand, not something you have been told about someone else's experience, not something you have read about somewhere. It has occurred in your own life. You can say with ringing assurance, "I know!"

The Christian faith indeed is one of personal experience. One doesn't need to take someone else's word on the matter. He or she may find out for himself or herself.

Very early in the ministry of Jesus, John the Baptist and two of his disciples were standing, talking, when Jesus came nearby. John said to the two, *"Look, the lamb of God,"* and the two men walked after Jesus.

Turning around, Jesus asked them what they wanted, and they responded, *"Rabbi . . . where are you staying?"*

Jesus replied, *"Come and you will see."*

That's the perfect personal invitation, which the Master tenders to all. "Come and see for yourself."

Changeable
August 09

If there is one single element that marks our world, it is the obvious fact that things are changeable. In business and industry, one of the most notable changes is called "downsizing." Many are unemployed because of that change. No one is fired any more, of course; your job has simply become "redundant"—but the change is just as severe, the pain as hurtful. And on the domestic scene, families are changing partners at the greatest rate in history.

There is one redeeming feature, I think, and it is that people, individually, are open to personal change. That has to be a plus.

Change means choices. I am reminded of Joshua, the great successor to Moses, the leader of the nation of Israel. Moses, you'll remember, had led his people out of four hundred years of slavery in Egypt, out towards the Promised Land—the new home God had assured them would be theirs. They were not an easy people to lead as Moses soon discovered. They wandered back and forth across the desert for forty years until Moses' successor, Joshua, led them across the Jordan River into that Promised Land. After many years, a huge number of battles, and continual quarrelling and difficulties, the nation had finally reached the objective—their own homeland.

Now an old man, Joshua assembled his people and addressed them, describing the pilgrimage they had taken over many decades. Finally, Joshua indicated that theirs was now a major choice in view of what God had done for them. *"Now fear the LORD and serve him with all faithfulness,"* Joshua advised his people. He also gave the following charge:

> *Throw away the gods your forefathers worshiped beyond the River and in Egypt, and serve the LORD. But if serving the LORD seems undesirable to you, then choose for yourselves this day whom you will serve, whether the gods your forefathers served . . . or the gods of the Amorites, in whose land you are living. But as for me and my household, we will serve the LORD"* (Joshua 24:14–15).

This choice still faces our world: the paths of success, material wealth, and pleasure or the way of God, who made us, and whose Son died to give us new and eternal life. God does not change.

Treasures—Old and New
August 10

One of the very shortest of Jesus' parables is contained in only one verse: Matthew 13:52.

> *"Every teacher of the law who has been instructed about the kingdom of heaven is like the owner of a house who brings out of his storeroom new treasures as well as old."*

There's always a danger that we who are older will cling to just the old ways . . . like Jim Jay in poet Walter de la Mare's little triplet:

Poor Jim Jay

Got stuck fast

In Yesterday.[4]

The disciples of Jesus' day had the Old Testament (old treasure) on which to draw, as have we. With Jesus now in their midst (new treasure), He offered them and us new ways— forgiveness, personal salvation, the promise of His Spirit to guide them and us in every activity of life, plus the assurance of the presence of God throughout all eternity. What further treasures! These spiritual treasures were like, explained Jesus, the owner of a house who brings out of his storeroom new treasures as well as old. And the treasures were not simply for show to be put on display, but to be given out and used.

The author of Hebrews speaks of *"a new and living way opened for us,"* noting that we also have *"a great priest over the house of God"*—our Savior Jesus Christ, who opened the new way by His death on the cross. Ours is a very personal faith, intimate and meaningful.

Said Jesus, *"A new command I give you. Love one another. As I have loved you, so you must love one another. By this all men will know that you are my disciples if you love one another"* (John 13:34–35).

So God's Word is to us both an old, cherished treasure, yet also a new gift from our Heavenly Father, enabling us to brighten our lives with new anticipation every day God gives us.

Competing According to the Rules
August 11

Sporting events are very popular. The World Cup of Soccer and the Olympics draw many thousands of spectators in person, and millions more watch on television.

Have you ever asked yourself why? I don't think there's a simple answer, but certainly in the athletic games men and women play, there are many elements. There can be change, challenge, accomplishment, strength, renewal, exhilaration, victory . . . even defeat, sometimes even when you've done your best.

The athletic event is a symbol of life itself. A goal is set, one goes into training; then in the event itself, one does his or her very best. Aren't our lives like that? We set our sights, we secure the best available training, and then we do our utmost to reach the goal.

The apostle Paul, who loved to use the athletic metaphor, wrote in his first letter to his young friend Timothy, in 1 Timothy 6:12a: "*Fight the good fight of faith. Take hold of the eternal life to which you were called.*" And again in his second letter to Timothy, chapter 2 and verse 5: "*If anyone competes as an athlete, he does not receive the victor's crown unless he competes according to the rules.*"

So, we are reminded, the good Christian, in the same way as the good athlete, chooses the goal of eternal life, competes according to the rules given in the Book of Life, God's Word, and will one day wear the victor's crown . . . not for himself or herself alone, but for the One who saved and trained him or her.

Living Water
August 12

On one occasion, Jesus and His band of disciples were traveling through Samaria. The Jews, who despised the Samaritans, rarely went into or through Samaria—except Jesus. Outside the town of Sychar was a public well. Jesus, tired from the journey, sat down by the well. The disciples had gone into town to get food.

A Samaritan woman arrived at the well to draw water. Jesus asked her for a drink. The woman was absolutely baffled by the fact that Jesus, obviously a Jew, would ask a despised Samaritan—and especially a woman—for anything. When she expressed this surprise, Jesus replied that if only she knew about God's greatest gift and who it was asking for a drink, she would have asked him for a drink of living water. This was an enigmatic answer, to be sure. As the conversation proceeded, Jesus turned it toward the meaning of living water. The woman still had trouble understanding what Jesus was talking about. She asked Him to give her this water so she wouldn't have to trudge many daily miles to the well to secure it.

Jesus switched His tactics a little, telling the woman to go to town and bring her husband back. *"'I have no husband,' she replied. Jesus said to her, 'You are right when you say you have no husband. The fact is, you have had five husbands, and the man you now have is not your husband. What you have just said is quite true'"* (John 4:17–18). Jesus, seeing into her very soul, told her what he saw, and she was distressed. She realized that Jesus was a prophet. After talking a little further with Him, He revealed He was the Messiah. The woman put down her water jar and rushed back to Sychar, crying out to all who gathered: *"Come, see a man who told me everything I did. Could this be the Christ?"* (John 4:29).

And a throng followed the woman back to Jesus. Many believed in Jesus because of the woman's testimony. Others believed when they came face to face with Jesus and the disciples. They saw and learned for themselves. They all then urged Him to stay, and He remained two days.

That's the Savior who then offered, and still does, a new way—the water of life for every yearning man or woman.

A Parable of Life
August 13

While walking along one of the beaches of the Oregon coastline as the tide was coming in, I came upon a parable of life. On the top of a ridge of sand left by the pounding waves, three youngsters were building a castle—not any old castle either, but one in a pyramid style, surrounded by a moat and walls.

The youngsters, two boys and a girl, worked diligently as the tide came closer by the minute. Sensing the task was hopeless, the girl and one of the boys left, with one boy remaining to build. Finally, the water got so close that some spilled around the edge, filling the moat. There's nothing wrong with that; moats are supposed to be filled with water. Then, however, a wave washed beyond the moat and lapped up one side of the castle. Thinking his effort was at an end, the boy pushed his foot against the castle, not knocking it down but damaging it. Then he walked away up the beach, disgusted I'm sure. I waited, watching the castle a little longer, and lo and behold, the tide began to fall back very slowly. Obviously, the tide had reached the high water mark and would do no more damage to the castle that day. But the boy had gone, sensing no hope.

Isn't that a little like life? Buffeted by the storms, we are sometimes sorely tempted to give up—to quit. Then almost imperceptibly, the tide turns; the buffeting ceases, and we are at peace. Yes, we've been hurt but certainly not beyond repair. If we stay around, the repairs too will come.

The Psalmist has something to say about the storms of life. Looking to his Creator, he writes: "*You rule over the surging sea; when its waves mount up, you still them*" (Psalm 89:9). Then in Psalm 107, the Psalmist describes vividly the feelings of those who are being crushed by life's storms: "*They reeled and staggered like drunken men; they were at their wits' end. Then they cried out to the LORD in their trouble, and he brought them out of their distress. He stilled the storm to a whisper; the waves of the sea were hushed*" (Psalm 107:27–29).

The Psalmist later adds: "*Let them give thanks to the LORD for his unfailing love and his wonderful deeds*" (Psalm 107:31).

May we do just that.

Training
August 14

There was a so-called "Miracle Mile" race at the Commonwealth Games held in Vancouver during the fifties. Roger Bannister nosed out John Landy to win the race and set a new world record. Both of them bettered four minutes for the mile—the first time two runners in the same race had done that. Bannister himself had broken the four-minute barrier only months earlier. Since those days, sub-four-minute miles happen quite regularly. Are the runners of today so much better than Bannister and Landy?

The answer is yes and no. Tracks are better, equipment (shoes, etc.) is better, but the biggest difference is training. World marks fall frequently as the training becomes better and better. One sometimes wonders what the limits are. The athletes are paying a price—sometimes a very high price—in actual physical pain that comes from heavy training. Discipline is rigorous, and the sacrifices are enormous.

What about the game of life (if I may dare phrase it that way)? The writer of the book of Hebrews has some interesting thoughts in this regard. He writes: *"Let us throw off everything that hinders and the sin that so easily entangles, and let us run with perseverance the race marked out for us"* (Hebrews 12:1). He goes on to refer to the discipline of training. *"Endure hardship as discipline"* (Hebrews 12:7a). Further on, he adds: *"Our fathers disciplined us for a while as they thought best; but God disciplines us for our good, that we may share in his holiness. No discipline seems pleasant at the time, but painful. Later on, however, it produces a harvest of righteousness and peace for those who have been trained by it"* (Hebrews 12:10–11).

Many of you have experienced God's loving discipline as you have traveled the track of life, and your lives show the fine results. For all, the clue to winning life's race is found in the following words in Hebrews: *"Let us fix our eyes on Jesus the author and perfecter of our faith."* (Hebrews 12:2a). He will pace our race of life.

Accompanied by the Master
August 15

There is a story concerning Jan Paderewski, the famous composer–pianist, and a small boy attending his concert. There is debate about its authenticity, but it does illustrate a point, like many stories.

The boy's mother had pressured him to come, with the hope that hearing the famous Paderewski would inspire the lad to practice on his own piano more. Before the concert was to begin, the mother turned to talk to some friends, and the restless boy slipped away unnoticed. He went up on the stage, sat down at the piano, and began to play "chopsticks." Drawing the attention of the crowd, some began to shout out to stop the boy. Backstage Paderewski heard the shouts, put together in his mind what was happening, and went onstage. Without announcement, he leaned over behind the lad and improvised a countermelody to harmonize and enhance chopsticks. As both of them played, Paderewski whispered, "Keep going. Don't Quit. Keep on playing; don't stop; don't quit."

Even when we are older, particularly when we are older, God gives us tasks to do to brighten our days . . . and someone else's days. Those tasks may be as simple as "chopsticks," and even so, we may falter and hesitate to go on. But God will take the little things we are able to do and enhance them, making them a valuable service in His kingdom, while the world may be trying to shout us down. God calls, always encouraging: "Keep it up; don't quit. I am with you to the end of time."

Perseverance
August 16

There are numerous examples throughout history of people overcoming disabilities and suffering to achieve a goal. The world of sports has many such examples. One in particular that comes to my mind is the story of Ray Ewry. As a boy, Ray was stricken with polio and confined to a wheelchair. He began exercising on his own to restore his body. A doctor told him that jumping from a standing position would help strengthen his withered limbs. His therapy gradually became his sport, and he grew up to become an outstanding athlete. He became so proficient that in one single afternoon in 1900, at the Olympic Games no less, he won the standing high jump, the standing long jump, and the standing triple jump. Four years later, he repeated the feat. In 1908, he won two more gold medals—eight Olympic gold medals in all.

What would drive such a person to persevere in the midst of dire suffering such as Ray Ewry obviously endured? Every person must speak for himself or herself, but it seems to me that the gaining of the goal, the fulfillment of the impossible dream, is truly a motivating factor, and suffering is an accepted part of that fulfillment.

In speaking about the race of life, the apostle Paul writes in Romans 5: *"We also rejoice in our sufferings, because we know that suffering produces perseverance; perseverance character; and character hope"* (Romans 5:3–4).

James puts it this way: *"Blessed is the man who perseveres under trial, because when he has stood the test, he will receive the crown of life that God has promised to those who love him"* (James 1:12).

Christ's Vineyard
August 17

One of the parables Jesus told was that of the vineyard grower who planted his acreage of vines, let it out to others (sharecroppers, if you like), and then went away for a long time. When the time of harvest came, the owner sent his servants to collect his proceeds. Instead of paying, the tenants killed one of the servants and attacked the others. The vineyard owner sent a second set of servants, and they were treated in similar fashion. The owner then sent his only son, reasoning "surely they will reverence him"—but no, they murdered him. *"What then will the owner of the vineyard do to them?"* Jesus asked. *"He will come and kill those tenants and give the vineyard to others,"* came His reply. Then the passage, as recorded in Luke, continues: *"When the people heard this, they said, 'May this never be.'"* Yet Calvary was just three days away.

Obviously, in this parable Jesus was referring to Himself as the Son who is to be thrust out of His Father's vineyard—the world. And His killers are His own people, the Jews of His day, and His Father is going to give the opportunity of salvation to others. As John writes: *"He came to that which was his own, but his own did not receive him. Yet to all who received him, to those who believed in his name, he gave the right to become children of God"* (John 1:11–12). That is what Calvary offers to you and me.

The first verse of Elizabeth Clephane's well-known hymn, "Beneath the Cross of Jesus," speaks for many:

> Beneath the Cross of Jesus, I fain would take my stand,
>
> The shadow of a mighty rock within a weary land;
>
> A home within the wilderness, a rest upon the way,
>
> From the burning of the noontide heat, and the burden of the day.[5]

Retired
August 18

Automobile license plates sometimes have interesting messages on them. One of the most interesting I have seen is a vehicle that had a front plate with "**RETIRED**" in bold letters in the center . . . and in the corners; "NO ADDRESS, NO PHONE, NO CLOCK, NO MONEY."

Likely, the last was the only one near the truth, but I'm sure that many of us can appreciate the owner's attitude to that ending of regular gainful employment, which we, with a measure of both dread and hope, call "retirement." I'm certain retirement hasn't been quite what we expected. Particularly for the early years of retirement, time has not dragged, and many of us sometimes wonder how we ever had the time to go to work. Gradually a change takes place, circumstances are altered, and sometimes time does hang heavy. How does one cope best?

One can get involved in many meaningful activities, if he chooses. There are friends and loved ones to visit and to host. Above and beyond all is time spent nurturing your personal Christian faith, with its assurance of the love and continued presence of a concerned and caring Heavenly Father.

The situation of the apostle Paul, when he wrote the little letter to the Christians in Philippi, was precarious and uncertain, to say the least. He was in prison for his faith. This is what he wrote about his life's uncertainties: "*I have learned to be content whatever the circumstances. I know what it is to be in need, and I know what it is to have plenty. I have learned the secret of being content in any and every situation, whether well fed or hungry, whether living in plenty or in want*" (Philippians 4:11–12). Then he adds this ringing note of absolute confidence in the future: "*I can do everything through him who gives me strength*" (Philippians 4:13).

This is a good motto, I suggest, for those of us who are truly retired, for there is yet much for each of us to do.

No Time to Listen

August 19

One of the real tragedies happening on the domestic scene in our day is that parents have become too busy—mothers as well as fathers—and the children suffer from a lack of parental attention. But I suppose it's hard to turn back the clock.

There is one true reassurance we have in life. God is never too busy to give us attention—to listen to us, whether we are very young or very much older. In the tenth Psalm, the Psalmist calls out: *"You hear, O LORD, the desire of the afflicted; you encourage them, and you listen to their cry, defending the fatherless and the oppressed, in order that man, who is of the earth, may terrify no more"* (Psalm 10:17–18). God loves you; He is listening.

In Psalm 34:6–7, David writes: *"This poor man called and the LORD heard him; he saved him out of all his troubles. The angel of the LORD encamps around those who fear him, and he delivers them."* Again in the same Psalm, in verses 17–18, *"The righteous cry out, and the LORD hears them; he delivers them from all their troubles. The LORD is close to the brokenhearted and saves those who are crushed in spirit."*

And if we respond to God's overtures, He promises peace. *"Peace I leave with you,"* said Jesus. *"My peace I give you. I do not give to you as the world gives. Do not let your hearts be troubled and do not be afraid"* (John 14:27).

The love of a gracious Father God is always assured if we look to Him in faith. Just call Him.

A Work of Art
August 20

Some of you, likely ladies, may have quilting as a hobby. Quilting is a marvelous hobby, calling for a great deal of creativity and all kinds of patience, as well as skill in sewing. The making of quilts is not only an individual effort but, especially in the past, was a cooperative one, where women in the rural areas had quilting bees and quilting clubs to make valuable and fulfilling use of the little spare time they had.

Quilters, of course, take material, having a variety of fabric, design and color, and work these pieces into a magnificent work of art.

God can do that with our lives—taking the bits and pieces of our lives and making them into something beautiful.

In one of the most heartwarming verses in the New Testament, the apostle Peter writes: *"Cast all your anxiety on him because he cares for you"* (1Peter 5:7). David the Psalmist writes of our Heavenly Father: *"When I consider your heavens, the work of your fingers, the moon and the stars, which you have set in place, what is man that you are mindful of him, the son of man that you care for him?"* (Psalm 8:3–4). But God does; He cares for every single one of us.

Jesus Himself, using a very simple illustration, made a strong statement concerning God's love for us. *"Are not two sparrows sold for a penny? Yet not one of them will fall to the ground apart from the will of your Father. And even the very hairs of your head are all numbered. So don't be afraid; you are worth more than many sparrows"* (Matthew 10:29–31).

Indeed, we are worth so much—you and I—that Jesus gave His life to make us whole. God cares.

Life's Meaning
August 21

At one time, I was pastor of a church in Sussex, New Brunswick. While there, I was also part-time chaplain at the nearby depot of the regular Army regiment. The depot was the center where nearby men (there were no women at that time in the infantry) took their first six weeks of training. Among my duties was leadership in a Padre's Hour once a week, and for me, at least, it was an interesting session. It was not a Sunday school class as you might imagine, for these young men were directly off the streets and farms of the Atlantic region. There was one aspect of their thinking that arose many times in the discussions we had. Most of them handled life fatalistically. If a little girl ran across the street and was knocked down by a car, that was the way it was to be. If, in the course of your career in the Army, you were killed in battle, that particular shell or bullet had your number on it.

But not everyone is a fatalist, seeing the world as a kind of massive clock that some power— God perhaps—has wound up and set in motion, and on it runs, without God or man able to do very much about it.

The difficulty with that point of view is that it absolves one of all sense of responsibility, and life becomes an unthinking experience, with very little meaning.

Jesus came into the world for the very purpose of showing life's true meaning: the fact that you and I can so live that we need not spin our wheels. He taught that we are alienated children of a loving Heavenly Father, who sent Jesus to redeem us and to give life clear meaning. That's the invitation He extends to all.

Sharing
August 22

I suppose on the larger world scene, the western part of the world, especially North America, has developed, to some extent at least, the fine habit of sharing. Millions upon millions of our citizens give many tens of millions of dollars every year to aid the underprivileged countries of the world . . . the dispossessed, the homeless, the refugees.

Not only Christians do this, of course, but a Christian does have a special reason to share. Christians give out of a heart of gratitude for what God has given us—life itself with its many blessings, new life through the sacrifice of Jesus, and a hereafter of surpassing love and beauty. But sharing does something for you too. Jesus put sharing this way: *"Give and it will be given to you. A good measure, pressed down, shaken together and running over, will be poured into your lap. For with the measure you use, it will be measured to you"* (Luke 6:38).

John the Baptist said this about sharing: *"The man with two tunics should share with him who has none, and the one who has food should do the same"* (Luke 3:11). The Master also said, *"Freely you have received, freely give."*

There is a West African Adinkra symbol, portraying interlocking crocodiles with a shared stomach, which being translated means, "If one eats, all eat." Wouldn't it be a wonderful world if all had such a vision?

Self-Sacrifice

August 23

Many incidents of self-sacrifice occur in wartime. One such incident is told by a chaplain who himself was experiencing war, literally in the trenches, in a fierce battle during the First World War. There was a shortage of water. An officer, ascertaining that the chaplain had some, asked the chaplain to locate a group of some forty men further along the trench, badly wounded and desperate for water. The chaplain found the casualties, and fortunately his bottle was full, although a military water bottle doesn't really hold much water. The chaplain went to the first man and gave him the bottle saying, "Here you are, lad—drink, but remember there are thirty-nine others who want it as badly as you." So it went from the first to the last, right along the line. "Do you know," he said afterwards, "it was the last man who got the most water."[6]

One of the noblest human characteristics is that of self-sacrifice . . . giving up your advantage so that someone else may have it. We do see sacrifices around us day by day. We see them in the seemingly "little" things of life, like a mother and father who sacrifice that their children might have a good education or might have the advantages in life denied to the parents. Most of you have been involved in making sacrifices like that.

The Christian faith, of course, is built on the theme of sacrifice, for that is how Jesus made possible our salvation—through His sacrifice on the cross. In turn, God calls on us to sacrifice. The apostle Paul writes to the Roman Christians: "*I urge you, brothers, in view of God's mercy, to offer your bodies as living sacrifices, holy and pleasing to God—this is your spiritual act of worship*"(Romans 12:1).

It is that kind of self-giving that makes a life.

Encouragers
August 24

There's an interesting footnote to the history of flight. The Wright brothers at first found it very difficult to do their experiments, for they needed a level field on which to practice flight. A farmer took pity on them and let them use one free of charge. It was the encouragement they needed. Equally important, another encourager, a Mrs. Beard, lived nearby and watched the men with a great deal of interest and concern. When the spindly craft landed abruptly and roughly—as it often did—Mrs. Beard would dash across the road with a bottle of her special lotion to soothe away their bruises.

She was not very important in the overall story of flight perhaps and yet so very vital to the well-being and attitude of the pioneering brothers.

Encouragement. In Romans, we find a list of gifts God gives to His followers, including the gift of encouragement, to enable them to be effective as Christians in this world. "*If it* [one's gift] *is encouraging, let him encourage.*" (Romans 12:8a)

"*Let us encourage one another,*" adds the writer of the book of Hebrews. When there was a major problem among the early churches in the book of Acts, the Jerusalem church wrote a letter, and as chapter 15, verse 31 notes, "*The people* [to whom the letter was sent in Antioch, Syria and Cilicia] *read it and were glad for its encouraging message.*"

Encouragement . . . a simple word with a world of meaning—not difficult to carry out, but vital in daily living.

A Ministry of Mercy

August 25

A person of high stature was talking to Mother Teresa about her work among the poorest of the poor in Calcutta, India. He asked her if she became discouraged when she saw so few successes in her ministry. "No," she answered, "I do not become discouraged. You see, God has not called me to a ministry of success. He has called me to a ministry of mercy."

Shakespeare has a marvelous passage on the virtue of mercy found in *The Merchant of Venice*.

> The quality of mercy is not strain'd, it droppeth, as the gentle rain from heaven upon the place beneath: it is twice blest; it blesseth him that gives and him that takes: 'tis mightiest in the mightiest: it becomes the throned monarch better than his crown . . . It [mercy] is an attribute to God Himself; and earthly power doth then show likest God's when mercy seasons justice . . . Consider this, that, in the course of justice, none of us should see salvation: we do pray for mercy; and that same prayer doth teach us all to render the deeds of mercy.[7]

Mercy never pays back what is deserved but instead shows compassion. We must be grateful that our Heavenly Father is a God of mercy; otherwise, none of us would be able to have salvation. We ourselves need to show mercy. The Lord and Savior Himself has said, *"Blessed are the merciful, for they will be shown mercy."*

The great apostle Paul, who had been a hateful persecutor of the little band of Christians before he came face to face with Jesus on the Damascus road, later wrote this to his young co-worker, Timothy: *"Even though I was once a blasphemer and a persecutor and a violent man, I was shown mercy because I acted in ignorance and unbelief"* (1 Timothy 1:13).

The world cries for mercy. Let us do our part to have a ministry of mercy today and every day.

True Beauty
August 26

There's an old story about a small boy who somehow got lost from his mother. The king of the land heard about the little fellow's plight and decided to help. The king asked the boy what his mother looked like. The reply came that she was the most beautiful woman in the world. The king ordered all the beautiful women in the land to parade before the lad, but alas, none turned out to be his mother. The king and the boy were both despairing when a knock came on the door, and in entered a decrepit, graying, and disheveled woman. Immediately upon seeing her, the boy leapt into her arms crying, "Mother."

There is, you see, a real element of truth in the old adage "Beauty is in the eye of the beholder." To a small lad, his mother will well be the most beautiful woman in the world, despite her inferior looks and tattered rags.

In the third chapter of 1 Peter, chapter 3, verses 3 and 4, the apostle writes in an intriguing fashion about the meaning of true beauty. He says: *"Your beauty should not come from outward adornment . . . the wearing of gold jewelry and fine clothes. Instead, it should be that of your inner self, the unfading beauty of a gentle and quiet spirit, which is of great worth in God's sight."*

"How beautiful on the mountains are the feet of those who bring good news, who proclaim peace, who bring good tidings, who proclaim salvation, who say to Zion, 'Your God reigns!'" writes the prophet Isaiah in Isaiah 52:7. A pair of feet, gnarled and callused, are hardly beautiful by any standard. Carrying the messenger who brings the good news of peace and salvation, they become angels' wings.

May our prayer today be to have the beauty of Jesus shine through us.

Our Reason for Hope
August 27

The way of the cross works. Along life's journey, we all have our difficulties, but the way of the cross, living the Christian life, holds up under the strain of life.

After a life with many ups and downs, traveling the way of the cross, Peter, the apostle, urges Christians: *"Always be prepared to give an answer to everyone who asks you to give the reason for the hope that you have"* (1 Peter 3:15b). And Paul rings in, as if responding: *"I know whom I have believed, and am convinced that he is able to guard what I have entrusted to him for that day"* (2 Timothy 1:12b). "That day," of course, refers to the Day of Judgment.

I too have found the way of Jesus to be like that. Not every difficulty disappears immediately; not all your prayers are answered in just the way you want every time (although they are answered in God's way and God's time). Life is not a bowl of cherries; however, there is a calmness, a peace, and an assurance that even if the world falls around you, you have the confidence of being in God's hands.

We make a serious mistake to assume that the Christian way brings instant and jubilant pleasure and prosperity. Jesus, before He went to the cross, prepared His followers for the situation to follow. *"I have told you these things,"* He said, *"so that in me you may have peace. In this world you will have trouble. But take heart! I have overcome the world"* (John 16:33).

Ode to Joy

August 28

Composer Ludwig Van Beethoven was just thirty-two years of age when he penned a very sad document. It was a will—that is what he called it. Most of the will did not deal with the settlement of his property but was used as a means of expressing Beethoven's bitterness toward life. "For six years I have been a hopeless case," he writes, ". . . cheated year after year in the hope of improvement . . . I am deaf. Ah, how could I possibly admit such an infirmity in the one sense which should have been more perfect in me than in others . . . this wretched existence."[8]

The year was 1802. Twenty-four years later, Beethoven was standing in a theatre in Vienna. A vast audience had risen to applaud him for the first performance of his Ninth Symphony—at the conclusion of which, the orchestra was joined by a chorus singing the composer's version of Schiller's "Ode to Joy."

Twenty-four years after his bitter complaint against life, Beethoven was able to compose a symphony symbolizing the spirit of joy. His deafness had not been cured. He was more cut off than ever from the world of sound. Yet here he was, one of the world's greatest composers. What had made the difference?

What had happened within him made the difference—despite, perhaps even because of, his severe handicap.

All of us would, no doubt, express great admiration and deep appreciation for a life like that —an ability to rise to the heights out of the depths of despair.

Stop the Frantic Search
August 29

Have you ever thought of how much Lao Tzu's simple little proverb, "Muddy water, let stand, becomes clear," applies to life?

Whether you let the mud settle if it is wet or the dust settle if it is dry, you will find it easier to examine the entire situation with some composure and to take some steps to correct the problem. It hardly ever pays to run around, as they used to say in that pithy description, "like a chicken with its head cut off."

That calmness, which we all cherish, is perhaps best described by the Psalmist in that most loved of all Psalms, the twenty–third. It begins, "*The* LORD *is my shepherd, I shall not be in want. He makes me to lie down in green pastures, he leads me beside quiet waters, he restores my soul.*" The prophet Isaiah adds in Isaiah 30:15b: "*In quietness and trust is your strength.*" The author of the book of Proverbs, with his usual, right-to-the point words of advice, puts it like this —very simply—"*Better a dry crust with peace and quiet than a house full of feasting, with strife*" (Proverbs 17:1).

Perhaps you will remember the time Jesus and His disciples were going by boat to the other side of the lake. Jesus, desperately tired, fell asleep in the stern. As he slept, a squall suddenly came down on the lake, and the disciples (fishermen though many of them were) became terrified. They woke Jesus. . . . *"Master, Master, we're going to drown!"* The Scripture continues: "*He got up and rebuked the wind and the raging waters; the storm subsided, and all was calm*" (Luke 8:24).

"Muddy water, let stand, becomes clear." So it is after the storms of life when the Master is aboard.

Measuring Another
August 30

We need to encourage one another more often. It seems the easier route is to be critical, but there's no doubt that being positive to one another pays dividends.

The apostle Paul, although he could be critical at times when necessary, always seized the opportunity to put in a good word for a deserving servant of Jesus Christ. Introducing a traveling deaconess to the church at Rome, Paul wrote in Romans 16:1-2: *"I commend to you our sister Phoebe, a servant of the church in Cenchrea. I ask you to receive her in the Lord in a way worthy of the saints and to give her any help she may need from you, for she has been a great help to many people, including me."*

Those to whom the letter was written must have felt very good about welcoming Phoebe. Phoebe herself would have been lifted up by Paul's positive note.

Paul's co-worker Barnabas was an encourager all his life. In fact, the name given to him by others, Barnabas, means just that—"son of consolation" or "encouragement." The very first mention of Barnabas in the New Testament finds him selling his own property and turning the money over to the apostles for the support of others. In fact, Paul owed his acceptance by the Christians in Jerusalem to Barnabas. After his striking conversion just outside Damascus, where he had gone to persecute the Christians, Paul went into Damascus.

After spending several days with the disciples there, Paul began to preach in the synagogues. After many days had passed, Paul was forced to flee when he heard about a conspiracy to kill him. Paul reached Jerusalem, hoping to link up with the Christians there. But, as Acts 9:26-27a, reads: *"When he [Paul] came to Jerusalem, he tried to join the disciples, but they were all afraid of him, not believing that he really was a disciple. But Barnabas took him and brought him to the apostles."* The recommendation of Barnabas cleared the situation. The one who was to become probably the greatest apostle and greatest missionary the world has ever seen was accepted.

We too, with our own words of recommendation and praise, can have a great impact on those around us.

Together for Good
August 31

There's a very promising verse in the book of Romans, to which many of us cling when disaster strikes. It's chapter 8, verse 28, which says, "*And we know that in all things God works for the good of those who love him, who have been called according to his purpose.*" You'll notice that the verse does not say that all things that happen to us are good or even pleasing to us. It does say that the various circumstances, events that happen in the life of the Christian, taken together, produce a good result or ending.

The story of Joni Eareckson Tada is a vivid reminder of this. A young Joni was out swimming when she had a diving accident so serious that she was left a quadriplegic. She was, and is, unable to care for even her simplest needs and is confined to a wheelchair. In a similar situation, many young people would simply call it quits. Not so with Joni. Joni does not spend her time doing little or feeling sorry for her situation. She travels the world on speaking engagements. She is often on a religious crusade platform with the Billy Graham Association and is a bestselling author—to name a few of her attributes.

Taken by itself, a diving accident that left a vibrant young woman almost useless could hardly be called "good." Yet God has given her the strength and ability to turn a desperate handicap into a life of tremendous accomplishment. God could have healed Joni Tada. Sometimes He does such healing, but not always. Instead, He gives the fortitude to turn seeming defeat to victory. And the final result is good. Glorious, in fact.

Thank God for Something to Do
September 01

Charles Kingsley, who lived in the eighteenth century, was a multi-talented man. He was a vicar, university professor, historian, and novelist. He wrote prolifically on social subjects. Charles Kingsley also left this little tidbit of advice: "Thank God every morning when you get up that you have something to do that day which must be done whether you like it or not. Being forced to do your best will breed in you diligence and strength of will, cheerfulness and content, and a hundred virtues which the idle never know."[1]

Sometimes, as seniors, we may feel that there is little to do, but it is possible to get quite involved in crafts, or painting, or reading, or perhaps in writing poetry or prose. And, of course, there arise opportunities to share with God and perhaps share God with others.

In one of Edward A. Guests' little rhyming couplets, he referred to a problem we all face— particularly when we are older.

> He started to sing as he tackled the thing
> That couldn't be done and he did it.[2]

This positive attitude towards life makes it possible for us to keep on growing— not in stature, but inwardly.

The apostle Peter closes the second epistle, which bears his name, in the following way: *"Grow in the grace and knowledge of our Lord and Savior Jesus Christ."* Earlier in the same epistle, Peter wrote: *"Make every effort to add to your faith goodness; and to goodness; knowledge; and to knowledge, self-control; and to self-control, perseverance; and to perseverance, godliness; and to godliness, brotherly kindness; and to brotherly kindness, love"* (2 Peter 1:5-7).

Life is still worthwhile, very worthwhile, and as Charles Kingsley said: "Thank God every morning when you get up that you have something to do."

Impressing
September 02

Making an impression! I suppose that has been the ambition of most, if not all, of us somewhere along life's way—to make an impression.

Athletes try to create a good impression on the coach, or scout, in order to make the team. Youngsters at school try to impress the teacher in order to get good marks. Salesmen try to make a favorable impression to garner a sale.

It seems to me that there is a critical question about all of this. Upon whom are we really trying to make an impression? The folks around us? Our neighbors perhaps? People who aren't easily impressed but make for a good challenge? The list could be endless.

The apostle Paul, writing to the Christians in Galatia, made reference to *"those who want to make a good impression outwardly."* Paul was referring to some Jewish Christians who wanted to impress some of their fellow non-Christian Jews by insisting that in order to become a Christian, everyone should become a Jew first, following all the Jewish regulations. Paul's advice was, *"May I* [we] *never boast except in the cross of our Lord Jesus Christ, through which the world has been crucified to me,* [us] *and I* [we] *to the world "*(Galatians 6:14).

After all is said and done, the ultimate One we must impress is our Heavenly Father. And *"what we are is plain to God,"* as 2 Corinthians 5:11 has it. Try as we might, we cannot fool God. We need to connect to God. He knows not only if the phone has yet to be connected—but even if it's off the hook.

Bobby
September 03

If you ever have a chance to visit Edinburgh, Scotland, and have a tour of that city, you will likely come across the statue placed in memory of a dog. Not many statues in the world memorialize a dog... and the Edinburgh dog was just an ordinary, little Scotch terrier.

A man named John Gray owned the dog, Bobby. Gray served as a night watchman for the police force, and Bobby would accompany John as he trudged the streets of Edinburgh. Part of their daily routine was to go to a local cafe for lunch, where master and faithful companion would both eat. John Gray suffered from tuberculosis and in 1858 passed away. Many attended his funeral, including Bobby. When all the people had gone, Bobby stayed on and lay down on his master's grave. For fourteen years, faithful Bobby kept a constant watch and guard over the grave, leaving only for food he received at the local café where he'd gone so many times before with John. In 1872, Bobby died and was buried beside his master. Later a British baroness, so deeply moved by Bobby's story, had a monument erected—a bronze figure of Bobby still keeping watch over his master's grave. On the plaque are these words:

> A tribute to the affectionate fidelity of Greyfriar's Bobby.
>
> In 1858, this faithful dog followed the remains of his Master to
>
> Greyfriar's Churchyard and lingered near the spot until his death in 1872.[3]

And Bobby was only a dog.

In his letters to the seven churches in the book of Revelation, the apostle John, quoting his Master, the Lord Jesus, wrote to the church of Sardis in chapter 2, verse 10: "*Be faithful, even to the point of death, and I will give you the crown of life.*" Few are asked to give their lives because of the beliefs they hold. All are required to be faithful.

A small Scotch terrier has illustrated the way.

Building Bridges
September 04

We need to ask ourselves some critical questions from time to time in our lives. Are we, or have we been, a stumbling block or a stepping-stone? Are we, or have we been, bridge destroyers or bridge builders? These questions do not refer to construction or engineering feats but instead to our interactions with people and more specifically to our spiritual interactions with people.

The apostle Paul was able, during his lifetime, to write to the Corinthian church: *"By the grace God has given me, I laid a foundation as an expert builder, and someone else is building on it. But each one should be careful how he builds"* (1Corinthians 3:10). None of us do all there is to be done in bridge building. We should, as Paul indicates, start the project and do it so well that others can pick it up. *"We who are strong,"* the apostle writes to the Roman Christians, *"ought to bear with the failings of the weak and not to please ourselves. Each of us should please his neighbor for his good, to build him up"* (Romans 15:1–2). We should build bridges to our neighbor.

A priest, in the Biblical sense, is one who represents God to man and man to God. In that sense, each of us may exercise that priestly function of being such a bridge over which our friends and neighbors may travel to God, to meet God.

That is a true function of the child of God, a "people person" who cares.

Insight
September 05

Insight is a most valuable commodity. Proverbs says this about it. *"If you call out for insight and cry aloud for understanding, and if you look for it as for silver and search for it as for hidden treasure, then you will understand the fear of the LORD and find the knowledge of God"* (Proverbs 2:3–5). A little later, the author of Proverbs writes: *"My son, pay attention to my wisdom, listen well to my words of insight"* (Proverbs 5:1).

The apostle Paul wrote the following words: *"This is my prayer: that your love may abound more and more in knowledge and depth of insight, so that you may be able to discern what is best and may be pure and blameless until the day of Christ"* (Philippians 1:9–10).

Insight is the eyes of the soul, seeing what you cannot see with your eyes. Insight is discernment, the ability to understand fully what is going on when very few others recognize the elements of the situation.

Jesus' enemies, the Pharisees and Sadducees, came to Him on one occasion, demanding that He show them a sign from heaven. His answer pointed to a fact, which we are all interested in— the weather *"When evening comes, you say, 'It will be fair weather, for the sky is red,' and in the morning, 'Today it will be stormy, for the sky is red and overcast.' You know how to interpret the appearance of the sky, but you cannot interpret the signs of the times"* (Matthew 16:2–3).

Many Old Testament passages, which the Pharisees and Sadducees knew well, pointed to the coming Messiah, but the Pharisees and Sadducees refused to recognize that Jesus was that Messiah, the Savior of the world. Well-educated, trained as they were, they had no eyes of the soul to see Him, no desire to discern Him.

We should not make the same mistake.

Struggles in Life
September 06

The struggles in life can get us down, but often the struggles in life make our faith stronger.

The classic struggle in the Old Testament is that of Jacob. Jacob had defrauded his twin brother Esau, who was the firstborn, of the special blessing due him from his father Isaac. Because of Esau's fury, Jacob had to flee to a distant land. There Jacob married, had children, and prospered.

Years later, Jacob wanted to return to his homeland. But how would Esau receive him? Jacob started out on his journey, but his fear reached a fever pitch as he learned that Esau was coming to meet him with four hundred armed men. Jacob had only his family and a few servants.

They came to the Jabbok River, which was a boundary to his homeland. At a place Jacob named Peniel (which means face of God), Jacob had wrestled physically with God's angel, struggling to prove his mettle, and the angel, in the morning, gave him God's special blessing. But the struggle had left Jacob's hip out of joint, and thereafter he limped all his life.

After the struggle, Jacob crossed the ford of the Jabbok, met Esau, and the brothers made peace.

Out of the struggle, a splendid relationship was born. I'm sure that has been the experience of many of us as, looking back, we see that out of our struggles, victories have been won, peace has been restored, and the blessings of God have been ours.

Very Special People
September 07

The story of Eliza Saunders is a very compelling one. Mrs. Saunders, who lived in Australia, had two young daughters, nicknamed Nellie and Topsy, who at a very young age answered the call to go and serve as missionaries to China.

Mrs. Sanders received a telegram one day informing her that a gang of rebels had murdered her two missionary daughters. Mrs. Saunders' extraordinary reaction was neither to criticize nor to condemn. She simply decided to go to China herself. For twenty years, she served the Chinese people until her death at the age of eighty-two.

I don't know about you, but I would have found such a reaction very difficult. To love and forgive her daughter's vicious murderers and to spend the last twenty years serving the people out of whom their murderers had come took a very special person.

Yet that's exactly what Jesus asks His followers to be—very special persons. Jesus taught: *"You have heard that it was said, 'Eye for eye, and tooth for tooth.' But I tell you, do not resist an evil person. If someone strikes you on the right cheek, turn to him the other also"* (Matthew 5:38–39). Then He added this: *"You have heard that it was said, 'Love your neighbor and hate your enemy.' But I tell you: Love your enemies and pray for those who persecute you"* (Matthew 5:43–44).

There is absolutely no place for revenge in the Christian way. As the apostle writes to the Roman Christians in the twelfth chapter: *"If your enemy is hungry, feed him; if he is thirsty, give him something to drink. Do not be overcome by evil, but overcome evil with good"* (Romans 12:20a–21).

The true Christian is not a man or a woman who simply lives a good, moral life. He or she does that too. The mark of the Christian is a radically different lifestyle where one does love and serve one's enemies, where one does not seek revenge but leaves it to God, where one does go the second mile.

That's the challenge Jesus leaves with His followers today.

Giving Up Too Soon
September 08

Two of the world's best armies at the time faced each other at the storied Battle of Waterloo. The Duke of Wellington's British force was victorious. Both armies were brave, both skillful, but as someone has noted, Wellington's army was persistent five minutes longer. Perseverance paid off.

The New Testament writer James has given us this little gem:

> *Consider it pure joy, my brothers [and sisters], whenever you face trials of many kinds, because you know that the testing of your faith develops perseverance. Perseverance must finish its work so that you may be mature and complete, not lacking anything* (James 1: 2–4).

I'm sure that many of us seniors can relate to those verses in James. Life has often been hard, sometimes painful. There has often been the temptation to drop out—to give in. The writer of Hebrews gives us some good advice in this regard.

> *So do not throw away your confidence; it will be richly rewarded. You need to persevere so that when you have done the will of God, you will receive what he promised. For in just a very little while, He who is coming will come and will not delay. But my righteous one will live by faith. And if he shrinks back, I will not be pleased with him.*

Then the writer says confidently, *"But we are not of those who shrink back and are destroyed, but of those who believe and are saved"* (Hebrews 10:35–39).

The persevering ones don't quit five minutes too soon.

Tests
September 09

We can't seem to get away from tests. Life is full of tests, whether we like it or not. As human beings, we all have to undergo tests of varying kinds and degrees. There are tests found in schooling, in the workplace, or for a license. Then there are, of course, medical tests, which you may experience a great deal as you age. There will be many tests that test our "character." Those who have long lifetimes have to endure many, many times of testing. Some tests will likely be intriguing and interesting. Some of the tests will be relatively easy ones. Some will be difficult ones. Some will be painful.

"Blessed is the man who perseveres under trial," writes James in his short epistle, "*because when he has stood the test, he will receive the crown of life that God has promised to those who love him*" (James 1:12).

"*Test me, O LORD, and try me,*" called David the Psalmist, "*examine my heart and my mind; for your love is ever before me, and I walk continually in your truth*" (Psalm 26:2–3). Here is a man who is sure of his faith . . . not boasting . . . simply relying on the God who made him and sustains him. Throw all sorts of tests at him and he consistently comes through victoriously.   As tested gold comes from the refiner's fire, so you and I are purified as we meet—and pass —the tests of life, both mental and physical. We can do it through the love of God.

Whatever Happened to Responsibility?
September 10

Do you ever think about how many irresponsible people we seem to have in our world? There are people who abandon their families, selfish drivers on the road, people at work not doing their job . . . and the list goes on. Why?

Undoubtedly, the greatest act of irresponsibility in history was that of a Roman governor. He literally washed his hands in front of a clamoring mob at the so-called trial of Jesus, saying in cowardly fashion, "*I am innocent of this man's blood, it is your responsibility!*" (Matthew 27:24b). But it wasn't; it was his—Pilate's. No amount of water would cleanse those hands.

Judas, who betrayed Jesus, was *"seized with remorse"* when he realized what he had done and, hoping to ease his terribly guilty conscience, hurried back to the chief priests who had rewarded him for betraying his Master. "'I have sinned,' he said, 'for I have betrayed innocent blood.' 'What is that to us?' they replied. 'That's your responsibility.'" (Matthew 27:4). And we can still hear the clink of the silver coins on the temple floor as Judas threw down the thirty pieces, the price of betrayal, then went out into the night and hung himself. For you see, it was his responsibility. Neither he nor Pilate could wash their hands of it.

God asked a son of Adam, named Cain, where his murdered brother Abel was? Cain responded rather flippantly, *"Am I my brother's keeper?"* God indicated very plainly that he was, and Cain paid a great price for his crime.

Ultimately, our responsibility is to God.

If we're rather clever, it might just be possible to pass off some of our responsibility to someone else. However, there comes a time when we're face to face with the ultimate responsibility to our Creator. It's wise to accept our responsibilities in life day by day. We'll have the peace of knowing that we have done our part before man and God.

Testing the Vibrations
September 11

The tuning fork has been used for hundreds of years to tune musical instruments. It's a small device made of high-grade steel, which, when tapped, gives a musical tone. Someone has said our heart works like a tuning fork. When our heart feels completely in tune with some thought or action we have taken, we feel good about it.

There is one major difficulty in all of this. What if our heart is not pure—if it is giving off the wrong vibrations, like a tuning fork made of inferior steel?

It may be a bit of a shock to discover that God's Word takes a very different view of our heart—that the heart is not always a good tuning fork to characterize our actions. Often it is just not trustworthy.

Jesus Himself put it all too plainly ... like this: *"A good man out of the good treasure of the heart bringeth forth good things: and an evil man out of the evil treasure bringeth forth evil things"* (Matthew 12:35 KJV). So we cannot depend upon the guidance of our hearts—unless the heart has been cleansed, made right by the power of God. And that's what happens if we heed the words that Jesus said to Nicodemus, *"You must be born again."*

Our Lord and Savior also said concerning our hearts, in the well-known Beatitudes, *"Blessed are the pure in heart, for they will see God."* The writer of Proverbs puts it this way, *"Above all else, guard your heart, for it is the wellspring of life."*

A good heart—a cleansed heart—will find, like a good tuning fork, good vibrations in the thoughts and actions of our lives. A cleansed heart truly can see rightly, feel rightly, and guide rightly.

A Mirror Maze of Self-Pity
September 12

People of all ages find mazes interesting. Apparently, in the Middle Ages, they were placed in the foyers of large churches, and some are in use even in churches of today. I can't understand why mazes should be popular in or near churches—except, perhaps, that the world outside is a maze.

There is a special type of maze called a mirror maze found in amusement centers. They are indoors, of course, and there are mirrors everywhere on walls and ceilings, and as you try to find your way, no matter where you look, you see one person—yourself, and that's not always flattering, especially if the image is distorted.

Sometimes in life we get lost in a mirror image of self-pity, particularly, it seems, as we get older. We get the impression that life is passing us by. It's hard not to begin to feel sorry for ourselves—to feel just a little bitter, perhaps. The next step is to blame God for our situation.

A person, old or young, lost in such a mirror image of self-pity, really has mistaken priorities. Life is not made up of I, me, and my. Instead, the focus should be away from ourselves. The focus should be on God and others. Happiness and fulfillment are never secured by seeking them directly, but rather they are the by-product of a focus on someone or something else.

"Ascribe to the LORD the glory due his name," cries the Psalmist (1 Chronicles 16:29a). From God, the spotlight turns to others. Wrote the apostle Paul, "*Each of you should look not only to your own interests, but also to the interests of others*" (Philippians 2:4). Probably the greatest tribute paid to Jesus was made by his enemies, not his friends, although they certainly didn't mean it that way. At the crucifixion, they shouted at him derision: "*He saved others; let him save himself if he is the Christ*" (Luke 23:35b). He could have saved himself, but He did not, for to Him others were of great importance.

So it is with us, if we would escape life's mirror maze, we must think first of our God and Savior, then others around us, then if there is any time left, ourselves.

Go and Do It for Somebody Else
September 13

If someone gives you something or does something for you, is that not a great incentive for you to give or do something for someone else? And to be given something of great value to you personally, something that actually changes your life for the best—isn't that certainly worth doing for someone else? It's called gratitude.

After many of the healings Jesus performed—opening blinded eyes, restoring the paralyzed, cleansing leprosy—He often asked those healed to go right home and not spread the news abroad . . . for He would have been inundated with vast crowds. But some of those so healed could not contain themselves, and they shouted for all to hear. They just couldn't hold it in. Something great had been done for them, and they thought the world must know too.

One of the greatest men of the ancient world, Paul of Tarsus, changed from a persecutor of the early church to a stalwart follower of the Master. He wrote to the church at Corinth, *"I am compelled to preach. Woe to me if I do not preach the Gospel!"* (1 Corinthians 9:16b). Such a valuable gift had been given him that he must, he must give it to somebody else.

Pass It On
September 14

There is a delightful story concerning the toll at the Golden Gate Bridge. It seems a motorist at the tollbooth decided to pay not only for himself, but also for the next person in line. He told that to the toll cashier as he gave his money and passed through the gate. Looking in his rear view mirror, much to his chagrin, he saw the toll collector taking money from the car behind him. The next day the benevolent motorist got the same cashier. There was annoyance in his voice as he questioned the cashier about what had happened to the money. The grinning cashier informed the motorist that the next driver had paid for the car behind him, and that driver in turn paid for the one behind him. Apparently, this went on for a few cars.

This story is a good illustration of how to "pass it on."

It is of great significance that the Greek word translated "gospel" in our English New Testament can also be translated "good news" or "glad tidings." The four Gospels of Matthew, Mark, Luke, and John could also be called the good news of those four writers, and the gospel of Jesus Christ is the good news or glad tidings of our Savior. The first thing we want to do with good news is to pass it on.

There is so much bad news flooding our newspapers, airwaves, and television screens these days that we have a longing for some bit of good news to cheer us up. Some of the papers are aware of this longing and have a small item, sometimes even on the front page, called "today's good news."

The good news that God sent in the person of His Son Jesus is much more permanent than any news item, as happy as it may be. God's offer of salvation and eternal life is not only good news for a tired and quarreling world, but also the greatest news of all time. We have a golden opportunity to pass it on.

Does God Believe in Me?
September 15

A person once stated, "I don't believe in God." The response from a listener was, "He probably doesn't much believe in you either."

Like the poet W.E. Henley, we may, if we wish, say proudly, "I am the master of my fate . . . I am the captain of my soul." But are we? Saying something doesn't necessarily make it so . . . does it?

David the Psalmist frequently questioned not God, but man. Consider his marvelous, short eighth Psalm, a little gem. David faces his problem head-on.

> *When I consider your heavens, the work of your fingers, the moon and stars which you have set in place, what is man that you are mindful of him, the son of man that you care for him? You made him a little lower than the heavenly beings and crown him with glory and honor* (Psalm 8:3–5).

God does believe in each of us, despite the response given to the person in the introduction who stated that he didn't believe in God. We are God's creation and His children.

Jesus said the following words to Nicodemus, a prominent member of the Jewish nation's ruling council: "*For God so loved the world that he gave his one and only Son, that whoever believes in him shall not perish but have eternal life*" (John 3:16).

Belief, however, is a two-way street—a mutual covenant. "*From everlasting to everlasting the Lord's love is with those who fear him, and his righteousness with their children's children—with those who keep his covenant and remember to obey his precepts*" (Psalm 103: 17–18).

As much as God loves us and believes in the potential we have, He does not force Himself upon us or compel us to believe in Him or to follow Him. The freedom to choose is ours. But if we turn Him down, eventually He must sadly turn away.

Comfort When Hurting
September 16

God does promise comfort when we are sorrowing and healing when we are hurting. The Psalmist writes in Psalm 119:50: *"My comfort in my suffering is this: Your promise preserves my life."* And what is God's promise? This is God's promise in the final verses of the great ninety-first Psalm: *"He will call upon me and I will answer him; I will be with him in trouble, I will deliver him and honor him. With long life will I satisfy him and show him my salvation."*

The prophet Isaiah quotes the Heavenly Father as promising His people: *"As a mother comforts the child, so will I comfort you"* (Isaiah 66:13a).

There is a real part for each of us in renewing life for others. The apostle Paul writes, *"Praise be to the God and Father of our Lord Jesus Christ, the Father of Compassion and the God of all comfort, who comforts us in all our troubles, so that we can comfort those in any trouble with the comfort we ourselves have received from God"* (2 Corinthians 1:3–4). Comfort one another.

You may be familiar with Joseph Scriven's hymn, "What a Friend We Have in Jesus." Part of the second verse is this:

> Have you trials and temptations?
> Is there trouble anywhere?
> We should never be discouraged;
> Take it to the Lord in prayer.[4]

Let us do just that. Take it to the Lord in prayer.

Someone to Love Me
September 17

I read one time about a fine young couple who wanted to adopt a little girl. After much waiting, the time finally came for the adoption, and the couple eagerly went to pick up their new daughter. They greeted her with open arms and then told her about the toys and clothes waiting for her at home. To their dismay, the little girl didn't seem terribly excited, so the couple said to her, "Is there something else you want?" She replied, "All I want is someone to love me."[5]

Many of us fall into that trap. Somehow we feel that the only way to win affection is to give things . . . all kinds of things . . . new things, bright and shiny.

As seniors, we have likely watched youngsters, after having received a host of new toys, become overwhelmed and begin to lose track of them. A short time later, the chances are good that they'll be back playing with a battered truck or an old doll because it's a familiar friend.

Many teenagers getting into trouble on the streets are there not because they are deprived, but because they are bored . . . bored with all the "things" they have . . . and little love.

The apostle Paul writes about the true kind of love in First Corinthians.

> *Love is patient, love is kind. It does not envy, it does not boast,*
>
> *it is not proud. It is not rude, it is not self-seeking, it is not easily*
>
> *angered, it keeps no record of wrongs. Love does not delight in*
>
> *evil but rejoices with the truth. It always protects, always trusts,*
>
> *always hopes, always perseveres. Love never fails*

(1 Corinthians 13: 4–8a).

That kind of love is sought by homeless girls and by you and by me. "All I want is someone to love me"—God offers it.

Loving Others
September 18

Sometimes we have difficulty saying the words "I love you." Sometimes we hesitate to use these words for fear of being misunderstood. One problem is that "love" seems to be the only English word for a whole range of things, and it seems to be getting worse with the passage of time.

We love apple pie, and we love the view we see so often as the sun sets in the west. We may love our job or love the way our neighbor cuts her hair or love the way a friend reads poetry. And on and on. So the very word love has been debased.

You may remember that an expert Jewish lawyer asked Jesus on one occasion which was the greatest commandment in God's Law. Jesus replied, *"'Love the Lord your God with all your heart and with all your soul and with all your mind.' And the second is like it: 'Love your neighbor as yourself.'"*

In his great first epistle, John writes:

> *How great is the love the Father has lavished on us, that we should be called children of God . . . This is the message you heard from the beginning. We should love one another . . . This is how we know what love is: Jesus Christ laid down his life for us. And we ought to lay down our lives for our brothers.*

At the very least, tell them you love them.

Filthy Rags
September 19

There is a verse in the Bible that some find very troublesome. In fact, there are many verses in the Bible that bother us—and for obvious reasons. But this statement in the book of Isaiah seems to create particular difficulty. It's in the sixty-fourth chapter, verse six. It's just a simple, but very potent statement. "*All our righteous acts are like filthy rags.*" Does that mean that the good things we do in this life are not acceptable to God? Just what was the prophet Isaiah getting at?

The truth of this verse is illustrated by the story of the counterfeit bill that seemingly did good as it circulated about the world, but when it arrived at the place where the real value counted (i.e., the bank), it was worthless. It did good, but it wasn't good.

The Bible is actually full of calls for righteousness. That is God's constant call to His creation. Isaiah himself writes, "*Tell the righteous it will be well with them, for they will enjoy the fruit of their deeds*" (Isaiah 3:10). In the Sermon on the Mount, Jesus speaks of good deeds and righteousness, but He carefully points to the difference between being good and simply appearing to do good.

"*I tell you,*" He said to the crowd, "*that unless your righteousness surpasses that of the Pharisees and the teachers of the law, you will certainly not enter the kingdom of heaven*" (Matthew 5:20). In a majestic call to each of us, the prophet Micah cries, "*He has showed you, O man, what is good. And what does the LORD require of you? To act justly and to love mercy and to walk humbly with your God*" (Micah 6:8a,b).

God is the difference. Are the good deeds done for the praise that will come to the person . . . or for our Savior's sake and in His name?

The Human Cry
September 20

A good many years ago in the days of the old Soviet Union, when atheism was much condoned, a play (blasphemous from Christians' point of view) called "Christ in Tuxedo," was about to begin in one of Moscow's theatres. The first act featured a church scene with the altar arranged like a bar. The second act featured a matinee idol, Comrade Alex Rostovsev, a fervent Marxist, who was supposed to read two verses from the Sermon on the Mount, and then remove his robe and cry, "Give me my tux."

Rostovsev began to read: *"Blessed are the poor in spirit, for theirs is the kingdom of heaven. Blessed are those who mourn, for they will be comforted . . ."* The actor stopped as if paralyzed. Then after an uneasy silence, he continued, shaking, *"Blessed are the meek for they will inherit the earth. Blessed are they who hunger and thirst for righteousness for they will be filled . . ."* and Rostovsev went on to finish the remaining verses of the chapter. Backstage the other actors called out to encourage Rostovsev to go on with his blasphemies, but he couldn't. He was no longer a blasphemer. Christ's words had conquered, and he had been changed. And there before the footlights, the man who had blasphemed the Crucified gave the sign of the cross and cried out the prayer of the penitent thief: "Lord, remember me when you come into your Kingdom."[6]

I don't know where or what had been the influence of Jesus in the actor's earlier life, but I do know that Jesus never gives up if He is calling you. He calls in the most unusual places and at the most unexpected times. The impact may shatter one's complacency.

David was called by God when, as a youth, he was tending his father's sheep. God called the prophet Amos when he was herding cattle and raising pigs. God's Son called Peter and Andrew when they were mending their fishing nets. In some respects, like Alex Rostovsev, the apostle Paul was just about to enter a new phase of his persecution of Christians when Jesus met him on the way.

Where was I when Jesus called? What did I do in response to that call?

Where Do You Want to Go?
September 21

As we get older, we sometimes develop a reflective mood, wondering what is going to happen to the world around us. The streets don't seem to be safe anymore... violence seems to be mushrooming. The media reflect the worst of it day by day. Then, too, we wonder about our part in all of this. There is an incident in Lewis Carroll's *Alice in Wonderland* that comes to mind.

Alice was traipsing through the woods and suddenly realized that, momentarily at least, she was a bit lost. Then she spied the Cheshire Cat sitting on the bough of a tree. So she asked, "Would you tell me, please, which way I ought to walk from here?" to which a very wise Cheshire Cat responded, "That depends a good deal on where you want to get to."[7]

A major factor in the difficulties so many face in our modern life lies right here. The psychologists would likely call it purposelessness. It can affect young or old, although it seems to appear mostly with some young people who just can't see much purpose in life... so they may even try to end it. That, of course, is no answer.

The Psalmist writes, *"I was young and now I am old, yet I have never seen the righteous forsaken or their children begging bread"* (Psalm 37:25). I am not suggesting a "prosperity gospel." The Bible does not suggest that if I follow God, I will automatically have everything I want, but Jesus does say, *"Seek first his kingdom and his righteousness, and all these things will be given to you as well"* (Matthew 6:33). And "these things" Jesus is talking about are not the luxuries, but rather our simple needs of food and clothing. He adds, *"Do not worry about tomorrow, for tomorrow will worry about itself"* (Matthew 6:34a).

God's kingdom and God's righteousness... that's the sure way of purpose, and thank God, He gives us a choice. Indeed, as the Cheshire Cat put it, the way ahead depends upon where we want to go.

God Laughs
September 22

Sometimes we wonder if God is in charge. We live in a world where there is very little recognition of God. The emphasis is on the world we live in instead of what will happen to us in eternity. In our world, we are becoming increasingly secular. Modern technology has become quite a force in our society. Never have people been so knowledgeable. Many diseases are being banished; leisure time is increasing. The world is shrinking with advances in communication. Why worry about a piece of pie in the sky by and by when you can have the whole pie now?

One might be reminded of a verse in one of the early Psalms, the second, where we read, *"The One enthroned in heaven laughs."* We don't normally picture God as laughing . . . and it's not a pleasant laugh. The Psalmist continues, *"The Lord scoffs at them."* The objects of his scoffing are humans like those who form their world and make their plans without Him.

James really puts the matter in proper perspective, when he writes:

> *Now listen, you who say, "Today or tomorrow we will go to this or that city, spend a year there, carry on business and make money." Why, you do not even know what will happen tomorrow. What is your life? You are a mist that appears for a little while and then vanishes. Instead, you ought to say, "If it is the Lord's will, we will live and do this or that"* (James 4: 13-15).

More than a century ago, in writing of their plans, people often wrote the letters D.V. at the conclusion. This was a good practice, for the letters in Latin stand for Deo volente—"God Willing"—a recognition that, after all, God is in charge.

Nearer Than Hands or Feet
September 23

In the book of Acts is an intriguing account concerning a visit that the apostle Paul, alone at the time, made to Athens, the heart of ancient Greece. There he found a country of idol-worshipping people. Yet Athens was still the greatest university city of the ancient world, and learned men came from everywhere. The Greek philosophers congregated there. Epicureans, Stoics, and others with differing philosophies gathered to talk and then talk some more, day and night.

That was the scene Paul entered, and he was soon in deep discussion (according to Acts 17) with a group of Stoics and Epicureans. They took him to the Areopagus—the name both for the place and for the select court that sat there. Paul was invited to speak, and as he began, he referred to the almost numberless gods he saw as he moved about the city, including an altar dedicated "to an unknown god."

From that starting point, the apostle began to tell them about his God, who was well known to him as the Creator of all. "*From one man,*" he said, "*he made every nation of men, that they should inhabit the whole earth; and he determined the times set for them and the exact places where they should live.*" Then he added this significant statement: "*God did this so that men would seek him and perhaps reach out for him and find him, though he is not far from each one of us. 'For in him we live and move and have our being'*" (Acts 17:26–28a).

God is here . . . nearer than hands or feet. The story of life is the story of a seeking God. We must be open to his call—to hear, to see, to feel. And as the Apostle said, "*reach out for Him.*"

Win a Bushel of Bucks
September 24

One morning in days gone by, I was driving to the office and decided, as we often do when alone, to flip on the car radio. I wasn't looking for anything in particular, so I tried three different stations, and within 15 or 20 seconds, two of them were advertising contests offering what they called "fabulous cash prizes." On the third, the announcer was saying loudly and excitedly something about "cash on the barrelhead." All within 15 seconds or so. Not so long before, I had seen an ad in a magazine about winning "a bushel of bucks."

Advertisers seem to assume that bucks are what everyone wants—bucks, big bucks. You have noticed, haven't you, that the bucks become less important as you get a little older? We've discovered that there are quite a few valuable items in this world that just cannot be bought. Meaning is one; happiness is another. Love, real love cannot be bought; concern and caring are two other examples. And one could go on.

All of these things have been secured for us and are available to us—bought, if you like, by the sacrifice of Jesus Christ on the cross—paid in full. Redemption is the term for it. The Psalmist writes, "*The LORD redeems his servants; no one will be condemned who takes refuge in him.*"

It seems to me that these things are a great deal more important than "big bucks."

"Towering O'er the Wrecks of Time"
September 25

In 1825, Sir John Bowring, then governor of Hong Kong, was inspired to write a hymn about the cross of Christ. The source of his inspiration was a remnant of a great stone cathedral on the nearby Macao Peninsula. The cathedral had been ripped apart by a devastating typhoon that left nothing standing except the front wall, bearing a great bronze cross. The title of the well-known hymn is "In the Cross of Christ I glory." In the second verse, he writes:

> When the woes of life o'er take me,
> Hopes deceive, and fears annoy,
> Never shall the Cross forsake me;
> Lo! it glows with peace and joy.[8]

John Bowring's hymn continues to speak to the world and to us as individuals. The world is still very much bothered by natural disasters—and by wars, near wars, and other human violence. As individuals, we are overtaken, sometimes daily, by life's woes—our hopes dashed, our fears magnified.

The cross is a beacon of continued hope. The cross should become a glorious torch of faith and trust. It was on that cross the Savior cried in victory, *"It is finished."* The goal accomplished, He rose again the third day and promised His followers, *"Because I live, you also will live."*

That heritage has been passed on to every succeeding generation.

Cold Iron

September 26

In the Rudyard Kipling poem "Cold Iron," the poet pictures a baron in his castle, boasting that the force of cold iron is master of all. So the proud baron makes rebellion against his king, using iron in the form of cannonballs as his weapons. But the baron is defeated and finds himself behind iron bars—cold iron bars. However, the king is forgiving and tells the baron another story of iron—the iron nails hammered into the feet and hands of the Son of God in Calvary. Finally, the baron sees it and cries that the "Iron out of Calvary is master of men all."[9]

The scene at Calvary after Jesus died was ominously quiet. The apostle John, who had been there, had taken the Master's mother, Mary, to his home. The other women who had been there had also gone. The soldiers had gone, as well as the mocking scribes and pharisees. Two prominent men, Joseph of Arimathea, who had received permission from Pontius Pilate to bury Jesus' body in his own new tomb, and Nicodemus, a member of the Jewish ruling council, came to the quiet cross together. Nicodemus brought burial spices with which to wrap Jesus' body for burial, and the two of them placed the body in the midst of the adjacent garden . . . in Joseph's new tomb.

What had happened? These men had not been conspicuous followers of Jesus when he was moving about the land. This is the first time Joseph of Arimathea is mentioned. And Nicodemus? Yes, he came to Jesus one night, slipping in under cover of darkness to question Him. The difference, of course, was the cross. As Kipling's baron said, "Iron out of Calvary is master of men all."

Calvary, you see is the watershed of life. At that hill, you either accept or reject God's pardon.

Like a Little Child
September 27

We seem to lose a great deal of our imagination as we get older. One only has to observe children at play, particularly the younger ones, to verify this. We who are very much older wish sometimes we could have retained some of that imagination. We become a little hardened, sometimes doubting a great deal. When anyone would suggest to the famous and unique evangelist of yesteryear, Gypsy Smith, that some of his views about the Christian faith were but figments of his imagination, he wouldn't argue but would simply reply, "Let me dream on if I'm dreaming."

Many strong and valid arguments can be made for the reality of our Heavenly Father. However, in the last analysis, they are not nearly as effective as the faith-in-action we see around us in so many lives, living examples of God at work in loving, caring, human lives.

Jesus put the matter in perspective when people bringing their children to Him were rebuked by the Lord's disciples. Jesus was indignant, and we read about his response in Mark 10:14–16: "*He said to them,* [His disciples], *'Let the little children come to me, and do not hinder them, for the kingdom of God belongs to such as these.'*" He added, "*I tell you the truth, anyone who will not receive the kingdom of God like a little child will never enter it.*" Mark concludes, "*He took the children in His arms, put his hands on them and blessed them.*"

No, not childish, but childlike. Not imagination, but faith.

Twisted Morality
September 28

There was a thief who had broken into the home of a widow and stolen a variety of things. Sorting through his loot, the thief came across a number of church offering envelopes that had money in them—money that the good lady had obviously intended to give to the church. So leaving them intact, the thief put them all in another envelope and mailed it to the church. It was rather ironic that he could steal from a widow, yet not steal from the church.

We love and show our respect for God by the way we love and respect those around us. Conversely, if we do not show regard for others around us, we have no real regard for God. In the twenty-fifth chapter of Matthew, Jesus Himself pictured the judgment scene, where men and women were divided into two camps. To those on the right, the Judge granted eternal life because, He said, they had fed Him when hungry, offered hospitality to Him when He was a stranger, and given Him clothing when He needed clothes. Surprised, the righteous ones on the Judge's right could not remember when they had done these things to Him. The Judge responded: *"I tell you the truth, whatever you did for one of the least of these brothers of mine, you did for me"* (Matthew 25:40). Or conversely, as is written in verse 45: *"I tell you the truth, whatever you did not do for one of the least of these, you did not do for me."*

To put it in more current vernacular . . . that's the bottom line or that's where the rubber hits the road. Rob a widow and you rob God . . . no matter how many church envelopes you forward.

In the Crises of Life
September 29

At one time, I was pastor of a church in Halifax, Nova Scotia. Early one morning, I went to visit one of our church members who was scheduled for surgery. In those days, at the hospital where my parishioner was, they would automatically call a minister if a patient was placed on the danger list or, if desired, when the patient was about to have surgery. Soon after I entered the hospital and was walking along a corridor, a nurse walked by pushing a patient in a bed. The nurse stopped, came over to me, and said, "You're a minister, aren't you?" And I pleaded guilty. "I'm taking a patient up to the O.R.," she then said, "and she doesn't want to go until she sees her minister. He's supposed to be here but hasn't arrived. Would you talk with her?"

I went over to the bed, learned that her church was not quite the same as mine, but she would love to have me pray . . . which I did, right there in the corridor, and then the lady was quite willing to be pushed off to the operating room.

You might say to me, "Why would she need a minister if her personal faith was strong?" Perhaps she didn't need a minister, but she did need God, as we all do when we face the crises of life.

As the Psalmist David writes, "*The LORD is near to all who call on him, to all who call on him in truth. He fulfills the desires of those who fear him; he hears their cry and saves them. The LORD watches over all who love him*" (Psalm 145:18–20a).

Writes the author of Proverbs, "*There is a friend who sticks closer than a brother.*"

That's the Friend who created us, who died for us, and who would save us . . . for now and for eternity. That's why it's so meaningful to call on Him at any time and especially in times of crisis. He's always there—waiting.

Fit to Play God's Music
September 30

To many of you who love music, the name of Antonio Stradivari is synonymous with the world's finest violins. If you own a Stradivarius today, you are wealthy or potentially so. Stradivari, who lived a long life, from 1644 to 1737, was, of course, an Italian violin maker. His method of violin making created a standard which succeeding generations have tried, generally unsuccessfully, to match. Stradivari insisted that no instrument constructed in his shop be sold until it was as near to perfection as human skill and care could make it. He once commented, "God needs violins to send His music into the world, and if any violins are defective, God's music will be spoiled."

I am reminded of that little tidbit of wisdom from the book of Ecclesiastes 9:10a: *"Whatever your hand finds to do, do it with all your might."* Paul has a similar word in his letter to the Colossians: *"Whatever you do, work at it with all your heart, as working for the Lord, not for men, since you know that you will receive an inheritance from the Lord"* (Colossians 3:23–24a).

God has given to those of us who believe in Him a message of reconciliation for a warring, hurting world. We are instruments of His love and healing. *"He [God] has committed to us the message of reconciliation,"* writes the apostle Paul in 2 Corinthians 5:19b. Paul adds in verse 20: *"We are therefore Christ's ambassadors, as though God were making his appeal through us. We implore you on Christ's behalf: Be reconciled to God."*

If the instrument is defective—as Antonio Stradivari put it—"God's music will be spoiled." The world will be poorer, and so will we.

Do As I Have Done
October 01

At one point in the very solemn occasion of the Last Supper, Jesus took a basin of water and a towel and began to wash His apostles' feet. In that country of dusty roads where the people wore sandals, it was a menial task for the very lowest of servants.

In a very modern example of that story, a missionary to Brazil that I know, carried out a similarly moving experience with his congregation. His object was to teach the lesson that Jesus taught—that of humble service. Everyone took part except one elderly, blind woman brought to church by her daughter. She always sat by herself. The reason she sat alone wasn't her blindness—her body reeked with neglect. The odor of her body kept people at a distance. Her hair was falling out in chunks, leaving large patches of scalp. Her feet were so crusted over that she could no longer wear shoes.

The day of the foot washing, no one paid very much attention to her—except one teenaged girl. The missionary's daughter got up from her seat, walked over to the woman, and spoke to her. There was a quiet murmur in the congregation, then a hush, then silence, as the girl led the old woman to the front of the church, knelt down and tenderly washed those crusted, filthy feet. Then the girl rose and led the woman back to her seat. The silence was broken by sobs as the Brazilian congregation grasped what the teenager had done . . . and they lined up to hug the elderly woman, offering no excuses, but love.

Jesus said the following words to His apostles on that original occasion: *"Now that I, your Lord and Teacher, have washed your feet, you also should wash one another's feet. I have set you an example that you should do as I have done for you"* (John 13: 14–15).

The important thing is not necessarily the physical act of foot washing (for as noted, foot washing was necessary in that dry and dusty land)—but similar services of loving outreach to those around us. *"Serve one another in love,"* we find in Galatians 5:13c. Or, as the Lord has commanded, *"Love your neighbor as yourself."*

Thanks for New Life
October 02

This time of year, the harvest season, gives us a great opportunity to give thanks. *"I will praise God's name in song,"* David the Psalmist writes, *"and glorify him with thanksgiving"* (Psalm 69:30). Later on in the same Psalm, verse 34, we read: *"Let heaven and earth praise him, the seas and all that move in them."*

The great prophet, Isaiah, adds to the chorus of thanks found throughout the Psalms:

"Give thanks to the LORD, call on his name; make known among the nations what he has done, and proclaim that his name is exalted" (Isaiah 12:4).

American, Oliver Wendell Holmes, noted physician, professor and author of the nineteenth century, wrote this about thankfulness.

"If one should give me a dish of sand, and tell me there were particles of iron in it, I might look for them with my eyes, and search for them with my clumsy fingers, and be unable to detect them; but let me take a magnet and sweep through it, and how it would draw to itself the almost invisible particles by the mere power of attraction. The unthankful heart, like my finger in the sand, discovers no mercies; but let the thankful heart sweep through the day, and, as the magnet finds the iron, so it will find, in every hour, some heavenly blessings; only the iron in God's sand is gold."[1]

So this harvest season, may we discover afresh how blest we truly are despite the difficulties the world delivers to us. We have new life where the old seems to have faded, and we have God's promised resurrection from death.

A Feeling of Uncertainty
October 03

The famous Scottish poet, Robert Burns, unlike most of his contemporary writers, was a man of the common people. One of his simplest, yet most gripping, poems is called, "To a Mouse." Apparently, Robert Burns had been crossing a farm field when he came upon a shivering mouse—its nest destroyed by the plow, then facing a bleak cold winter. He writes in the last verse.

> Still, thou art blest, compared wi' me!
> The present only toucheth thee:
> But och! I backward cast my e'e
> On prospects drear!
> An' forward, tho' I canna see,
> I guess an' fear![2]

The feeling of uncertainty, as we look back on our lives or wonder just what the future offers, is somewhat common to much of mankind, particularly if you live in what we call the third world, the underdeveloped world. The Christian message of hope resonates in this sort of world and with this sort of person. True, not one of us is entirely satisfied with our own performance in the past. However, we can be forgiven both for those things we have done that we ought not to have done and for leaving undone those things we ought to have done.

This is how David the Psalmist describes the situation as stated in Psalm 103: "*As far as the east is from the west, so far has he* [i.e. God] *removed our transgressions from us.*" Forgiven— blotted out. Then hear the great apostle Paul's statement in Philippians 3:13-14: "*Forgetting what is behind and straining toward what is ahead, I press on toward the goal to win the prize for which God has called me heavenward in Christ Jesus.*"

No lack of hope there!

In Ephesians 1:18, Paul prays, "*that the eyes of your heart may be enlightened in order that you may know the hope to which he has called you.*"

No need to guess or fear. This is God's promise!

Mastering the Difficulties of Growing Old

October 04

Some of you may be familiar with the works of Francisco Gaya, one of the foremost European painters. For many seniors, however, the chief interest in Francisco Gaya would be his behavior during the declining years of his life. As he aged, like some of you, he was one of those very determined and courageous people who mastered many of the difficulties of growing old.

One of his last paintings shows an old, bearded man, bent over and supporting himself on two canes. Gaya's courageous philosophy of life is clearly shown in the title that he gave the work: "Aun Aprendo," which means "I am still learning."

The world's greatest Teacher issued this invitation to join Him in learning. This is how He put it when He walked among men and women and taught "as one having authority"—that was the way His hearers put it. *"Come to me all you who are weary and burdened."* He said, *"Take my yoke upon you and learn from me, for I am gentle and humble in heart, and you will find rest for your souls"* (Matthew 11:28a–29). The souls of many folks are not finding much rest nowadays, either. There is not much real food for the soul; other appetites have taken over.

"Take my yoke upon you," He said. Some of you, perhaps, may know about the use of yokes on the farms of yesteryear. A yoke, of course, is a heavy piece of curved wood with attachments, to couple or link together draft animals such as oxen, enabling them to pull well as a team. Lest you be fearful of the weight of Jesus' yoke, He adds, *"My yoke is easy and my burden is light"* (Matthew 11:30).

"Learn from me" is an invitation, very personal, to the finest lessons on life and eternity, but you have to be linked with Jesus to enjoy the lessons.

Singing Again
October 05

There's an old traditional story about three monks whose monastery was burned to the ground by an invading army. The monks found refuge in a nearby forest, built a shelter, and found a beautiful glade where they worshipped God every day. Their voices were old and cracked, but they tried to sing praises to God. One day a stranger with a magnificent voice joined them in their singing, but soon the monks stopped singing. Sometime later, an angel appeared and asked them why they had stopped. They explained that their new arrival's singing was much better than their singing could ever be. "Yes," said the angel, "it is beautiful, but that man does not sing to praise the Lord, but for the pleasure of hearing his own voice. The Lord wishes you to start singing again."

As we age, our voices are not as strong and true as they once were. Perhaps we feel that we can hardly present our best to God. We might take it to extremes and sing very little or even stop altogether. The important part, however, is not the quality of the singing but the continued praise to the Lord through our singing.

The book of Psalms, which was the Hebrew hymnbook, mentions the word "praise" well over two hundred times. Many of the Psalms were written by Israel's great King David—and praises to God were on his lips when he was a young man, middle-aged, and especially when he became well-advanced in years. Before he became King, when David was hard-pressed as a young man, his very life in jeopardy, he sang out to God, *"The LORD lives! Praise be to my Rock! Exalted be God, the Rock, my Savior!"* (2 Samuel 22:47).

When David fled from Saul and hid himself in a large cave, David again lifted his eyes heavenward, *"Be exalted, O God, above the heavens; let your glory be over all the earth"* (Psalm 57:5).

If you and I have stopped singing God's praises, then we need to apply the message of the Psalmist and start singing again.

Music in the Soul
October 06

While driving an acquaintance to a meeting, he told me about his first visit to the beautiful Lake District in England, the country of the poets. Visiting the estate where William Wordsworth lived and eyeing the surrounding countryside, he told me he had said to himself, "Why, anybody could write poetry amid these surroundings." Apparently, he soon changed that opinion, for as he walked the roads of that village, he saw a man working by the side of the road, breaking rock with a heavy hammer. As his hammer beat a steady crack upon the surface of the rock, the man never looked up. My friend said he decided that day, that poetry was of the soul . . . and there was no music in the heart of the hammerer.

I suppose it is not easy to look up and break your rhythm as you do a heavy job like breaking rock. In our day, you'll never see anyone doing it . . . it's all handled by machinery.

But I know what the professor meant. Poetry . . . music . . . appreciation of the beauty of the world that God has made—these are deep in the heart and soul. Someone has said that "poetry is music in words and music is poetry in sound." The French writer Joseph Joubert has said that, "You will find poetry nowhere unless you bring some of it with you." That, I think, was what my friend was saying . . . trying to tell me.

Do I have the music, the poetry of God, in my soul? The Psalmist asked this question in the middle of the night when, like so many of us do when we are sleepless, he tossed and turned. Then in expectation, he turned to his God: "*I remember the days of long ago; I meditate on all your works and consider what your hands have done. I spread out my hands to you; my soul thirsts for you like a parched land*" (Psalm 143:5, 6). And a line or two later in his poem he cries, "*Let the morning bring me word of your unfailing love, for I have put my trust in you. Show me the way I should go, for to you I lift up my soul*" (Psalm 143:8).

With that kind of poetry and music in the soul, one may always look up . . . in appreciation and thanksgiving, whether or not he ever writes it down in verse.

Stuck
October 07

Did you ever get stuck? If you have driven a car, I can guess that you have become stuck more than once. I once read of three loggers who got their truck stuck in the mud right up to the axles. The reaction to this happening was quite different for all three. One cursed and stormed out of the truck. Another decided to go take a nap under a pine. The third grabbed an ax and saw and set about cutting wood to slide under the wheels. Within an hour, the third man managed to pull the truck out of its mud hole, and they were on their way.

There are some similarities in the situations where you and I are mired, bogged down in some problem or difficulty. It's like being stuck in the mud . . . right up to the axles. We don't have the luxury of sleeping under a pine tree. We're stuck. We of course can become angry, violently angry . . . but that does no good.

The Psalmist David was in that sort of situation on more than one occasion. He writes of one such instance in Psalm 69: "*The waters have come up to my neck,*" he writes, "*I sink in the miry depths, where there is no foothold.*" A little later he admits that the trouble may be of his own making as he says, "*You know my folly, O God; my guilt is not hidden from you.*" Then, like the third logger, David approached the difficult situation wisely. He decided to do something about it. He cried out to his Heavenly Father, as recorded in verses 17 and 18a. "*Answer me quickly, for I am in trouble. Come near and rescue me.*" And God answered.

God always answers . . . not as soon as we would like perhaps. Sometimes his answer is "yes," once in a while "no" for God knows better than we do what is good for us. Sometimes His answer—if it is for our benefit—is "wait a little while." However, God does come to our rescue as He did for David. He pulls us out of the mud holes of life.

Let us, then, call on the name of the Lord.

Thank Him
October 08

Jean Francois Millet was born in 1814 into a peasant family in rural France, and until the age of nineteen, he spent his youth working on the land. Later, he became an established artist. Many of his paintings depict peasant farmers, based on memories of his childhood. One such memory became the inspiration for his painting, "The Angelus," his best-known work. As a boy, he was entranced by the sweet-voiced church bell that would ring each day as the sun was setting. When the workers in the field heard the bell ring, they would stop their work and say a prayer of gratitude.

This time of year, Thanksgiving is very much on our minds. Thanksgiving Day is a day set apart by our government to foster the spirit of gratitude, and in our country of today, it is a reminder that many need. We are inclined to take for granted the many good things that come our way and grumble about the bad. A land of self-made men and women is not a thankful land . . . you have no one to thank but yourself. The writers of the Psalms obviously never felt that way. Some twenty-five times, the giving of thanks to the Heavenly Father for His goodness is mentioned directly and many, many more times indirectly. Psalm 107 begins in this typical fashion: *"Give thanks to the LORD, for he is good; his love endures forever."*

Today, may we hear the Angelus bell ring.

"Thank Him . . . thank Him" . . . and bow.

Small Forces
October 09

Those of you who are of a scientific turn of mind will not be at all surprised by a method used by a professor of physics to demonstrate the effect of very small forces on large masses. In his classroom, the professor would suspend from the ceiling, a heavy lump of metal. He would then take a basket of small paper pellets and begin to bombard the heavy iron mass with them. This would always cause his first-time students to smile . . . even to laugh. What did the professor think he was doing? How could he expect to make even the slightest impression on that heavy piece of metal with tiny, almost weightless paper pellets?

At first, nothing happened, and the smiles grew broader. Then after a time, the iron mass would begin to tremble, then begin to move . . . and finally would swing in a wide arc—all because of many repeated pecks of tiny paper pellets.

God's prophet Zechariah asks the question: *"Who despises the day of small things?"* God had called upon Zechariah's people to rebuild God's destroyed Temple. They had started, slacked off, and the prophet was encouraging them to take up the work that had started and faltered. And he asked the question, *"Who despises the day of small things?"*—the intimation being that God doesn't. He promises strength to all with vision, who try to bring the vision to fruition—perhaps only paper pellets attacking a piece of metal. Like the pellets, they finally accomplished their end—God's end.

Each of us, through a word here or there or a tiny action here or there, can help make the lives of others brighter.

Peace and Quiet
October 10

A man was visiting a lighthouse keeper. As the two of them were looking out at the rough seas, the lighthouse keeper told his friend to look down and see how completely still it was at the place where three currents met. Three separate currents from three different directions were swirling about, but where they met in the center . . . all was peace . . . all was still.

I think there's a parable of life here. There are all sorts of currents swirling about us in our world—violent acts of all sorts, competition, hatred, self-centeredness, misunderstandings, separations, etc. But there is a center of peace and quietness.

"Be still and know that I am God" is written in the Psalms. Knowing God brings quietness and calmness of mind, even in the midst of very troublesome times.

The prophet Elijah was running for his life in fear of the furious Queen Jezebel of Israel. Elijah had been the means used by God to destroy the priests of the false gods she worshipped, and she had vowed to take his life. In fleeing Jezebel, Elijah found himself in desert country . . . then finally alone, dreadfully alone, on Mount Horeb. He had traveled forty-one days to get there. There on the mountain, God spoke to him. *"What are you doing here, Elijah?"* Pouring out his troubled soul, the prophet described his struggles and grief, saying that he was the only one of God's followers left and that his enemies were after him. Hidden in a cave at the time, God told him to go out on to the mountain where God would reveal Himself. Elijah went out and waited. In a demonstration of power, God sent a great wind that shattered rock, but God was not in the wind. Then a violent earthquake, then a fire—but no God. Then after the fire . . . just a whisper or a still, small voice. That was God.

Very often God speaks to us out of the stillness of life . . . into the rather hectic aspects of the world in which we are so often caught up.

So whenever you are troubled, seek the stillness . . . the peace of God.

God's Hand in Ours
October 11

Have you ever completed dot-to-dot pictures or watched your children or perhaps your grandchildren do them—or even assisted them? If the person doing the dot-to-dot doesn't connect the dots in the proper order, it makes quite a mess. Of course, some parallels can be made with our journey through life. Perhaps the first is that as old as we are, we don't know all the answers to the riddles of life. When we move ahead on our own, the picture of our life . . . the one we are trying to sketch . . . is not very clear. Like an unraveled ball of yarn, our life might be a little confusing to an onlooker.

It seems to me that the Master of this life, our Creator God, has not only mapped out the best possible pathway, but has also placed a large number of dots or markers along the way. The prophet Isaiah in his chapter 30 had something like this in mind when he wrote: "*Whether you turn to the right or to the left, your ears will hear a voice behind you, saying, 'This is the way; walk in it'*" (Isaiah 30:21). Earlier, the writer of the book of Proverbs had said: "*In the way of righteousness there is life; along that path is immortality*" (Proverbs 12:28).

God has not only made and marked the path through His Word, but He also speaks to us through our inner voice. If we're listening, His hand is there to guide us.

Deep Roots
October 12

The various kinds of trees that grow in our forests have different kinds of root systems. The pine is a fast-growing tree, with shallow roots that spread widely in every direction, lapping up the surface water. The maple is said to be slow growing, sending its roots much deeper for the moisture far into the earth. Both root systems obviously give life to the trees, but when the winter winds come and the gales blow, the maple with its deep roots will stand. Often, the pine, with its shallow base, will topple.

I remember as a youth, standing on a hill opposite a British Columbia forest, with a large clearing between the woods and me. It was wintertime and a very stormy day. As I watched the woods, the trees swaying violently in the wind, frequently a tree would fall—just like a pin in a bowling alley.

I think I appreciated the value of deep roots that day. A deep root system enables the tree to withstand the buffeting of the storms. Applying the concept to our lives, a deep spiritual root system allows us to face the fiercest gales that life may throw at us. We may not only survive, but also come through the tempest better men and women. The secret of personal victory in life is a good, deep root system.

Paul, writing to the Romans, put it very simply and also very succinctly: "*If the root is holy so are the branches*"(Romans 11:16b). The very first of the Psalms refers to the importance of a good root system. *"Blessed is the man,"* the Psalmist writes, *"who does not walk in the counsel of the wicked or stand in the way of sinners or sit in the seat of mockers. But his delight is in the law of the LORD, and on his law he meditates day and night."* Then the secret of that life: "*He* [she] *is like a tree planted by streams of water, which yields its fruit in season*"(Psalms 1:1–3a).

Enjoyment to the Full
October 13

Many people, especially in our culture it seems, are overly concerned about possessions and are envious of people who have an abundance of this world's goods. We don't have to possess something to enjoy it.

You don't have to own a glorious sunset to enjoy it to the full, nor own a forest with its quiet restful glade, nor own a mountain to experience the thrill of majestic greatness.

In that sense, we all are rich, even the poorest of us. You don't have to be a millionaire to enjoy to the full a million-dollar view of God's world. You don't have to be a millionaire to possess fully the wonders, the glories of God's salvation and eternal life. Speaking for God, the prophet Isaiah said:

> "*Come, all you who are thirsty* [spiritually parched], *come to the waters; and you who have no money come buy and eat! Come, buy wine and milk without money and without cost. Why spend money on what is not bread, and your labor on what does not satisfy? Listen, listen to me, and eat what is good, and your soul will delight in the richest of fare. Give ear and come to me; hear me that your soul may live.* (Isaiah 55:1–3a).

The glories of God's natural and spiritual world are available to all without money and without price, as the Scriptures promise—"the richest of fare," as Isaiah puts it. And all of this is available whether you live in a mansion on a hilltop or in a little shack.

Come in Here With Me
October 14

Abraham Lincoln attended the New York Avenue Presbyterian Church in Washington when he was president. The story is told that Mr. Lincoln was in his pew one Sunday morning when an older man, evidently a stranger, was looking quite intently for a place to sit in the crowded church. He was well forward, but still did not see a place to sit. He then turned to walk back. Just as he was passing Mr. Lincoln's pew, the president put out his arm and invited the stranger to come and sit with him. It certainly shows the character of the president who, though heavily burdened with the affairs of state, was considerate enough to say to a stranger, "Come in with me."

In a different sort of way, isn't that just what God says to us . . . to you and me? As we wander up and down the aisles of life, with the ushers all busy and the seats all occupied, the One who made the world and indeed holds the whole world in His hands invites, "Come in here with me."

And He could add, "It's cold outside." That much we know . . . we've felt it.

Very early in His ministry, Jesus was passing by the place where John the Baptist was preaching, and John remarked to two of his own followers, *"Look, the Lamb of God!"*—the Son of God. Intrigued, the two men (one of them Andrew who later became one of the twelve apostles) ran after Jesus and asked Him, *"Where are you staying?"*

Jesus' answer was most significant. *"Come and you will see."* His words sound like, "Come in here with me."

That's an invitation to every stranger.

Wailing Walls
October 15

The Wailing Wall in Jerusalem is believed to be the outer western wall of the temple that was originally built by Solomon and later destroyed and rebuilt a couple of times. It was last destroyed by Roman legions under Titus in 70 AD and has yet to be rebuilt.

Prayer and the somber wailing at the wall continue to this day, of course, not only lamenting the destruction of the temple, but other trials and adversities that the Jewish race has had to endure throughout the ages. And many mourn in sympathy for a people who have suffered so much.

The Old Testament in the Bible is the story, an all-too-often sad story, of that brilliant race of people who have contributed so much to our world. Who of us can judge them as a nation when the faults of our own nation are as great or greater?

We sometimes forget that our Savior, Jesus, was Jewish. Over Jerusalem one day, He cried out in rejected pain.

> "O Jerusalem, Jerusalem, you who kill the prophets and stone those sent to you, how often I have longed to gather your children together, as a hen gathers her chicks under her wings, but you were not willing! Look, your house is left to you desolate. I tell you, you will not see me again until you say, "Blessed is he who comes in the name of the Lord." (Luke 13:34–35).

To those who mourn at the Wailing Wall and at the Wailing Walls in life—east, west, north, and south—God calls, *"Turn to me and be saved, all you ends of the earth; for I am God, and there is no other"* (Isaiah 45:22).

The Empty Cross
October 16

The Rev. G.A. Studdert-Kennedy was an English clergyman, well-known poet, and writer of very perceptive religious verse. A chaplain in WW I, he tells of walking one night in 1917 in the woods near a battleground when he stumbled over something. He came upon an underfed German boy with a wound in his stomach and a hole in his head. Then he writes that the boy's face faded away and, in his mind's eye, Studdert-Kennedy saw the figure of Christ on the cross. Said he: "From that moment on, I have never seen the world as anything but a Crucifix. I see the Cross set up in every slum, in every filthy, overcrowded quarter, in every vulgar, flaring street that speaks of luxury and waste of life. I see Him staring up at me from the pages of the newspaper that tells of a tortured, lost, bewildered world."[3]

His words portray a desperately sad picture of a lost world, heightened by the tragedy of a man he had stumbled upon in the woods that night. Many, many years later, in our day and age, we have to admit that there hasn't been a great deal of improvement. Indeed, sorrow is a great deal more widespread, despite the fact that we in the Western world are not in a world war. The chaplain was right. All the poverty, the terror, the bewilderment and the hopelessness is encapsulated in that cross on the windy hill outside Jerusalem's gate. There the Son of God bore all the hatred and violence that men could muster. Yet He said, *"Father, forgive them, for they do not know what they are doing"* (Luke 23:34a).

That's not the end of it all. After Calvary, it was an empty cross, an empty tomb, and angelic voices repeating: *"He is not here; he is risen, just as he said"* (Matthew 28:6a). He is a living Savior.

Earlier to His disciples, grief-stricken at the prospect of His death, Jesus had said, *"Take heart! I have overcome the world"* (John 16:33c). So may you and I. So concerned about the plight of people in our bewildered world, we must do our part to correct it. We are able to live above the strife in personal spiritual victory, and the world needs such men and women to show the way. That we can do, even in our senior years.

Does Jesus Care?
October 17

If I might be pardoned a personal impression, I really don't think that there are many folk around who really believe that there isn't a God out there somewhere. Quite a few more, however, do find it difficult to accept that the God out there cares a great deal about us. How could a God of billions of people care for little old me? Is God really nearby when I hurt, when you hurt, when the burdens and trials of life press in on us? Does God really care? Does Jesus care?

Frank Graeff, who lived in the late nineteenth and early twentieth centuries, asked that very question as the title of one of the many hymns that he wrote. Like many of us, he was called upon to go through many difficult experiences in his life—experiences that tried his faith. During one of those experiences—perhaps like those you and I have from time to time—he wrote the hymn, "Does Jesus Care?" The first verse and chorus go like this

Does Jesus Care?

Does Jesus care when my heart is pained
Too deeply for mirth and song,
As the burdens press and the cares distress
And the way grows weary and long?

Refrain

O yes, He cares, I know He cares,
His heart is touched with my grief;
When the days are weary, the long nights dreary
I know my Savior cares.[4]

Particularly comforting to Frank Graeff and helping to inspire the hymn were the words of the apostle Peter in his first letter, chapter 5 verse 7: *"Cast all your anxiety on him* [i.e. God] *because he cares for you."*

That's a promise of caring that God always keeps.

Early Failure
October 18

There are numerous examples of early failures in life. Winston Churchill did very poorly at school. Canada's John Diefenbaker tried numerous times to be elected to public office but failed. Later Diefenbaker succeeded and went on to be elected prime minister. Babe Ruth set records not only in home runs, but also in strikeouts. The interesting thing, however, is not that these people were failures, but they learned from their mistakes and went on to bigger and better things.

John Mark, who appears many times on the pages of the New Testament, was a similar failure—at first. He was chosen to accompany the apostle Paul and Barnabas on the very first missionary trip around the eastern Mediterranean. The journey was hardly underway when Mark quit and went back to Jerusalem as recorded in Acts 13:13: *"From Paphos, Paul and his companions sailed to Perga in Pamphylia where John* [Mark] *left them to return to Jerusalem."* Perhaps it was homesickness or simply discouragement. Regardless, when they were to leave on the second journey, Paul refused to take Mark along as recorded later in Acts: *"Barnabas wanted to take John, also called Mark, with them, but Paul did not think it wise to take him, because he had deserted them in Pamphylia and had not continued with them in the work"* (Acts 15:37–38).

Paul and Barnabas separated, Paul taking Silas and Barnabas taking Mark. Later the disagreement was settled, and Mark became valuable to Paul. Indeed, Mark became the author of the second Gospel, which bears his name—a famous man in Christian history.

Peace Not of This World
October 19

Henri Nouwen is a Catholic priest, famous theologian, author, and educator. In the 1980s, Henri moved to a little community near Toronto called Daysbreak. Daysbreak is a L'Arche community. L'Arche is an international movement of communities that welcome people with disabilities. Henri moved into one of the homes that housed people with disabilities.

Among the people Henri worked with was a twenty-five-year-old man named Adam. He could do very little for himself, as he suffered from severe epilepsy. The young man made a profound impression on Henri. He writes: "Out of this broken body and broken mind emerged a most beautiful human being, offering me a greater gift than I would ever be able to offer him." In the seemingly hopeless Adam, Henri found "a peace rooted in being." Henri goes on to say, "Adam is teaching me about peace that is not of this world."[5]

Henri's words echo those of his Master Jesus in the well-loved fourteenth chapter of John. *"Peace I leave with you,"* Jesus said, *"My peace I give you. I do not give to you as the world gives. Do not let your hearts be troubled and do not be afraid"* (John 14:27). And they remind us of this promise in the book of Philippians: *"And the peace of God, which transcends all understanding, will guard your hearts and your minds in Christ Jesus"* (Philippians 4:7).

That peace of soul is available to all, whether a renowned theologian or an Adam in a loving group home in Daysbreak.

Forgiveness
October 20

Some of you are familiar with Corrie ten Boom. She lived in Holland during World War II, where she and her family hid Jews from the occupying Nazis. Later, Corrie and her family were arrested and put in Nazi concentration camps, the last one being the Ravensbruck camp, where her beloved sister, Betsie, passed away painfully.

In 1947, two years after her release from the Ravensbruck camp, Corrie ten Boom returned to visit the camp and gave a message of forgiveness to those who had been her enemies and had treated her family so cruelly. After her address, a man, whom she recognized as one of the guards at the time of her imprisonment, came forward to speak to her. The man, who by now had become a Christian, asked for her forgiveness. She was reluctant at first to forgive him, wrestling with extreme difficulty with her thoughts, but finally took the man's hand in hers and forgave him.

Forgiveness. It is such a wonderful thing to be forgiven. And it is such a wonderful thing to be forgiving . . . to forgive someone else of his transgressions against you.

"*Bear with each other,*" writes the apostle Paul in his letter to the Colossian Christians, "*and forgive whatever grievances you may have against one another. Forgive as the Lord forgave you*" (Colossians 3:13).

Speaking about prayer to His apostles, not long before the crucifixion, Jesus added this important corollary: *"And when you stand praying, if you hold anything against anyone, forgive him* [or her], *so that your Father in heaven may forgive your sins"* (Mark 11:25).

Both forgiving and being forgiven are vital to spiritual growth.

Caring
October 21

The name of Mother Teresa is known to most. She, having spent most of her life reaching out to the poor and downtrodden in India, is the epitome of humility and servanthood. Her influence has spread far beyond the borders of India. She has spoken of her work in this way:

> There is always the danger that we may just do the work for the sake of the work, This is where the respect and the love and the devotion come in—that we do it to God, to Christ, and that's why we do it as beautifully as possible.[6]

The epistle of James is one of the most practical, down-to-earth books one can find anywhere. It talks about the temptations you and I face, the relation of faith to deeds—the things we do every day. It even recommends the best method of taming our tongue—sometimes a problem. It ends its five brief chapters with a prayer of faith.

The definition of pure religion is this according to James: *"Religion that God our Father accepts as pure and faultless is this: to look after orphans and widows in their distress and to keep oneself from being polluted by the world"* (James 1:27). Faith and good living plus a loving concern for others are the essentials of religion, and James adds, *"I will show you my faith by what I do"* (James 2:18b).

This is not to say that we earn God's salvation or even brownie points by our good deeds. Rather, God's salvation within has to break out in service to others.

Sitting On It
October 22

A traveler tells the story of sitting in an international airport beside a very distraught female. She had apparently lost her plane ticket. With nowhere to go and no one to turn to, the girl had been sitting in the terminal for hours, not knowing what to do. The traveler and a couple of others offered to buy the girl lunch and talk to the airline. As she stood up to go with them, she suddenly screamed. There, lying where she had been seated, was the ticket. She had been sitting on it all the time.

"Sitting on it," used figuratively in our language, is a colloquialism for doing nothing about a situation when we have it in our power to correct the problem.

Jesus told a remarkable little story—one of His parables—about a man who, in effect, did nothing in an investment situation when he had an excellent opportunity.

Four men were involved in the parable—an employer and three of his employees. The employer was going away for a lengthy period, and he called in three of his trusted workers. He gave each man quite a sum of money to handle for him. To the first, he gave five thousand; to the second, two thousand; and to the third, one thousand. After a long time, the master returned. He called the three workers before him and asked each how he had made out. The first doubled his five thousand to ten thousand, the second likewise doubled his two thousand to four thousand, and both were suitably rewarded. Then the third. Giving the impression that he thought his master was a hard man, he told the master that he was afraid and buried his one thousand to protect it and had now dug it up. The employer was furious at the third . . . not that he had lost the money, but that he simply hadn't used it. He had not gained any interest. He had sat on it.

Is it just possible that we might be sitting on our ticket today? It could be a ticket to glory . . . whether we know about it or not.

Please Sound the Note
October 23

Back in the days when the New York Symphony made regular radio broadcasts, a Wyoming man who raised sheep wrote to the conductor of the time asking an unusual favor. Winter was coming, and he wouldn't be able to get into town to get batteries for his radio. The only comfort he would have would be his fiddle, and it was desperately in need of a tune. The man asked the conductor if he would be so kind as to sound the note "A" on an upcoming broadcast, so that he could be sure that his fiddle was up to standard pitch. The conductor complied and on the ensuing broadcast had the pianist sound the note.

You'll notice that when the symphony orchestra is tuning up, led by the concert master and just prior to the conductor's entrance, the oboe is call upon to sound that standard, for the oboe is reputed to have perfect pitch.

The Wyoming shepherd's eagerness for standard pitch, and the eagerness of the orchestra, indicate humankind's cry for standards. Even today, when so many standards have gone by the board, you do hear a faint cry for a return to some sort of normative living. People are tiring of a life with few standards. As the apostle put it in his letter to the Corinthians: "*If the trumpet does not sound a clear call, who will get ready for battle?*" (1 Corinthians 14:8).

God give us that clear call—that standard note!

Blest Be the Tie
October 24

John Fawcett, who lived in the eighteenth and early nineteenth centuries, began his ministry in a tiny Baptist church in a small village in Yorkshire, England. He toiled diligently there for seven years and then received an invitation to become pastor at a church in London—both an honor and an opening for enlarged opportunities. He accepted the call. He and his family readied themselves to go. People of the congregation came to bid a tearful farewell. In reaction to the tremendous outpouring of emotion from his congregation, they decided to stay. It was a quick decision, and emotional, but it was firm. Fawcett continued in that Yorkshire pastorate until he died, fifty-four years later.

John Fawcett is best remembered, for one hymn, known around the world, that reflected on the family's inability to part from their beloved congregation. I'm sure many of you know the first verse:

> Blest be the tie that binds
>
> Our hearts in Christian love;
>
> The fellowship of kindred minds
>
> Is like to that above.[7]

"If you have any encouragement from being united with Christ," writes the Apostle to the Church at Philippi, *"if any comfort from his love, if any fellowship with the Spirit, if any tenderness and compassion, then make my joy complete by being like-minded, having the same love, being one in spirit and purpose"* (Philippians 2:1–2).

The fellowship of which both John Fawcett and the Apostle wrote is two-dimensional . . . fellowship with God and fellowship with one another. That's truly living.

The Process of Making New
October 25

Life is a journey, a building process for those of us of the Christian faith. Oftentimes we wonder about and misunderstand the Master Builder's plans and methods. At times, life's happenings may be quite painful, and we question their purpose and the means that have been used.

Life has not always been as beautiful as a bowl of roses or as tasty as a bowl of cherries. There have been difficulties and attacks. We may wonder why these things happen. The author of the book of Hebrews writes: "*Our fathers disciplined us for a little while as they thought best; but God disciplines us for our good, that we may share in his holiness*" (Hebrews 12:10). And he adds in verse 11: "*No discipline seems pleasant at the time, but painful. Later on, however, it produces a harvest of righteousness and peace for those who have been trained by it.*" Not all the problems and trials of life are God's means of discipline, but they may be used by God to enable us to grow. Yes, we can grow—even when we are older. We can grow more loving, more kind, more forgiving, more gracious, or unfortunately, perhaps the opposite.

British writer Elizabeth Barrett Browning, an eminent poet and wife of the well-known Robert Browning, was thinking of the same problem . . . and to its solution, when she wrote:

"Where Christ brings His cross, He brings His Presence, and where He is, none are desolate, and there is no room for despair. As He knows His own, so He knows how to comfort them— using sometimes the very grief itself, and straining it to the sweetness of a faith unattainable to those ignorant of any grief."[8]

Reconciliation
October 26

Isn't it wonderful to hear stories of reconciliation? Doesn't it warm your heart when you hear of a father and a son reconciling, a husband and wife on the verge of divorce reconciling, two friends reconciling, or someone reconciling with God? The very simple definition of reconciliation is "to bring back to friendship." The definition may be simple, but the action to get it done may not be. There might even be years of bitterness to overcome.

Is there someone that you need to reconcile with? Perhaps you even need to reconcile with God. Reconciliation happens best at the foot of the cross, whether reconciling with God or reconciling with your fellow man.

The apostle Paul has written some marvelous words on this very meaningful matter of reconciliation in Second Corinthians, where he writes: *"God was reconciling the world to himself in Christ, not counting men's sins against them. And he has committed to us the message of reconciliation"* (2 Corinthians 5:19). Then Paul adds this thought in verse 20, a challenge to every Christian: *"We are therefore Christ's ambassadors, as though God were making his appeal through us. We implore you on Christ's behalf: Be reconciled to God."*

That reconciliation is vital for each of us . . . in this world and the next.

Cling and Wait
October 27

Without a doubt, in terms of creature comforts and the ability to entertain ourselves, we have the highest civilization in mankind's time on planet Earth. We have aircraft that can get us to our destination very quickly, cars that we can help us travel our highways in splendid comfort, air-conditioned homes and offices in which to work, televisions that bring in the world (and the junk), computers that pour out more information than we'll ever use . . . or need. And on and on.

However, are we satisfied, fulfilled, or happy? There's a malaise abroad in the land, and we are having a hard time coping. Our problems are becoming too big for us, our debt is huge, and violence has become a way of life.

Arnold Joseph Toynbee wrote a ten-volume commentary on the story of mankind. In this vast work, Toynbee traced the rise and fall of civilization after civilization. In concluding his work, he makes a very stirring statement that we should well heed. Toynbee describes a dream he once had. He dreamt that he was in one of England's great abbeys where, a huge cross was suspended above the altar . . . and in his dream, he was clutching the foot of the cross. A voice was saying to him in Latin, "Cling and wait." And that's the message Toynbee leaves with his readers in concluding his massive study of history: cling to the cross and wait.

Toynbee's advice is very pertinent, very forceful: "Cling to the cross and wait." Waiting is not simply folding our hands and doing nothing. We need to follow the example of Christ and keep busy doing our part to make the world a better place—a place where God rules.

Peer Pressure
October 28

Remember Aesop's fable about the miller and his donkey. In a nutshell, a miller and his son set out for the fair, walking beside their donkey. They came upon a group who said that they were foolish to walk—one of them should ride. Obligingly, the miller placed his son on the donkey, continuing on their way. Soon they came upon a group of folks who berated the son for riding while allowing his father to walk, so they changed places. Shortly thereafter, they came upon a group who lectured the father for allowing his son to walk. Ever eager to please, the man pulled his son up on the donkey and continued. This time an angry group stopped them, charging the miller with cruelty to the animal, so they got off, found a pole, tied the donkey's feet to it, and continued on their way. Soon they came to a bridge, and the donkey, frightened by noise of the crowds who were watching the sight and laughing, fell into the river. The miller concluded that by trying to please everybody, he ended up pleasing nobody.

Those around us in this world often feel that they know how we should live and act. If we live differently, there is a strong influence to conform. Among younger people, it is called "peer pressure," and such pressure by schoolmates and friends is often much more penetrating that that of the home, the school, or the church. Even dress differently, and you may be ridiculed.

Peer pressure not only affects youth. It can affect all of us.

Romans 12:2 has an excellent word of wisdom. *"Do not conform any longer to the pattern of this world, but be transformed by the renewing of your mind. Then you will be able to test and approve what God's will is—his good, pleasing and perfect will."*

As we travel life's roadway, the guidance of the Heavenly Father is much more trustworthy than that of any passer-by.

The Peace of God
October 29

Each of us, as we get older, is inclined to grow increasingly critical of the scene around us in the community and in the world. As seniors, it seems we often long for the "good old days." Sometimes we are inclined to idealize those days, and we forget that they too had their share of problems. When we look to the future, we may become fearful; we may be cynical and easily slip back into nostalgia.

When the problems of the world—our world—and its future are getting us down, we can look to God's Word for some help.

Philippians 4:7 says this: *"And the peace of God, which transcends all understanding, will guard your hearts and your minds in Christ Jesus."*

Isaiah 30:15 reminds us about the benefits of rest and quietness as he tells us what the Sovereign Lord says: *"In repentance and rest is your salvation, in quietness and trust is your strength."*

Romans 12:18 tells us to, *"If it is possible, as far as it depends on you, live at peace with everyone."*

Ephesians 4:15 reminds us that, *"Speaking the truth in love, we will in all things grow up into him . . . that is, Christ."*

And David the Psalmist concludes: *"I was young and now I am old, yet I have never seen the righteous forsaken"* (Psalm 37:25).

These verses contain some excellent advice from God's Word to help keep us in a positive frame of mind today and every day.

The Road of the Loving Heart
October 30

Famous author, Robert Louis Stevenson, in later life settled on the island of Samoa due to his declining health. Here Stevenson became quite a local legend, a man of considerable influence. Among other things, he befriended some Samoan chiefs who had been put in prison for political activism. A few months before his death, these chiefs, upon securing their release from prison, were responsible for building a badly needed road to Stevenson's country home. At the corner of the new road that was built, the chiefs erected a sign bearing their names and that of Stevenson's Samoan name with this message:

> Remembering the great love of his highness, **TUSITALA**, and his loving care when we were in prison and sore distressed, we have prepared him an enduring present, this road which we have dug to last forever.[9]

They named it "The Road of the Loving Heart."

As I think of this story, it seems to me that God has done something like that for us. There's a difference, of course, for He has built the road to us—not we to Him. He not only rescued us from the prison of sin when, like the Samoan chiefs, we were "sore distressed," but He also provided the way back home. It is quite significant, I think, that the Christian faith is described as the Way at least half a dozen times in the book of Acts and spelled with a capital "W" in the modern NIV translation of the Bible.

Jesus said, "*I am the way and the truth and the life. No one comes to the Father except through me*" (John 14:6).

"The Road of the Loving Heart" is a beautiful expression to describe the way Jesus has opened up for us. It is God's enduring present . . . a road dug to last forever.

The Capacity to Love
October 31

Jules Léger, who served as the governor-general of Canada from 1975 to 1979, and his brother, Cardinal Paul Emile Léger, were both men of faith. On one occasion, they were both honored by the University of Sherbrooke in Quebec. At the convocation address, the governor-general made some pertinent personal observations.

Of his father, Jules Léger said this: "He imbued each [his sons] with a belief in God and assured them that this was all the inheritance they needed to make their way in life." And he said this of faith: "Only with faith is the capacity to love and persuade, to live and to die with dignity possible."[10]

The little book of Habakkuk near the end of the Old Testament echoes these thoughts. *"The righteous will live by his faith.* "But what is faith?" you say. The New Testament book of Hebrews gives the simplest answer. The author writes, *"Now faith is being sure of what we hope for and certain of what we do not see"* (Hebrews 11:1). The author goes on to give a host of illustrations of faith, all the way from Abel (Adam's son), to Gideon, Daniel, Samuel and the prophets. They all had great faith in God . . . lived in that faith, loved God and their fellowmen, and persuaded others that the way of God was the good way. They died in that faith, sure that the Heavenly Father had prepared for them a fine eternity.

Irish poet, Anna Elizabeth Hamilton, put it like this.

> Faith is a grasping of Almighty power;
> The hand of man laid on the arm of God;
> The grand and blessed hour
> In which things impossible to me
> Become the possible, O Lord, through Thee.[11]

The Sound of Your Name
November 01

These days we seem to take polls on every aspect of life. There was a poll taken a while ago that asked a sampling of people what the most pleasant sounds they heard in life around them from day to day were. You might be surprised at what ranked first. According to that survey, the most pleasant sound in the world is that of your own name.

The most touching scene surrounding the crucifixion and resurrection of Jesus involved the Master and one other person. The apostle John describes the picture at the tomb when His followers discovered that it was empty and the stone rolled away. Mary Magdalene was there early that morning and, finding the tomb vacant, ran to tell the apostles. Peter and John rushed off to see for themselves and, in wonderment, left again for their homes. But Mary Magdalene remained at the sepulcher, weeping. Looking into the tomb again, she saw two angelic figures who asked her why she was crying. *"'They have taken my Lord away,' she said, 'and I don't know where they have put him'"* (John 20:13). And she turned around and saw a man standing before the grave. Through her tears, Mary couldn't see very well and thought the man to be the gardener. When He asked her why she was weeping, she replied, *"Sir, if you have carried him away, tell me where you have put him, and I will get him"* (John 20:15b).

Then the risen Savior said one word—*"Mary."*

That did it. Her name on the lips of the Lord of life. The sweetest word in the language.

Entertaining Angels—Without Knowing It
November 02

Queen Victoria, who reigned from 1837-1901—sixty-four years, appears regally in statue before the Parliament buildings in Victoria, British Columbia . . . the city that bears her name.

There is an interesting story about her that took place when she was younger and staying at her summer palace in Balmoral, Scotland. She liked to take long walks there, and while on one of those trips, she was caught in a heavy rainstorm. Noticing an old cottage, she ran toward it for refuge. In the cottage lived an elderly peasant woman who opened the door to the Queen's knock. The Queen asked her if she might loan her an umbrella. The woman, not recognizing the Queen, said that she had two umbrellas—one almost new and the other worn and much older. She told the Queen that she could take the old one for "the new one I don't lend to nobody—for who knows whether I would ever get it back." The Queen accepted the old umbrella, politely thanking the woman.

The next day a servant in the royal livery brought the old umbrella back and returned it with thanks and the assurance that Her Majesty had received good service from it. How sorry was the woman that she had offered her queen not her best, but the oldest and most dilapidated umbrella she had. Repeatedly, she cried, "If only I had known. If only I had known."

The book of Hebrews has a very solitary word that speaks to that point. We are exhorted, *"Keep on loving each other as brothers* [or sisters]. *Do not forget to entertain strangers, for by so doing some people have entertained angels without knowing it"* (Hebrews 13:1-2).

Crisis

November 03

On one occasion when speaking about the word crisis, President John F. Kennedy said, "When written in Chinese, the word crisis is composed of two characters—one represents danger, and the other represents opportunity."

Danger and opportunity. The two don't seem to have very much in common, although I must admit the Chinese have stumbled onto something.

Jesus said, after rebuking Peter for drawing his sword and cutting off a man's ear when the armed guards of the high priest rushed into the Garden of Gethsemane to arrest Him, *"Do you think I cannot call on my Father, and he will at once put at my disposal more than twelve legions of angels?"* Jesus continued, *"But how then would the Scriptures be fulfilled that say that it must happen in this way?"* (Matthew 26:53–54).

There had been a crisis in Jesus' life, a crisis of immense proportions. However, the crisis had come before His arrest, and He saw all the rest that followed as opportunity.

Following the holding of the Last Supper with His apostles in Jerusalem, Jesus led them into the Garden of Gethsemane. Jesus then took Peter, James, and John—the inner circle of the little band—further into the garden. Asking them to watch and wait a little while, He moved still further into the garden alone. Jesus fell face down on the ground and, in agony, prayed, *"My Father, if it is possible, may this cup be taken from me. Yet not as I will, but as you will"* (Matthew 26:39). Three times Jesus prayed this prayer while the sleepy disciples nodded off. Then He turned to face the soldiers who had come to arrest Him. The crisis was over . . . opportunity loomed.

Jesus opened the way of opportunity for you and for me when He accepted the way of the cross. Forgiveness, new life, and eternal life—all are ours if we simply accept.

Crisis equals both danger and opportunity for us too. Danger if we say "no"; rich opportunity if we say "yes."

Will You Have a Cup of Tea?
November 04

In one of his books, author and missionary Charles Harvey describes the appearance of a major item in his rural New Brunswick kitchen of many years ago.

"In the days before inflation, insulation, and airtight stoves," he writes, "the kitchen 'range' formed the centerpiece of rural hospitality. To the right of the firebox and toward the back of the cooking surface sat a teapot. Out in front of it was a large, spouted water-heating device, we still call a teakettle. These two permanent residents on kitchen stovetops made a cup of tea a warm possibility any time. When the potent brew was tempered with thick cream, it made a molasses cookie taste fit for the queen."[1]

Have you ever asked someone to drop by for a cup of tea? "Just a cup of tea?" you say. However, it is obvious that a cup of tea is a mark of hospitality and friendship in many parts of the world.

"*Share with God's people who are in need,*" writes the apostle Paul to the Christians at Rome, the heart of the empire, adding, "*Practice hospitality*" (Romans 12:13). Similarly, Peter has a word for daily living, offering the same advice. "*Above all,*" he writes, "*love each other deeply, because love covers over a multitude of sins. Offer hospitality to one another without grumbling*" (1 Peter 4:8–9). The apostle John, writing to his friend Gaius and commending him for welcoming visiting strangers into his home, missionaries of the Gospel, concludes, "*We ought therefore to show hospitality to such men so that we may work together for the truth*" (3 John 1:8). The author of Hebrews pleads for similar hospitality, writing, "*Keep on loving each other as brothers. Do not forget to entertain strangers, for by so doing some people have entertained angels without knowing it*" (Hebrews 13:1–2).

"Will you have a cup of tea . . . or share one?"

Humble Service
November 05

Dr. Rufus M. Jones was a well-known and respected American Quaker. As well as being a writer, editor, professor, and preacher, he was a major factor in the American Friends Service Committee, which was prominent during World War I.

A former student of Dr. Jones, tells of a guest lecturer staying at the home of Dr. Jones, who upon retiring for the night left his shoes outside the door. Being an experienced traveler in Europe, Jones knew exactly what that meant, so the next morning the guest found his shoes outside the door, neatly shined. The same thing happened the next morning and the morning after that. When leaving, the guest took out a coin, gave it to Rufus Jones, asking him to give it to the person who had shined his shoes each night. With a smile, Jones pocketed the coin, and the lecturer never did know that someone more famous than himself had shined his shoes.[2]

That sort of humility, that sort of attitude to personal service, surprises us—even shocks us a bit. It shouldn't, for many of us are followers of a Man who took a basin of water one day, wrapped a towel around His waist, and washed his apostle's feet –a job for a menial servant.

Afterward Jesus asked His followers: *"Do you understand what I have done for you? You call me 'Teacher' and 'Lord,' and rightly so, for that is what I am. Now that I, your Lord and Teacher, have washed your feet, you should also wash one another's feet"* (John 13:12b-14).

In hot and dusty Palestine, foot washing was a sign of loving hospitality . . . even as shining shoes was for Rufus Jones. In a similar vein, Paul, writing to Christians at Philippi, says this about his Master:

> *Who, being in very nature God, did not consider equality with God something to be grasped, but made himself nothing, taking the very nature of a servant, being made in human likeness. And being found in appearance as a man, he humbled himself and became obedient to death—even death on a cross!* (Philippians 2:6-8).

And Paul prefaced these remarks with the following words: *"Your attitude should be the same as that of Christ Jesus!"*

Proclaiming
November 06

Those of you who have done some scientific study or tinkering, particularly in the field of physics, will readily recognize the name and the genius of Michael Faraday. Faraday, born in the late eighteenth century, was the discoverer of electro-magnetic induction and other significant conceptions having to do with electrical and magnetic phenomena. In practical terms, Faraday's discoveries made possible the development of electrical machinery for industry.

Although best known for his scientific genius, Michael Faraday also had some very significant, seldom-mentioned aspects of his life. To me, the most intriguing element to his life was that for twenty-seven years the great scientist preached every other Sunday to the congregation of a small church . . . and nothing would deter him. Faraday looked on his scientific endeavors as an act of cooperation with God. He indicated that if he failed in that work, he would be failing God. However, he believed it would be an even greater failure to be absent from the pulpit when he was scheduled and, therefore, to fail to proclaim the good news concerning the Light of the World, his Savior.

The apostle John had a similar dedication to proclaiming the Light of the World, the Light of Life. In the first chapter of his first epistle, John writes: *"That which was from the beginning, which we have heard, which we have seen with our eyes, which we have looked at and our hands have touched—this we proclaim concerning the Word of life. The life appeared; we have seen it and testify to it, and we proclaim to you the eternal life . . ."* (1 John 1:1-2).

That's good news, whether proclaimed by the apostle John, Michael Faraday, or even you or me.

Victorious Over Suffering
November 07

Arthur Henry Hallam said, "Pain is the deepest thing we have in our nature." He added, "Union through pain and suffering has always seemed more real and holy than any other."

Many seniors, particularly the older ones, can say that both of these statements are true, as many have experienced both personally. For pain is not always, but often, the companion of the elderly. Pain does lie very deep in our nature, and often we have gained the finest friendships with others who have suffered.

How does God help us with the pain and suffering that we have to endure? Prayer will bring relief on many occasions . . . even a cure. Concerning prayer, James writes, *"Is any one of you in trouble? He* [or she] *should pray"* (James 5:13a). Then there is hope.

God does not promise immediate healing for all the pain and suffering in the world. Yet as the apostle wrote to the Roman Christians, suffering becomes a means of spiritual growth: *"We also rejoice in our suffering,"* he writes, *"because we know that suffering produces perseverance; perseverance, character; and character, hope. And hope does not disappoint us"* (Romans 5:3–5a).

The New Testament writer James adds these examples of patient suffering or suffering patiently. *"Brothers,"* he writes, *"as an example of patience in the face of suffering, take the prophets who spoke in the name of the Lord. As you know, we consider blessed those who have persevered."* He goes on, *"You have heard of Job's perseverance and have seen what the Lord finally brought about. The Lord is full of compassion and mercy"* (James 5:10–11).

We sometimes forget that in the Garden of Gethsemane, Jesus—God's Son—prayed three times to his Heavenly Father that He might not have to face the cross. *"My Father, if it is possible, may this cup* [this cup of overwhelming pain and grief] *be taken from me. Yet not as I will, but as you will."* (Matthew 26:39).

God's will was done. It was necessary for your salvation and mine. Jesus gave His life, but the final answer was given by angels at His tomb at the resurrection: *"He is not here; he has risen."*

The resurrection made it possible for you and me to be victorious over the hurts, the bruises, the pains, and the sufferings of this life . . . and finally and totally victorious in eternity.

Sacrifice and Honors
November 08

June 6, 1944, will long be remembered. It was D-Day, the date of the Allied invasion of Europe through Normandy in World War II. One word comes to mind when thinking about the events of that day—sacrifice—surely one of the noblest human qualities. An anonymous author has put it aptly, "Self-preservation is the first law of nature; self-sacrifice is the highest rule of grace." And it happens in many areas of life.

During the building of the great Boulder Dam on the Colorado River, an amazing engineering feat, eighty-nine men lost their lives. At the dam site, this simple inscription honors those sacrifices: "For those who died that the desert might bloom."

One of the thrilling stories of outstanding self-sacrifice in Old Testament days is found in 1 Chronicles, chapter 11. It tells of David and his army going out to battle the Philistines, Israel's traditional enemies. The Philistines were encamped in a nearby valley, while David and his army were near the cave of Adullam, which had been David's hiding place as he fled from Saul. In a lull in the proceedings, David became very thirsty and, perhaps more to himself than to anyone else, muttered aloud: *"Oh, that someone would get me a drink of water from the well near the gate of Bethlehem!"*

Three of David's finest officers overheard his remark, and holding him in the highest regard, they decided to try. The three officers broke through the Philistine ranks, drew water from the well at the gate of Bethlehem, and took it back to David.

The King was so moved by their dangerous act that he could not drink the water for which they had risked their lives. Rather, he poured it out as an offering to the Lord in thanksgiving for a very brave and honorable act by three of his chosen leaders.

In the battle of life, high honors go to the one who serves God and his or her fellowman. This is how Jesus put it in John 12:26. *"Whoever serves me must follow me; and where I am, my servant also will be. My Father will honor the one who serves me."*

The world is not likely to salute you, but the God of glory does. He honors you for serving faithfully His Son.

Well Done!
November 09

As we look back on our lives, perhaps some of us feel that we were passed over when the awards of this life were given. I once watched an episode of a TV documentary called "Quiet Heroes" that illustrates that feeling.

The hero of the story was a veteran of World War II, whose daughter obviously loved him very much. Her father, a Canadian, had been a bomber pilot, attached for some reason to Britain's R.A.F. All his service had been in the Far East where he had flown—and loved— Liberator aircraft. He and his crew flew many, many missions up and down the coast near India, defending the shipping lanes against Japanese planes and submarines. They and their fellows were very successful in their missions, and after moving on to other transport units at the end of the war, the father returned to Canada.

To the present, he had remained satisfied with his accomplishments, except for the lack of any sort of recognition from the R.A.F. or the British Government. The daughter had recently learned that at the regular air show held in Walla Walla, Washington, many vintage planes take part, including the Liberator. She went to work. First, she approached the R.A.F. concerning her father's unrecognized squadron. Then she learned that one of her father's crew members was living, but in England. She communicated with him and learned that he would be delighted to attend a reunion. Then she arranged with the air show authorities for her father to fly in a Liberator . . . all of this unknown to her father.

It was not hard to persuade her father to go to the air show, where he successively watched a Liberator in flight, flew in it, then became stunned when he came face to face with his British crew mate. After all of these surprises, he was in tears when a squadron leader from the present R.A.F. was introduced and read a splendid proclamation from the R.A.F. concerning his own fine service and that of his now—recognized squadron.[3]

As many have said, we all like a little praise and recognition.

For those of us who, like the pilot, feel that we were passed over when the awards were given, remember that we—you and I—were so important that God sent His Son to die that we might have eternal life. Then one day, when we stand before Him on the Day of Judgment, God will say to those who have served Him, "Well done, good and faithful servant." People, even governments, may neglect to honor good service . . . God always remembers.

The Supreme Sacrifice
November 10

Despite all that is wrong with our world, most of our citizens have deep appreciation for the sacrifices that have been made on our behalf through world wars and smaller conflicts. Many have paid the supreme sacrifice so that the rest of us might have freedom . . . yes, life itself. Jesus Himself puts such a sacrifice in the category of the very best: *"Greater love has no one than this, that he lay down his life for his friends"* (John 15:13).

We hear a great deal of complaining all around us in our day. No one seems satisfied. People appear to want more and more. This is a good week to take stock, I think, both physically and spiritually. First, we should be ever thankful that we are here, materially blessed, thanks to the sacrifice of those who gave all to save us. Second, we should give thanks to Almighty God for the offered gift of eternal life through the sacrifice of His Son on the cross of Calvary. The first—the gift of life—becomes worthwhile for time and eternity when we reach out to God and accept His loving forgiveness.

Many have given their lives in battle so that we have freedom. God sent His Son, who gave His life, that all who come to Him may live eternally.

The Final Peace
November 11

The Victoria Cross, Great Britain's and other Commonwealth countries' highest military honor, is presented not for just ordinary valor, but for the extraordinary. Daniel Laidlaw was one who did something extraordinary in the First World War that earned him the Victoria Cross. It was the First Battle of Loos, and Laidlaw's fellow soldiers were tired, shaken, and uncertain because of the desperate fighting and ravages of battle. Danny did something about it. And the instrument he used was the bagpipes. During heavy enemy bombardment, he, a piper with the king's own Scottish Borderers, marched up and down the parapet, exposed to enemy fire. He so inspired his shaken comrades that they dashed out of the trench and assaulted. Piper Laidlaw continued to pipe them along until he was hit and wounded. Unlike so many Victoria Cross winners, Piper Laidlaw survived the moment that brought him the great honor.

Today we honor those who paid, many with their lives, for the freedom we enjoy. May that freedom never be lost, and may young men and women not be called upon to make further sacrifices in causes that bring the world to war.

Peace depends upon each of us. Peace, however, is not simply absence of war. It is much deeper; it's inward—in the heart, if you like.

Of the many titles of Jesus found in the Bible—Counselor, Mighty God, Everlasting Father, and many more—not a single one I can think of refers to war and His prowess in battle. Isaiah does call Him the Prince of Peace. In forecasting His coming, Luke writes that He is *"to guide our feet into the path of peace."* When He was about to leave the world, Jesus assured His followers: *"Peace I leave with you; my peace I give you. I do not give to you as the world gives. Do not let your hearts be troubled and do not be afraid"* (John 14:27).

He is the One through whom you and I and the world may find that "peace of God, which transcends all understanding," as the Apostle Paul describes it.

Sharing
November 12

One should never underestimate the importance of sharing. Along life's way, we do share many similar adventures, and in that respect, perhaps the older we are, the more we have to share. Sharing one another's trials and tribulations, the loss of loved ones, illnesses, etc., can be good for the soul.

Have you ever realized that the Bible is a book of sharing and that God through His Son Jesus wants to share in our times, to bring healing of mind and peace of soul. *"Your word,"* writes the Psalmist in Psalm 119:105, says, *"is a lamp to my feet and a light for my path."* If we see clearly, brightly on the pathway of life, there is no need to stumble or to fall.

After over four hundred years in Egypt, many of those years spent as virtual slaves, the Israelites of the Old Testament were miraculously freed by God. With Moses as their leader, they escaped across the Red Sea on dry land. Although, they had their newly found freedom, they had to cross difficult and dangerous territory in order to reach the Promised Land. By day God gave them a pillar of cloud to guide them, a pillar of fire by night. As Exodus 13:22 has it, *"Neither the pillar of cloud by day nor the pillar of fire by night left its place in front of the people.*

God's guidance in life is sure and sufficient. We can trust Him completely. Jesus Himself made this promise in a verse that was quoted in the previous devotion and applies here as well. *"Peace I leave with you; my peace I give you. I do not give to you as the world gives. Do not let your hearts be troubled and do not be afraid* (John 14:27).

That from the "greatest story ever told." Let's be sure to share it.

Prayer Like a Telephone
November 13

Mark Twain was one of America's greatest humorists. He could make outrageous remarks and get away with it. He once wrote, "It is my heart-warmed and world-embracing hope that all of us . . . may eventually be gathered together in a heaven of everlasting rest and peace and bliss . . . except the inventor of the telephone."

I'm sure the humorist wasn't engaging in a vendetta against Alexander Graham Bell personally, but he wanted the world to know that in his estimation, the telephone was more bane than blessing.

Sometimes I'm inclined to agree with him, particularly when someone phones at precisely 6 p.m.—knowing that's the sure-fire time to catch you home . . . and the caller waxes for many minutes on the tremendous merits of the product they are selling. Or you might receive a call from one of the pollsters, asking you some trite questions.

Of course, one needs to look at the other side. A telephone is of tremendous value in the middle of the night when someone takes sick or there's an accident. Also, it's marvelous to hear from one of the members of your family or a dear friend over the phone. Business, of course, really depends on the telephone. In short, we couldn't get along without it.

Have you ever realized that prayer is like a telephone? Handy and right at your side. All you have to do is pick up the receiver. You don't even have to dial. God is always ready, waiting at the other end of the prayer line. But do not, as so many of us as are prone to do, take over the conversation. Like the telephone, prayer is a two-way conversation. Actually, you'll likely do much better if you let God do most of the talking.

Psalm 145:18 says this, "*The LORD is near to all who call on him, to all who call on him in truth.*"

May I say the following words reverently: "Let us give God a ring!" Whereas the telephone may be a win/lose situation, prayer is win/win.

Doing For Others
November 14

Anne of Green Gables, the novel written by Canadian author Lucy Maud Montgomery, is a perennial favorite. Similar success is enjoyed by the musical version put on in Charlottetown, P.E.I., in the summer. The TV series has been a hit as well. Indeed, "Anne" has achieved much international acclaim, particularly in Japan.

Those of you familiar with the story, set in rural P.E.I. many years ago, will recall that a brother and sister (Matthew and Marilla Cuthbert) tried to secure a lad from an orphanage in Charlottetown to help the elderly Matthew with the farm work. They were told that the lad would arrive on a certain day and train, and when Matthew went to pick the lad up at the train station, the lad was, much to his amazement, a girl. With some misgivings, Matthew drove the buggy home with the new arrival, to be met by stern sister Marilla. After Anne had gone to bed, brother and sister talked to decide her fate. Marilla was bent on sending the orphan girl back.

"What good would she be to us?" asked Marilla, to which her brother perceptively responded, "We might be some good to her." And of course, Anne did stay.[4]

If you were to think of one word that sums up the life and three-year ministry of Jesus, it might very well be "others." His whole outlook was one of doing, caring for others. Indeed, His bitterest enemies . . . those who put Him on the cross . . . added it all up without meaning to do so. Mocking Him while He hung on the cross, the chief priests, the teachers of the law, and the elders jeered, "He saved others, but he can't save himself."

That is the core of the gospel. The Son of God could easily have saved Himself, but not without denying salvation to us. Therefore, he chose to die because of His eternal and loving concern for spiritual orphans like you and like me.

Faith in God
November 15

To have full faith in people sometimes ends in disappointment as, once in a while, people let you down. They don't justify the faith you have put in them. On the other hand, not to have faith, for fear of being hurt, often leaves one in a very negative situation. You don't trust anyone, and life becomes joyless. There is no fear of this dilemma when your faith is placed in God.

There's a fine definition of faith in the eleventh chapter of Hebrews. It goes like this: "*Now faith is being sure of what we hope for and certain of what we do not see. By faith,*" the author adds, "*we understand that the universe was formed at God's command, so that what is seen was not made out of what was visible*" (Hebrews 11:1,3). Simple faith realizes that the hand of God was prominent in all of creation . . . that we are made according to God's plan, and like the great St. Augustine, we believe that the hearts of men and women are restless until they rest in the God who created us all.

Sir Humphry Davy, the famous English scientist who made many discoveries of worldwide importance in chemistry in the eighteenth century, referred to faith this way: "I should prefer a firm religious belief to every other blessing. For it makes life a discipline of goodness; creates new hopes, when earthly hopes vanish; and throws over all decay, the destruction of existence . . . awakens life even in death."[5]

Put your faith in God and experience His fullness.

Glory in the Cross
November 16

The cross of Christ is all-important to the Christian. Writing to the followers of the cross in Galatia, the apostle Paul wrote, *"May I never boast except in the cross of our Lord Jesus Christ, through which the world has been crucified to me, and I to the world"* (Galatians 6:14). Paul realized that boasting—for a Christian—was a non-starter. The cross of Jesus is the central aspect of life for every Christian, calling for a sacrificial offering from each of us. Jesus had earlier invited, *"If anyone would come after me, he* [or she] *must deny himself* [or herself] *take up his cross,* [or her cross], *and follow me"* (Matthew 16:24). The cross for every follower of Jesus is a small—very small—replica of the cross on which Jesus Himself suffered. During His short three-year ministry of healing, serving, and saving, Jesus was often persecuted, often ridiculed, and His cross was the most fiendishly designed death ever devised by man. And all the while He was bearing your sins and mine—redeeming us.

What hardship then if you are given a small replica of that cross to bear? Jesus did not promise His followers a lifetime spent on a bed of roses. *"In this world,"* He said, *"you will have trouble. But take heart! I have overcome the world"* (John 16:33b).

The cross draws us to a suffering Jesus. More than that, it draws us to a suffering world for which He died. To share in that suffering is our rich privilege.

God's Caring
November 17

Queen Victoria was a passenger on a train that was racing through the foggy night when a strange phenomenon occurred. All of a sudden, the engineer saw, in the beam of the engine's powerful headlight, a shadowy figure standing in the middle of the track waving its arms. The engineer managed to bring the train to a grinding halt. He and a trainman stepped down to see what had stopped them, but there was no trace of the figure. When the engineer walked a short distance further up the track, he came upon an incredible sight. Where there was supposed to be a bridge, there was simply space. The bridge had been washed out into the swollen stream. A few hundred yards more, and the speeding train would have gone into the stream.

What was the shadowy figure? Upon further investigation, the engineer discovered that the "flagman" who had saved their lives was merely a huge moth that, magnified on the headlight beam, appeared to be a phantom figure waving its arms. When told of the strange happening, Queen Victoria said, "I'm sure it's no accident. It was God's way of protecting us."

God cares for us. It's such an assurance to know that we have someone who constantly watches over us. God does care for those who are part of His family, and He makes no distinction between rich or poor, black or white, royal or commoner, French or English. He does show His caring in a multitude of ways—sometimes the ways are great, sometimes seemingly insignificant.

"*Come, let us bow down in worship,*" sings the Psalmist, "*let us kneel before the LORD our Maker; for he is our God and we are the people of his pasture, the flock under his care*" (Psalm 95:6–7).

Peter writes, "*Cast all your anxiety on him* [God] *because he cares for you*" (1 Peter 5:7).

Ours is a loving, caring God. We are His cared-for children—if we only ask.

Meekness
November 18

There is a lot to be said about the true humility of the human spirit when moved by the love and power of God. Jesus termed this true humility as "meekness." *"Blessed are the meek,"* He said in the Beatitudes, *"for they will inherit the earth."*

Meekness is lacking in our world. So much of advertising is addressed to pleasing you and me . . . satisfying not only our every want, but also most of our wishes.

Meekness is not the picture of the hesitating, self-deprecating, hopeless little guy who used to appear in comic strips ages ago—Mr. Milquetoast. He was a parody of meekness. That sort of meekness inherits neither earth nor heaven.

True meekness is one of the very finest human qualities, that of reverence and humility before God, possessed by a man or woman fully under God's control. There are, as far as I can discover, only two men in the Bible of which the word "meek" is used in their description. The first is Jesus Himself, and the other, surprisingly, is Moses. Numbers 12:3, in the King James Version, says this, *"Now the man Moses was very meek, above all the men which were upon the face of the earth."* Moses could be angry, very angry—but at the right times and never selfishly. He could be stern and unrelenting—again at the proper times. Moses was a man who was fully under God's control.

If we ourselves seek meekness, following the example of Moses will point us in the right direction.

A Staggering Finish
November 19

The marathon is a very grueling race, requiring a lot of mettle and grit. This determination was very much evident in something that took place in the marathon at the Commonwealth Games held in Vancouver. With thousands watching in person and millions more on television, an English marathoner, Jim Peters, staggered onto the track in the stadium, almost at the end of the twenty-six mile, three hundred eighty-five yard race. He collapsed into the arms of one of the English trainers, just about two hundred yards short of the finish line. He made a last-ditch effort toward what he thought was the finish line, but it was, in fact, a finish line for shorter races. The finish line for the marathon was a short distance further across the track.

Jim Peters should have won the marathon easily, but he didn't. He was a great distance ahead of his nearest competitor. Seemingly, he didn't pace himself and had nothing left at the end.

In the epistle of Galatians, some Galatian Christians were having similar problems in the race of life. They were in danger of failure in their lives—not making it spiritually—staggering over the track. Paul wrote to them pointedly, "*You were running a good race. Who cut in on you and kept you from obeying the truth?*" (Galatians 5:7). Then writing to the Corinthians, the apostle expressed the fervent wish that, "*After I have preached to others, I myself will not be disqualified for the prize*" (1 Corinthians 9:27).

May we be great finishers.

A Striking Conversion
November 20

Today I just wanted to underline the richness of the conversion of Saul of Tarsus to the apostle Paul—the experience that completely turned his life around.

Saul of Tarsus would have undoubtedly been considered, by many, to be one of the world's great men. Tarsus, his proud birthplace, was capital of Cilicia and center of the Roman government of that region. Mark Antony had granted every inhabitant of Tarsus a deeply cherished Roman citizenship. Saul, though a Jew, valued the privileges it gave. Indeed, the name Paul, by which he was later and best known, is Roman.

When Saul was about twenty, he attended Pharisees' school for rabbis at Jerusalem. He first appears in the New Testament in the book of Acts, standing approvingly by, minding the clothes of the mob who stoned Stephen, the first Christian martyr. Popular with the high priest, he became a fanatical leader of the persecutors of the new Christian sect.

But God was working in Saul's heart. While on his way from Jerusalem to Damascus to persecute Christians there, Saul came face to face with the risen Jesus, and he experienced the most dramatic conversion recorded anywhere in Scripture.

Saul, with the fanatical zeal of the persecutor, became Paul, the even more zealous ambassador of Christ. To trace even a few of his missionary journeys will leave you wondering how one man could have been so effective.

God can do that with people. He can turn their lives completely around.

Dramatic conversions continue.

Thanksgiving Day
November 21

American writer, Sarah Hale, was left a widow with five little children when still very young. She opened a small millinery store to support her family and somehow found time to do some writing. The success of her writing gave her opportunity to become editor of a small women's magazine, "Godey's Lady's Book," That magazine increased its circulation greatly under her guidance.

Godey's was a secular magazine, but as editor, Sarah Hale would frequently pick up religious matters and support causes which she favored as a Christian. One of her major interests concerned Thanksgiving Day. For many years, she wrote congressmen, governors, and presidents, seeking a national holiday—at least one day a year—for the nation to give thanks to God.

In 1863, still striving for her cause, Sarah Hale wrote to President Lincoln. As the editor of the nation's most popular magazine, she could not be ignored entirely. Interestingly, in her letter to the President, she quoted Nehemiah 8:10a, where Nehemiah, said, *"Go and enjoy choice food and sweet drinks, and send some to those who have nothing prepared. This day is sacred to our Lord."* On October 3 of that year, 1863, President Lincoln issued a proclamation calling on his people to "set apart and observe the last Thursday in November next as a day of thanksgiving and praise to our beneficent Father who dwelleth in the heavens."

Canada's first Thanksgiving Day was proclaimed in 1879, when November 06 was so marked; the date was later changed to the second Monday in October.

May we be truly thankful for all the blessings our Heavenly Father has given us.

Outreaching Love
November 22

In the last book of the Bible, Revelation, chapters two and three contain a total of seven letters written to seven churches in Asia Minor. These churches were quite different from one another and thought by many to represent churches of different standing throughout history—and even today.

The first letter was to the church at Ephesus. Ephesus was the capital of the Roman province of Asia, one of the leading cities in the Roman Empire. The Apostle Paul had spent three years there on his third missionary journey. The church there was obviously one of his best loved. One of his epistles is addressed to that church. Yet some years later as John pens the book of Revelation, things have gone down among the Ephesian Christians. The letter contains both praise and criticism. God is speaking:

> *I know your deeds, your hard work and your perseverance. I know that you cannot tolerate wicked men, that you have tested those who claim to be apostles but are not, and have found them false. You have persevered and have endured hardships for my name, and have not grown weary. Yet I hold this against you: You have forsaken your first love. Remember the height from which you have fallen!* (Revelation 2:2-5a).

Hard work, perseverance, discernment, endurance . . . all these for God, and yet those Christians have "forsaken their first love." They've been so busy doing things that they have forgotten their duty to love. And that is an outreaching love—for if we love God, we love those around us, our brothers and our sisters. *"This is how we know what love is,"* writes John in his first epistle, *"Jesus Christ laid down his life for us. And we ought to lay down our lives for our brothers"* (1 John 3:16). A sober, challenging thought.

Letters
November 23

There are a good number of references in the Bible to the sending of letters, of course always delivered by hand by a special messenger. The first such mention is in the book of Second Samuel, where a letter was used very tragically—to send the bearer to his death. The apostle Paul wrote many letters—to the Christians in Rome, Corinth, Galatia, Ephesus, Philippi, Colosse, and Thessalonica, as well as personal letters to Timothy, Titus and Philemon. In God's Word, they are called epistles—another word for letters. James wrote letters, so did Peter and John.

Letters of recommendation were often carried by the person being recommended. In his second letter, or epistle, to the church at Corinth, Paul uses a delightful figure of speech concerning letters of recommendation. In the third chapter, he asks the Corinthians, *"Do we need, like some people, letters of recommendation to you or from you?"* And he goes on: *"You yourselves are our letter, written on our hearts, known and read by everybody. You show that you are a letter from Christ, the result of our ministry, written not with ink but with the Spirit of the living God"* (2 Corinthians 3:1b–3a).

Paul is saying that we show more clearly by our lives, by the way we live, that Christ is in us, than by all the letters we may send. When you come right down to it, a letter delivered because it bears a postage stamp is not as meaningful or personal as a message you bear or live. All around us every day, there are people who see us, watch us, and read us. Thus, we understand Paul's view: "Do others see Christ in us?" What message do they read?

The Silence of God
November 24

Is God sometimes silent? If He is indeed silent, how do we deal with it? From time to time, many of us feel that there seems to be silence in Heaven for an hour or two . . . sometimes a day or two . . . or perhaps longer. Sometimes there is a little difficulty in "getting through."

David the Psalmist shared our experience. For example, in the first and second verses of Psalm twenty-eight, David cries out, "*To you I call, O LORD my Rock; do not turn a deaf ear to me. For if you remain silent, I will be like those who have gone down to the pit.*" David continues in verse two: "*Hear my cry for mercy as I call to you for help, as I lift up my hands towards your Most Holy Place.*"

That's Israel's greatest king talking . . . sensing for a time the silence of God. At another point in his career, pursued by his enemies, David cried, "*O LORD, you have seen this; be not silent, Do not be far from me, O Lord. Awake, and rise to my defense!*"(Psalm 35:22-23a).

In the twenty-fifth Psalm, verses 16–18a, David prays, "*Turn to me and be gracious to me, for I am lonely and afflicted. The troubles of my heart have multiplied; free me from my anguish. Look upon my affliction and my distress.*"

However, in Psalms 42 and 43, which are linked as one Psalm in many Hebrew Bibles, the Psalmist asks and answers this meaningful question three times: "*Why are you downcast, O my soul? Why so disturbed within me? Put your hope in God, for I will yet praise him, my Savior and my God.*"

And in Psalm 28, where he first expressed fear as to God's silence, David soon concludes, "*Praise be to the LORD, for he has heard my cry for mercy. The LORD is my strength and my shield; my heart trusts in him, and I am helped. My heart leaps for joy and I will give thanks to him . . .*" (Psalm 28:6-7).

God will speak to the human soul—to you and to me—out of His seeming silence.

Press On

November 25

As seniors, we realize that most of our life lies behind us rather than ahead of us. However, seniors may fall into the trap of spending too much time dwelling on the past, rather than looking to the future. We too, need to press on into the future. We can take some lessons from Paul in this regard, in his letter to the Philippians.

Paul was still languishing in a Roman prison when he wrote this letter to his dear friends at Philippi, who had been so supportive of his missionary work. As he writes, Paul looks back over his life, thanking God for little victories and yearning to become more like his Savior. He writes:

> *Not that I have already obtained all this, or have already been made perfect, but I press on to take hold of that for which Christ Jesus took hold of me . . . One thing I do: Forgetting what is behind and straining toward what is ahead, I press on toward the goal to win the prize for which God has called me heavenward in Christ Jesus* (Philippians 3:12–14).

Here is a man growing older who has accomplished more than most, who wants to forget all his achievements and look only toward an indescribable future. There is a word here for each of us too as we look ahead rather than back. It can make such a splendid difference in our lives.

Press on.

"Leave Me My Men"
November 26

Andrew Carnegie was truly a rag to riches story. He began work as a bobbin boy in a cotton factory. After stints in various occupations, he established a number of steel companies that eventually merged into the massive United States Steel Corporation. Carnegie became one of the world's richest men.

When Carnegie was at the pinnacle of business success, someone asked him what he believed about the future of his vast industrial empire.

Carnegie replied, "You can take from me all my plants. You can take from me all my money. You can take from me all my equipment. But if you leave me my men, I will build it all again."[6]

As the life of Jesus moved swiftly toward the cross of Calvary, the work that Jesus had come to undertake would have been described as in serious jeopardy. He had chosen twelve men to be his close associates and to carry forward the task after He left them. He already knew that one of them was a traitor and would betray Him, and another—one of His little inner circle—would deny that he even knew Jesus when the pressure came. In the incident in the Garden of Gethsemane, an armed posse was sent by the Jewish leaders to arrest Jesus. In the book of Matthew, it is written, *"Then all the disciples deserted him and fled."*

Not much was left to build on there. Yet following the resurrection of Jesus and the empowerment of God's Holy Spirit on the day of Pentecost, those same 11 men (Judas, the traitor had hanged himself) literally turned their spiritual world upside down.

When before the Sanhedrin, the highest Jewish Council, Peter and John presented such a powerful defence that, as the book of Acts records, *"When they saw the courage of Peter and John and realized that they were unschooled, ordinary men, they were astonished and they took note that these men had been with Jesus"* (Acts 4:13).

So it has been throughout the centuries—ordinary men and women in God's Kingdom have significantly affected our world.

Time and Eternity

November 27

God has put in all of us a longing responsive to God's yearning for us, His children... His creation.

In the beginning of the third chapter of the sometimes-puzzling little book of Ecclesiastes, the author has written that:

> *There is a time for everything,*
> *and a season for every activity under heaven:*
> *A time to be born and a time to die,*
> *A time to plant and a time to uproot...*
> *A time to tear down and a time to build*
> *A time to weep and a time to laugh*
> *A time to mourn and a time to dance...*

The author then goes on to list many more contrasts in relation to time, and then he says this in verse 11a of chapter three. "*He* [God] *has made everything beautiful in its time. He has also set eternity in the hearts of men.*"

The whole of sacred history, as recorded in the Bible, is the story of God's loving search for humankind from the moment of Adam and Eve's sin in the Garden of Eden, recorded in the book of Genesis, to the call of Jesus almost at the very end of the book of Revelation: "*The Spirit and the bride say, 'Come!' And let him who hears say, 'Come!' Whoever is thirsty, let him come; and whoever wishes, let him take the free gift of the water of life.*"

May He find a responsive chord in your heart and mine.

High Ways Are By-Ways
November 28

I read one time of a person who, like so many others, drove over the same monotonous freeway day after day to his city office and to a job that he also found dreary. One day he took a different route. He was amazed at the beautiful scenery he found along the way. Passing through a village, he noticed a sign that said "Clerk Wanted." He enquired about the job, found out it was just what he needed, and took the job.

Some of you perhaps know the English poet John Oxenham's little ten-line verse "The Ways," which describes the choice that everyone must make as he or she travels life's freeway:

> To every man there openeth
> A Way, and Ways, and a Way,
> And the High Soul climbs the High Way,
> And the Low Soul gropes the Low,
> And in between, on the misty flats,
> The rest drift, to and fro.
> But to every man there openeth
> A High Way and a Low,
> And every man decideth
> The Way the soul shall go.[7]

Jesus, describing what John Oxenham calls the "High Way," put it like this: *"Enter through the narrow gate. For wide is the gate and broad is the road that leads to destruction, and many enter through it. But small is the gate and narrow the road that leads to life, and only a few find it"* (Matthew 7:13–14).

There are broad, modern freeways where the crowd is always on the move, the traffic dense. Then there are the High Ways of which Oxenham writes.

If you, like the person on the freeway, are willing to leave life's hustle and frenzied bustle to find peace and wonder in the by-ways, come to the One who is the way, the truth, and the life. He'll be expecting you.

With Jesus
November 29

Author Joseph Conrad in his book *The Mirror of the Sea*, quotes from a letter of Sir Robert Stopford, who commanded one of the ships with which Nelson chased to the West Indies an enemy fleet nearly double in size. Describing the desperate hardships of that daring adventure, Stopford wrote: "We are half-starved and otherwise inconvenienced by being so long out of port, but our reward is that we are with Nelson."[8]

Another man with a great deal of seafaring experience tells it like this in 2 Corinthians 11: 26b–27a:

> *I have been in danger from rivers, in danger from bandits, in danger from my own countrymen, in danger from the Gentiles; in danger in the city, in danger in the country, in danger at sea; and in danger from false brothers. I have labored and toiled and have often gone without sleep. I have known hunger and thirst and have often gone without food.*

And he continues, concluding later on in the next chapter: "*For Christ's sake, I delight in weaknesses, in insults, in hardships, in persecutions, in difficulties. For when I am weak, then I am strong*" (2 Corinthians 12:10). The man in the passages of Scripture, the apostle Paul, was with Jesus.

That can be our assurance too as we sail the seas of life, no matter how tempestuous: we can have our Master with us.

Andrew and I
November 30

You may not know it, but today, November 30, is St. Andrew's Day. It is likely familiar to those of you of Scottish origins, for St. Andrew is, of course, the patron saint of Scotland—and I find this most interesting—also of none other than Russia. Andrew was an apostle, brother of Simon Peter. He, in fact, first introduced Peter to Jesus. Like others of the Apostles, Andrew was martyred, and it is traditionally held that he was crucified on an X-shaped cross. That X-shaped cross is today part of Great Britain's flag, the Union Jack; representing Scotland, it is a white St. Andrew's cross on a blue field.

A well-known poem, later to become a hymn, was written to mark St. Andrew's Day in 1852 by Cecil F. Alexander. Despite the male-sounding name, Cecil Alexander was Mrs. Alexander, the wife of Dr. William Alexander, who later became archbishop for all Ireland. Dr. Alexander asked his wife to write a poem that would go with the sermon he was going to preach on St. Andrew's Day.

Here are the first two verses from that hymn, "Jesus Calls Us O'er the Tumult.

> Jesus calls us; o'er the tumult
> Of our life's wild, restless sea,
> Day by day His sweet voice soundeth,
> Saying, 'Christian, follow Me.'

> As, of old, Saint Andrew heard it,
> By the Galilean lake,
> Turned from home and toil and kindred,
> Leaving all for his dear sake.[9]

Jesus is calling you today. Are you willing to follow him?

Going the Second Mile
December 01

Once while walking, I passed a man who was doing something that didn't seem that remarkable at first glance. He was in a green area through which the sidewalk ran, alternately kneeling and then walking over to a bucket by then piled high with greenery. The man was removing the weeds from a public park area, just to make it more pleasant for everyone. As I passed, I remarked that not many do such weeding for the city for free, and he just smiled and said that the city maintenance workers were not doing it, so he thought he would.

Not very exciting really . . . just a man pulling weeds—someone else's weeds—doing it voluntarily and obviously enjoying it. In short, a good citizen.

Jesus said something about "going the second mile." Jesus originated the saying; in fact, although He didn't use the word "mile," he used the Hebrew or Aramaic equivalent. Matthew 5:41 quotes Jesus as saying: *"If someone forces you to go one mile, go with him two miles."* That experience goes all the way back to Persian times, when the success of the mail service, established by that empire, depended upon forcing people to provide assistance in carrying the mail. The Romans continued the practice and sometimes also required assistance to soldiers as they traveled the roads with their heavy packs.

The Jewish nationalists fought such forced labor under the Romans, but Jesus urged His followers not only to cooperate with the Roman authorities, but also to do twice what was demanded, shocking the pagans by such an act of grace. Jesus encouraged His followers to be good citizens, in other words, but doubly good citizens as Christians.

Following Jesus causes a Christian to go the extra mile, even to digging up weeds for others voluntarily . . . Jesus' doctrine of the second mile.

River of Delights
December 02

The story is told of a little girl who, while standing in the bathroom, inquisitively asked her mother, "Where does water come from before it gets into the pipes?"

"From the rivers, dear," her mother replied. "We've got two rivers near here, and our water comes from both."

"I see," said the little girl. "And which of them is the hot river?"

This story brings to mind the importance of rivers from the dawn of history until this present day. The second chapter of Genesis describes a river that watered the Garden of Eden. As it flowed from that garden, it broke into four parts, becoming the headstream of four important rivers—one of which was the great River Euphrates, another the Tigris, these two being joined at one point today. Since early times, the Euphrates has been an important means of transportation and travel as it makes its way from Mesopotamia to the Persian Gulf.

Another well-known river, of course, is the Nile, which is a major feature of the northeastern part of Africa. Then, of course, we have the Amazon, the Congo, the Mississippi, the Ganges, the St. Lawrence and so on . . . all important, not only as a means of carrying people and goods, but also as the very lifeblood of many countries as they irrigate the nearby land.

David the Psalmist is exultant about rivers in Psalm 36:8b, where he says metaphorically, "*You* [God] *give them drink from your river of delights."*

Well, a river may not be the complete source of hot water, but God's "river of delights" offers a veritable cornucopia or horn of plenty of fine gifts, both physical and spiritual, to all who will simply take them. The secret? Jesus put it this way: *"Seek first his kingdom* [God's kingdom] *and his righteousness, and all these things will be given to you as well"* (Matthew 6:33).

Gold or God
December 03

Roger W. Babson, founder of the Babson Institute for the training of business executives, was talking one day to the president of one of the South American republics. Babson was wondering why South America, with all of its abundant supply of natural resources and other advantages, was so far behind North America, and he posed the question to the president: "Mr. president, what do you think is the reason?" The president became thoughtful and finally responded, "South America was settled by the Spanish, who came in search of gold, but North America was settled by the Pilgrim Fathers, who went there in search of God."[1]

Gold or God! In English, there is only a one letter difference. Take the "L" out of "gold," and you have "God." But the two are literally worlds apart. One is the symbol of a grasping, materialistic culture; the other is the Author of a totally new way of life. One is centered on this present world . . . the other on eternity.

The pursuit of gold is very prevalent in our modern Western world, and it is, ironically, particularly widespread during the Christmas Season. Amazing, isn't it, how the simple story of the Christ child, who made the day possible, has been literally swamped by the rush for gold? A foul-smelling stable has become a gilded replica, and jolly old St. Nick, as loveable as he is (and I hesitate to fault him), presides in place of the One who came to show us how to live, then died and rose again to make it all possible.

We don't normally picture God as a humorous God. Indeed, humor is of several types, one of them being bitter irony, which we find in Psalm 2, and is relevant to what we are talking about:

"*Why do the nations conspire and the peoples plot in vain? The kings of the earth take their stand and the rulers gather together against the LORD and against his Anointed One* [Jesus]. *'Let us break their chains,' they say, 'and throw off their fetters'*" (Psalm 2:1–3). But then this in verse 4: "*The One enthroned in heaven laughs; The Lord scoffs at them.*"

Has gold conquered God? Don't let it happen in your life.

Is That All There Is?
December 04

As the Christmas Season approaches with all its hustle and bustle, I am reminded of a song that I believe was high on the music charts at one time. The song expressed sentiments of a lonely girl, apparently at the end of her rope, and was called "Is That All There Is?"

Those words—Is that all there is?—seem to be a warning, a kind of danger signal as the Christmas season approaches. Most stores at this time of year are already decked out in their Yuletide finery and expecting the crowds to get larger. But we need to ask, "Is that all there is?"

Ralph Waldo Emerson, the American poet and philosopher, put it like this:

> Things are in the saddle
>
> And ride mankind.

It's always dangerous when the things of life, the things we covet, swallow us up.

Listen to these words of wisdom from the author of Ecclesiastes found in chapter two.

"I denied myself nothing my eyes desired; I refused my heart no pleasure. My heart took delight in all my work, and this was the reward for all my labor. Yet when I had surveyed all that my hands had done and what I had toiled to achieve, everything was meaningless, a chasing after the wind; nothing was gained under the sun" (Ecclesiastes 2:10–11).

It's as if the writer was asking, "Is that all there is?" Of course not. We simply need to heed the words of the Master: *"If anyone is thirsty, let him come to me and drink"* . . . that's the spiritual water of life of course.

Faith's Good News
December 05

I read somewhere about a little girl who pestered her father with endless questions about a rhinoceros. Finally, tiring of her too frequent questions, he presented her with a magnificent, detailed book on the rhinoceros that even included detailed photographs and drawings. When she finished the book, the girl thanked her father, then added, "But it told me more about the rhinoceros than I really wanted to know."[2]

That story strikes a sympathetic chord in our day. It seems that everything about us is open to question, so much so that we are absolutely surfeited with answers, most of them unsatisfactory . . . and most people are not interested in hearing.

How do you measure a sunrise or gauge the bubbling laughter of a two-year-old? If you could count the stars in space or indicate the number of shimmering droplets in a waterfall, how knowledgeable would you be?

Certainly, the most brilliant scholastically of the early followers of Jesus looked at the situation. His response? We can look to the words of the apostle Paul as found in

1 Corinthians chapter 13 verse 12: *"Now we see but a poor reflection as in a mirror; then we shall see face to face. Now I know in part; then I shall know fully, even as I am fully known"* The word then in this instance means in the eternal hereafter, with the God who created it all.

That we do not have the answers to all of life's perplexing questions is no cause for fear or despair. This is where our faith enters in—your faith and mine—a faith so vitally important that the apostles of Jesus asked of Him on one occasion: *"Lord, increase our faith."* Christ responded that faith no bigger than a tiny mustard seed could remove mountains—mountains of fear, mountains of doubt, and mountains of blighted dreams.

We already know more than we really want to know from this world's blackened historical pages, but there is yet simple "good news" from the God–revealed book of life.

Trust and Faith
December 06

Trust and faith are two of the most important qualities missing from our world, and they are the very qualities we need in our relationship with God.

The small child is very trusting. Those with young children or grandchildren are very much aware of that fact. The small child is not expecting to be lied to and generally accepts things as presented—at face value. Later on in life, growing children discover that you cannot trust everyone. They discover that some try to fool you . . . some take advantage of you. They conclude—at first reluctantly—that there are some things that are not what they seem to be. Putting it plainly, some people just cannot be trusted.

Sometimes we become a little bitter.

Then there's faith, which is really "trust plus." Faith is absolute trust, a willingness to put everything into a cause or a person. Someone has said that it is like betting your life on it. You may remember the incident when Jesus and a number of His disciples were traveling by boat on a lake in the evening. While the experienced fishermen manned the boat, Jesus was asleep in the stern. A furious squall came up, and the disciples were terrified. Waking Jesus, they asked Him, *"Don't you care if we drown?"* Jesus stilled the seas, then asked, *"Why are you so afraid. Do you still have no faith?"*

When Jesus is with you on the seas of life, there is no need to fear . . . you may have complete trust and full faith.

An Overgrown Path
December 07

A missionary working in a remote jungle area told a simple, but meaningful story. To meet the need for prayer and quiet time, the practice grew for the Christians there to make their way into the nearby jungle, walking through the long grass to find a suitable spot. Soon everyone recognized the hut of a Christian because of the well-worn path from the hut into the jungle. Of course, if the quiet time of the Christian fell by the wayside, the path was soon overgrown because of the rapid growth in the jungle.

We don't have to be natives in some small, remote village in the jungle to have an "overgrown" path. Even when we have a good deal of spare time, we sometimes allow the difficulties of life—the problems, the weariness, the fears, and the worries—to banish our own quiet time, the time so necessary for our spiritual well-being.

I'm sure you have realized that even our Master, Jesus, felt compelled from time to time to go off to some quiet place to meditate and to pray. Sometimes He went alone. Sometimes He went with a few of his disciples. When word reached Jesus that John the Baptist had been beheaded by the evil King Herod, we find the response of Jesus: *"When Jesus heard what had happened, he withdrew . . . to a solitary place"* (Matthew 14:13a). It was during such a prayer, with the apostles Peter, James, and John accompanying Him, that the Transfiguration occurred.

After the miracle of the feeding of the five thousand, Mark records: *"Immediately Jesus made His disciples get into the boat and go on ahead of him to Bethsaida, while he dismissed the crowd. After leaving them, he went up on a mountainside to pray"* (Mark 6:45–46). He also said to his disciples on another occasion: *"Come with me by yourselves to a quiet place and get some rest."* (Mark 6:31b).

That was His invitation then . . . and so it remains. We simply cannot afford to neglect our quiet time or let the pathway to it become overgrown.

At The Door
December 08

There's an old, old story of a German prince who longed to possess a Cremona violin, one of the world's very finest, and he offered a vast sum to anyone who would sell him one.

For a long time, he had no success. Then one day an old man appeared at the castle gate with a worn case under his arm. He wasn't very presentable, so the servants wouldn't agree to take him before the prince as he requested. He persisted, and they finally and grudgingly agreed to take the old man's message to the prince. It was the simple message, "Heaven's music is waiting at your door."

Intrigued, the prince had the old man admitted to his presence. The stranger drew from its shabby case a perfect violin. He created such marvelous music with it that the enthralled prince offered the old man any price he would name for the instrument, but the man just shook his head. "The violin may only be yours," he said, "on condition that I pass my life within your house and use the instrument every day." The prince accepted the princely gift on those terms.

There is a parable here . . . particularly apropos at this season of the year. "Heaven's music" is truly "waiting at our door," but all too few recognize that the Giver is the major part of the Gift. As poet James Russell Lowell puts it, "The gift without the giver is bare."

That night in Bethlehem, everyone shut Him out . . . multitudes still do . . . wanting the joy of the season without the Savior. Yet He still stands knocking.

In Revelation 3:20 John quotes Him, *"Here I am! I stand at the door and knock. If anyone hears my voice and opens the door, I will come in and eat with him, and he with me."*

Flower of Holy Night
December 09

In Mexico, it is the Christmas custom for worshippers to gather at the church on Christmas Eve, each bringing a gift to be laid upon the altar for the Christ child.

Legend has it that many years ago in one Mexican village, a young boy too poor to bring a gift nevertheless wished to hear the beautiful Christmas music and catch something of the essence of the season. After the doors of the church had been shut and the service had begun, the boy remained outside but found a window to peer in. Looking in, he knelt in the soft earth, and as the congregation prayed, he prayed too. After the boy got up from his knees, he looked down, and there in the spot where he had been praying was a beautiful flowering red plant. He stooped down and picked up one of the red flowers, reverently went into the church, and placed the flower on the altar—his gift for the Christ child.

Years later, the first American ambassador to Mexico, Joel Roberts Poinsett, saw the flowering red plant. Recognizing its rarity and beauty, he took one of the plants back to the United States. The plant he introduced to the rest of the world was the poinsettia, "The Flower of the Holy Night."

These many years later, "The Flower of the Holy Night" graces many Western homes at Christmas. May its message grace our hearts.

Taking Notice
December 10

Are you familiar with the story of a certain famous president's humble birth? He was born in a log cabin near Hodgenville, Kentucky, in February of 1809. About the date of February 12, 1809, a neighbor hailed a man from town:

"Any news down't the village, Ezry?"

"Well, Squire McLain's gone t' Washington t' see Madison swore in, and ol' Spellman tells me this Bonaparte fella has captured most o' Spain. What's near out here neighbor?"

"Nuthin," was the response, "nuthin' a'tall, 'cept fer a new baby born t' Tom Lincoln's. Nuthin' ever happens out here."[3]

Nothing . . . except that on that day and at that place, Abraham Lincoln was the baby in Tom Lincoln's log cabin. And not many people were taking notice.

Not many people were paying attention over 2000 years ago when a baby was born in a stable's manger in a little town called Bethlehem. The event was not very important to most of the passers-by, but the Son of God was born that day into the human race. Only a few noticed . . . a few shepherds on a hillside . . . two or three, perhaps four, magi from a distant land . . . a wicked King who sought to destroy Him. That is all.

No wonder that later, the beloved apostle, John, was constrained to write in his Gospel: "*He came to His own, but His own did not receive Him.*" Thankfully, John was able to add the following words: "*Yet to all who received Him, to those who believed in His name, He gave the right to become children of God.*"

Abraham Lincoln brought freedom of body to a multitude of enslaved people. Jesus Christ opened the way for all mankind—men, women and children—to have freedom of soul and conscience for all eternity. He offers it to you and to me this Christmas, which marks His human birth. Are we taking notice?

Comfort Ye
December 11

In one of Shakespeare's plays, "Love's Labour Lost," one of his characters, musing about this time of the year, says: "At Christmas I no more desire a rose than wish a snow in May's new-fangled mirth."

Those of us who have lived all or most of our lives in the Northern Hemisphere—particularly in the northern part of the Northern Hemisphere—can readily appreciate those sentiments.

There is something almost indefinable about this time of year . . . the glowing fire . . . the decked-out evergreens . . . the twinkling lights. Above all, Christmas spells comfort—not only the comfort of putting up your feet in your easy chair, but also the mental and spiritual comfort of knowing all is well. "It is well with my soul," the hymn writer puts it.

The prophet Isaiah forecast Christmas many centuries before it happened, as is written here from the King James Version. This familiar passage was also used by Handel in Messiah.

> *Comfort ye, comfort ye my people, saith your God. Speak ye comfortably to Jerusalem, and cry unto her, that her warfare is accomplished, that her iniquity is pardoned: for she hath received of the LORD's hand double for all her sins. The voice of him that crieth in the wilderness, Prepare ye the way of the LORD, make straight in the desert a highway for our God. Every valley shall be exalted, and every mountain and hill shall be made low: and the crooked shall be made straight, and the rough places plain: And the glory of the LORD shall be revealed, and all flesh shall see together: for the mouth of the LORD hath spoken it* (Isaiah 40:1–5).

May our Lord and Savior be a comfort to you today.

Have We Forgotten?
December 12

Apparently, newspaper publisher William Randolph Hearst had an insatiable desire for the world's best artwork. The story has it that a beautiful, expensive work of art captured his interest on one occasion. Hearst decided he must have it, no matter what the cost. He didn't know where the piece was, so he sent his agents to look for it. After months of searching, they finally found the original painting in one of Hearst's own warehouses. Most likely Hearst, or his agents, had not thought to check the catalogue of his possessions.

This story reminds me that although Christians are rich spiritually, we have sometimes forgotten the vast extent of those riches that have slipped back into the storehouse of our minds. One of those blessings is the joy of our salvation.

Peter in his first epistle, right at the beginning, refers to some of those sometimes forgotten blessings found in following Jesus Christ: "*Though you have not seen him,*" Peter writes, "*you love him; and even though you do not see him now, you believe in him and are filled with an inexpressible and glorious joy, for you are receiving the goal of your faith, the salvation of your souls*" (1 Peter 1:8–9).

Have we forgotten the salvation of our souls . . . our adoption into the family of God?

If we are inclined sometimes to forget the multitude of blessings God has promised, may I suggest we do as William Randolph Hearst should have done—look them up in the catalogue. The catalogue of God's blessings, of course, is God's Word, the Bible. There we shall find not only what we know we have, but also many other blessings hidden from us. Beyond these, as Peter has noted, we have "an inheritance that can never perish."

Because He Lives
December 13

One of the best of the hymns of our times is entitled "Because He Lives," written by the song-writing American husband and wife team of Bill and Gloria Gaither. It was written when the songwriters were going through a "kind of dry spell." The United States was going through a rough period because of the Vietnam War, racial tension, etc., and Gloria was expecting their child. Bill remembers that they thought, "Brother, this is really a poor time to bring a child into the world."[4] But their son came, and the lyrics followed, part of which include:

> How sweet to hold a new born baby,
> And feel the pride and joy he gives.
> But greater still the calm assurance:
> This child can face uncertain days because He [Christ] lives.[5]

A verse from God's Word that is sometimes associated with the hymn is John 14:19. Jesus is quoted by the Gospel writer as saying, *"Before long, the world will not see me anymore, but you will see me. Because I live, you also will live."*

These words of the Savior were spoken in either the upper room in Jerusalem, where Jesus was holding the Last Supper prior to His crucifixion, or just following this event as they were on their way to the Garden of Gethsemane. Jesus, knowing that the cross was just ahead, was far more concerned about His apostles than Himself. They just could not seem to absorb the fact that He was soon to leave them. They had been with Him now for three years. Jesus had taught them; He had endeavored to prepare them for His departure for He knew that on them depended the future of His mission and the leadership of His Church.

So He said, *"You will not see me anymore,"* but He gave this tremendous promise, *"Because I live, you also will live."* He did live again on the resurrection morn. In the strength of that resurrection, a weak, defeated, apostolic band proceeded to set their world on fire.

And for us, as the Gaithers say in the chorus of their great hymn...

> Because He lives, I can face tomorrow.
> Because He lives, All fear is gone.
> Because I know He holds the future,
> And life is worth the living just because He lives.

Doing Christmas Right
December 14

Like Scrooge and Marley, most of us have been involved in many Christmases past. We don't really know how many in the future are to be ours. We do have this one, and we need to make sure that we manage it properly.

There are many ways of doing Christmas "wrong." We just need to look around us. When one watches the frantic buying and selling, the spending of lots of money on gifts, one is reminded of the words from the Epistle of James, the 4th chapter, verses 13–15.

> "Now listen, you who say, 'Today or tomorrow we will go to this or that city, spend a year there, carry on business and make money.' Why, you do not even know what will happen tomorrow. What is your life? You are a mist that appears for a little while and then vanishes. Instead, you ought to say, 'If it is the Lord's will, we will live and do this or that.'"

Actually, the only excuse for all the merchandising that goes on is to provide the means of securing gifts for those we love. Love neither requires nor requests the multitude upon multitude of gifts that pour over the shelves and display cases of our emporiums at the season to mark His birth.

Might it just be that we have our priorities wrong. The emphasis should be on the One whose birthday we celebrate and on the gifts given to Him or in His name. The angels sang of those gifts so long ago—"Peace on earth, good will to men."

Kneeling in Prayer
December 15

Some representations of the nativity show an ox and other animals kneeling. Indeed, Thomas Hardy, one of England's literary masters and author of many novels, short stories, and poems, wrote a well-known poem, called "The Oxen," that refers to the oxen kneeling in the presence of our Lord.

Around the centerpiece of history, the human birth of the Son of God in a crude Bethlehem stable, many legends have grown—including this one that oxen knelt in His presence. Perhaps they did; the idea is intriguing.

Far more important, however, is that we should kneel. The Psalmist writes: "*All the ends of the earth will remember and turn to the LORD, and all the families of the nations will bow down before him, for dominion belongs to the LORD and he rules over the nations*" (Psalm 22:27–28).

May that be our prayer as Christmas approaches. Rather than bowing, many of the nations are at war, either without or within. Others are involved in the mad race for the almighty dollar, pound, ruble, or yen. Peace will come in your heart and mind, and in the hearts and minds of all, when they and we bow before the One who came as a baby in Bethlehem and when we all acknowledge Him as Savior and Lord.

Expectations
December 16

William Carey was the forerunner of the modern missionary movement that began at the start of the nineteenth century. William Carey was raised in a rural village and began his working life as a cobbler, a shoemaker. He also did some church work on the side as a lay preacher. The walls of Carey's cobbler shop were covered with various maps of the world because William Carey had a dream—the sharing of the gospel with the far corners of the world.

William Carey preached a poignant sermon, which was to become his motto: "Expect great things from God. Attempt great things for God." As a result of Carey's dream, the first overseas missionary society was formed in England. William Carey himself became the first missionary to India, serving there with distinction for the rest of his life.

I don't suppose that William Carey ever had any money or very many possessions to call his own, but he did have the very great satisfaction of seeing his expectations realized in great measure as God rewarded his diligence and his optimism. He had attempted great things for God, and His God rewarded his greatest expectations.

Trees
December 17

Many legends exist about the origin of the Christmas tree. However, it is generally believed that the Christmas tree is of German origin and dates back to the sixteenth century. Later on, the custom of putting up a decorated evergreen tree spread to Europe and North America. It has become one of the symbols of Christmas—for Christians and non-Christians alike.

Be that as it may, trees do play a prominent part in the economy of God—all the way from the tree of life and the tree of the knowledge of good and evil in the second chapter of Genesis to the tree of life again near the end of the book of Revelation. Eating fruit from the tree of the knowledge of good and evil brought about humankind's downfall. In Revelation, those who overcome evil are promised the right to eat from the tree of life. Trees, almost without number, are mentioned in God's Word.

The balsam fir is a variety of the fir, which is common among our basic Christmas trees. Balsam is also the source of the balm of Gilead, a resinous gum ointment used in healing. Thus, a variety of balsam is used for healing, and a variety of balsam is used for our Christmas trees. Healing as used in God's word may mean spiritual healing as well as physical.

May we thus see beyond the tinsel, the colored lights, and the baubles on our tree to the tree of God's word, the symbol of healing for the nations and for each one of us individually—healing of soul as well as the mind and body. May this Christmas mean God's gift of healing to our stricken world.

Willing to Share
December 18

Christmas is a time of giving and sharing and hopefully generous giving to those who are less fortunate. We live in a needy world, and there are many, both at home and abroad, who could use our help. We need to be willing to share what we have.

In the sixth chapter of First Timothy, Paul talks plainly about a subject we sometimes like to avoid—money. Money itself is not harmful; it's neutral of course. The use or misuse of money is what causes problems. It can be used for good purposes, or it can be used for bad ones. Wealth is not necessarily a bad thing. Some wealthy people in this world do much good with their wealth.

There were some wealthy people in the congregation at Ephesus, where Timothy was serving. "*Command them,*" Paul writes, "*to do good, to be rich in good deeds, and to be generous and willing to share. In this way they will lay up treasure for themselves as a firm foundation for the coming age, so that they may take hold of the life that is truly life*" (1 Timothy 6:18–19).

God, of course, has promised life that is "truly life," to each one of us who expresses his or her love for God in being generous to those in need, both here at home and in the many needy areas of the world.

The Greatest Golden Text
December 19

Many Sunday schools of yesteryear had a special verse with each lesson called the "golden text." Students were often encouraged to learn it during the week, to be repeated in class the next Sunday.

I think that most will agree that the greatest of them all, the "golden text of the golden texts," would be John 3:16, which in the King James Version reads: *"For God so loved the world, that he gave his only begotten Son, that whosoever believeth in him should not perish, but have everlasting life."*

The background for this "golden text" is an incident in the life of Jesus Himself, an occasion when a member of the Jewish nation's supreme council, the Sanhedrin, was sufficiently impressed by what he had heard about Jesus that he wanted to find out more. Not wanting to be seen by his influential friends in the act of calling upon Jesus, he went at night to where the Master was living.

Received graciously by Jesus, the Pharisee indicated that he believed that Jesus was a teacher sent from God, for no man, he said, could do the miracles Jesus did unless God was with him.

With this opening, Jesus told the man the way to salvation—the way to reconciliation with God, indicating that God had shown His love to the world by the gift of His Son and that whoever believed in Him would have eternal life.

The writer, John, in this third chapter of his Gospel, makes no mention of the conclusion of that night's interview or what sort of impact it had on Nicodemus . . . for Nicodemus it was. Later in John's gospel in chapter 19, in the story of the crucifixion and burial, Joseph of Arimathea, who asked Pilate if he might bury the body of Jesus in his own private garden tomb, was accompanied by the same Nicodemus. It took the cross to bring Nicodemus out to confess Jesus as his Lord and Savior.

Christmas, the birth of Jesus, was God's way of giving to the world, but it took the cross and the empty tomb to convince many to accept God's Son.

As we come closer to the great day of His birth, may we see Christmas in the context of Jesus' whole life, culminating in His death and resurrection—all a gift from God.

A Wheelbarrow for Christmas
December 20

Many years ago, so the story goes, an English dean in his cathedral one morning overheard a small boy who was kneeling in front of the nativity scene, praying, "Please, can I have a wheelbarrow for Christmas?"

The dean made inquiries and found out the lad was from a poor family. He needed the wheelbarrow to collect wood to keep the fire going for his mother in their home. With some help, the dean produced a wheelbarrow, filled it with clothing and other Christmas fare, and left it outside the boy's door on Christmas Eve.

Early the next morning, the dean saw a curious sight. The boy pushed his new empty wheelbarrow up to the manger scene. Then he gently picked up the doll representing the baby Jesus and wheeled it around the room. The puzzled dean asked the youngster what he was doing.

"Well, sir," responded the boy, "I asked Him for it. It's only right that He should have the first ride."

David the Psalmist once observed in Psalm 8:2, "*From the lips of children and infants you have ordained praise.*"

The disciples were arguing on their way to Capernaum, and Jesus asked them what they were arguing about. No one said a word. They were ashamed to admit they had been arguing as to which one of them was the greatest—the most important. Jesus sat down, called them all around him, and said, "*If anyone wants to be first, he must be the very last, and the servant of all*" (Mark 9:35). Then He took one of the children of the house in His arms and said to His followers, "*I tell you the truth, unless you change and become like little children, you will never enter the kingdom of heaven*" (Matthew 18:3). So much for their pride.

The boy with the new wheelbarrow wasn't much of a theologian, of course, but he did the only thing he knew. He made a true response to the gift he was given, which he fully believed had come from God. It had come from God, of course, because God often uses others in giving answers to prayer.

We can match the boys' enthusiastic gratitude by carrying His Son in our hearts. That's the greatest response we can make to the God who gave and still gives.

Through the Furnace
December 21

I read an interesting article one time of someone who had visited a china factory. He saw some of the china before the final touches had been applied. A drab looking blue had been applied, as well as some touches of a dirty red paint—even a little black. The design was smudged in spots. In short, it looked a mess. Then the china was put in the furnace for the colors to be burned in.

When the china was removed from the furnace, the design was clear, and a bright gold color shone against the black, the blue, and the marvelous red of the china.

China can be expensive, but it is hardly worth the price until it's been put through the furnace.

As Christmas approaches, I'm sure some of you feel that you continue in a furnace of difficulty despite the music, the decorations, and all the seeming joyousness all around. Continual disability is a trial, and so are the pangs of sorrow and disappointment.

Isaiah, the Old Testament prophet who looked forward on a number of occasions to the coming of Christ that first Christmas, has something powerful to say about what he calls the "furnace of affliction." He writes, quoting the Heavenly Father, *"See, I have refined you, though not as silver* [or fine china, he might have said]*; I have tested you in the furnace of affliction."*

Isaiah was writing to his own people initially, but his word has a much wider implication and touches even us. He means, I believe, that although the "furnace of affliction" is difficult and sometimes hard to bear, God will bring out of it a character, a person of beauty, glory, and serenity, who will be truly blessed himself and be a blessing to all who are around.

Caring for Each Other
December 22

This season reminds us of our responsibility and privilege in caring for each other. At Christmas, even our own secular world demonstrates some of that virtue of caring.

There is an old fable by Aesop that tells of a woodsman who went into the forest to find suitable wood to make a handle for his axe. He consulted with the trees, asking them which tree could be used to make his handle. The larger, stronger trees conferred together and decided the woodsman could use the younger, smaller Ash. The woodsman felled the Ash and fashioned an axe handle that he attached to his blade. Then he began to cut down the grandest and noblest trees of the forest. Aghast at what he saw, the old Oak complained to a neighboring Cedar that having surrendered the rights of the weak to the destroyer, they themselves would suffer the same evil.

We are called to reach out to those in need. We are called to care for our neighbor. As God showed His caring love for us in sending Jesus, we are called to care for one another. Our expression of caring love for our neighbor reflects our relationship with Him who promises our standing for the eternal ages.

The Gospel of John in chapter 13, verses 34 and 35, quotes Jesus as putting it like this:

> "A new command I give you: Love one another. As I have loved you, so also you must love one another. By this all men will know that you are my disciples, if you love one another."

May we show this very day His love and care for us by showing our love and care for others.

Let Your Light Shine
December 23

One of the legends surrounding Christmas has it that a shepherd boy, transfixed in wonder at the nativity, stayed all night, assisting in providing warmth for the newborn Christ child by holding his lamp above the crib. When dawn broke, he left the stable. Then, according to legend, he tried to blow out his lamp but couldn't. It is said that the lamp continued to burn until the very end of his life as a token of his loving act that first Christmas night.

Only a legend . . . not factual . . . and yet it bears a truth that is very important. Lights are of vital significance as we travel the Christian way. Lights, indeed, are very much a part of the true Christmas celebration, and so they should be. As the prophet Isaiah said of the coming of the Messiah: *"The people walking in darkness have seen a great light; on those living in the land of the shadow of death a light has dawned"* (Isaiah 9:2). Picking up the theme, the writer of John's Gospel said of the coming of Jesus: *"In him was life, and that life was the light of men. The light shines in the darkness, but the darkness has not understood it"* (John 1:4–5).

Jesus is the "light of the world." So are you and so am I if we are His followers. Jesus Himself said so. This is how he put it in the Sermon on the Mount. *"You are the light of the world,"* Jesus said. *"A city on a hill cannot be hidden. Neither do people light a lamp and put it under a bowl. Instead they put it on its stand, and it gives light to everyone in the house."* He added, *"In the same way, let your light shine before men, that they may see your good deeds and praise your Father in heaven"* (Matthew 5:14–16).

The light that the Lord has given us is to be held high this Christmas, to bring glory and honor to the One whose birth we celebrate.

That light should never go out until our journey is over, our work done.

Doing Without the Baby
December 24

There is a story told about a man and his son who went to purchase a baby Jesus for their nativity scene. Somehow, the piece had got broken or lost, so they went looking for a replacement. They were unsuccessful in their search again, as they had been looking for this particular replacement piece for a number of years. The man turned to the boy and said, "I guess we'll just have to do without the baby Jesus for another year."[6]

Unfortunately, that's the way the world is going in our day and age: "We'll have to do without Jesus for another year." The years come and the years go, and Jesus is pushed far into the background, soon to be forgotten, soon to be, as Shakespeare described one situation, "a tale told by an idiot . . . signifying nothing."

It won't really happen quite that way. God will not be banished from His world. You can easily forget or neglect to replace a baby Jesus in a manger scene, or you can do as most Western governments are doing—refuse to allow a manger scene in a public place at all. You can put all the focus of Christmas on the trappings, the tinsel, the bright lights, and all the rest. But Christ will always remain in Christmas, especially if you and I and the millions of others who follow Him keep our perspective clear—that if Jesus had not come, there would be no Christmas.

He was born in a manger, as there was "no room for them in the inn." The family had to escape to Egypt to escape the sword of Herod. The Scriptures say that He came to his own, but his own did not receive Him. The high priest and the other religious leaders brought monstrous pressure on the Romans, and the Romans put Him on a cross . . . to die. Die He did, only to break the bonds of death and rise victoriously the third day. With most of the then–known world against Him, He lived, and He lives and says to us as He said to His disciples then, "Because I live, you too shall live."

That's the wondrous gift of Christmas: new life. You don't have to do without Jesus—now or ever.

No Vacancy

December 25

> *"And she gave birth to her firstborn, a son. She wrapped him in cloths and placed him in a manger, because there was no room for them in the inn"* (Luke 2:7).

No room in the inn. Have you ever felt just a hint of empathy for the innkeeper? After all, the city was crowded and accommodation hard to come by, but he did find a spot for the couple in his stable. He didn't know that the Son of God was about to be born.

Things are different today of course. But are they? Not long ago, a cabinet minister in a provincial government gave directions to a choir—not a church choir—that was to sing at a tree-lighting ceremony outside the legislative buildings. They were not to include the name Jesus or Christ in any of their carols. The minister had to back down when some of his fellow cabinet members were critical, but his attitude is not so very different from many who would take Christ out of Christmas. There are governments of local communities that are banning nativity scenes from public property. There is simply no room . . . no room in the inn.

How do you take Christ out of Christmas? You would have to change the very name of the day.

The name Jesus is the Greek equivalent of the Old Testament Hebrew name Joshua, and means "Jehovah is salvation." The name Christ is the Greek equivalent of the Hebrew Messiah, meaning "anointed." Thus, Jesus Christ is the One anointed to bring salvation. That's exactly what the angel said to Joseph concerning Mary: *"She will give birth to a son, and you are to give him the name Jesus, because he will save his people from their sins"* (Matthew 1:21).

Despite the "no vacancy" sign at the inn those two millennia ago and the many similar "no room" signs around us this Christmas, salvation through Jesus is the true message that goes out to the world.

I wonder if the world is listening.

The Key
December 26

We have always heard that Christmas is a time of giving, but we have to admit that getting is part of the process. Undoubtedly, the following well-known words are true: "It is more blessed to give than receive." Yet there are some things that we may receive at this season of the year that really make life shine. For example, there was a young woman who had a very generous aunt who gave her niece all sorts of wonderful things every Christmas. One year, the aunt gave her a key . . . a plain, ordinary key. The key was to the aunt's house and came with the instructions for the niece to use the house as though it were her own.

You will have seen the parallel already, I'm sure. God's gift to the world that first Christmas was and is a key, the key to the Father's House. The baby in that crude bed of straw, surrounded by wondering shepherds and later by adoring Wise Men, is the Key, the Way. Jesus was later to say, *"I am the way and the truth and the life. No one comes to the Father except through me"* (John 14:6). When in victory He cried on His cross, *"It is finished,"* the door was opened, the way to the Father's house . . . through Him.

Entrance to the Father's house is just the beginning, the first of a veritable treasury of good things. Paul wrote, *"The gift of God is eternal life in Christ Jesus our Lord"* (Romans 6:23b). In addition, he wrote, *"For it is by grace you have been saved, through faith—and this not from yourselves, it is the gift of God—not by works, so that no one can boast"* (Ephesians 2:8–9).

Salvation . . . eternal life . . . yes, life itself—these are the gifts of God to you and to me. However, we must receive them. And there are more—many, many, more—gifts from God.

You may offer one gift in return. It too is a key . . . the key to your heart.

These keys, yours and God's, are the greatest gifts of Christmas.

Hopelessness
December 27

Hopelessness, unfortunately, is all too prevalent in our land. It can be found in the young, the middle-aged, and the old. It is even found in people who, by the world's standards, are very successful. Why is there such a pervasive mood of hopelessness in our land? We have the highest standard of living in our history. We have many conveniences and have made great advances in the medical, technological, and other fields. We have entertainment at our fingertips. Why this feeling of hopelessness?

Do you know that the King James Version of our English Bible has some eight hundred thousand words? Not once does the word hopeless appear. It does show up once in the New International Version in the book of Isaiah, where God has been chiding his people through the prophet for their wicked ways. *"You were wearied by all your ways,"* he writes, *"but you would not say 'It is hopeless.'"*

Nothing is hopeless with God and—what is more important—no one is hopeless with God.

Hope, in fact, is one of the great themes of the New Testament. To a persecuted band of Christians in Rome, Paul wrote, *"We also rejoice in our sufferings, because we know that suffering produces perseverance; perseverance character; and character, hope. And hope does not disappoint us, because God has poured out his love into our hearts"* (Romans 5:3–5). *"And we rejoice,"* Paul writes earlier in the same chapter, *"in the hope of the glory of God."*

Humility
December 28

In a *Peanuts* comic strip, written some years ago, the little character Linus is musing. "When I get big," he says, "I'm going to be a humble little country doctor. And every morning I'll get up, climb into my sports car and zoom into the country! Then I'll start healing people . . . I'll heal everybody for miles around! I'll be a world famous, humble little country doctor!"[7]

Perhaps most of us, as we get a little older, don't have too much trouble with pride. Humility, perhaps, comes a little more naturally, but there are moments, I'm sure, when it wouldn't be too hard to emulate Linus, wishing somehow that we might be able to claim some of the world's fame. But as the old aphorism states it, "If wishes were horses, beggars would ride"—or zoom along country roads in a brand new sports car.

In that marvelous and very personal invitation of Jesus at the end of the eleventh chapter of Matthew, the Lord of life says, *"Come to me, all you who are weary and burdened, and I will give you rest. Take my yoke upon you and learn from me, for I am gentle and humble in heart, and you will find rest for your souls."*

Not many could say with a completely clear conscience, "I am gentle and humble in heart," and prove it from their way of life. I have known and you have known people who feel and say that they are most humble. They take pride in their humility, and pride cancels humility.

Jesus taught, *"If someone strikes you on the right cheek, turn to him the other also. And if someone wants to sue you and take your tunic, let him have your cloak as well. If someone forces you to go one mile, go with him two miles"* (Matthew 5:39b–41). That's humility.

Our Need: a Savior

December 29

Roy Lessin, a Christian writer, wrote this gem.

> If our greatest need had been information,
> God would have sent us an educator,
> If our greatest need had been technology,
> God would have sent us a scientist.
> If our greatest need had been money,
> God would have sent us an economist.
> If our greatest need had been pleasure,
> God would have sent us an entertainer.
> But our greatest need was forgiveness,
> So God sent us a Savior.[8]

In that simple masterpiece that we call the Lord's Prayer, given in response to Jesus' Apostles' plea, "Lord, teach us to pray," the Master first directs our thoughts to our Heavenly Father: "Our Father, who art in heaven, hallowed be thy name, thy kingdom come, thy will be done on earth as it is in heaven." Then he directs our thoughts to our survival needs: "Give us this day our daily bread." Then the next clause has to do with forgiveness: "Forgive us our trespasses." We need forgiveness for spiritual survival . . . and ultimately for physical survival too.

In 1 John 1, verse 9, the apostle writes, *"If we confess our sins* [to Him]*, he is faithful and just and will forgive us our sins and purify us* [or cleanse us] *from all unrighteousness."*

That is the real meaning of Jesus' coming that first Christmas and of His death on the cross and the empty tomb, the first Good Friday and Easter—the gift of a Savior who forgives and gives a great start for the New Year.

Missed

December 30

Some of us may be disappointed if we missed the real opportunities put before us in the Yuletide season now passing. The real meaning of the season is not the bright lights, the shimmering tinsel, nor the sound of the cash register, but the story of a loving God breaking in on the human scene. There is much more to the season than the well-depicted manger scene in ancient Bethlehem. The manger birth is the beginning of an extraordinary life, that of the Son of God, who emptied Himself of His godly qualities to become human—like you or me. It was just a beginning because, after living an exemplary life of caring, He gave up his life. He sacrificed that life so that you and I might find forgiveness and have new life. Then He rose again to defeat the death we all must face.

Christmas, Good Friday, and Easter—all are joined in the greatest story ever told.

We don't have to face eternal disappointment when we have the Babe of Bethlehem in our hearts. His salvation is open to all who call on Him. Wise Men of every age invite us to come with them and worship. May this be our resolution as we approach the beginning of another year.

Why Don't You Lay Down Your Load?
December 31

At times in life, we seem to give God only half of a burden instead of the whole or some of our burdens instead of all of them.

One of the most familiar and often-quoted verses in the Psalms is David's advice in Psalm 55: "*Cast thy burden upon the LORD, and he shall sustain thee: he shall never suffer the righteous to be moved*" (Psalm 55:22, King James Version). "Cast thy burden upon the Lord" means throwing your burden down, whether it's a burden of guilt or a burden of worry, and trusting God with it.

In the well-known parable of the sower, Jesus pictures a farmer sowing his seed by hand, as they did in those days. Some of the seed fell on the path, and it was trampled on. Some fell on rock, and when the plants came up, they withered. Some fell among thorns, which choked the plants, and some fell on good, fertile ground.

Jesus' disciples asked Him what the parable meant. He explained that the seed was the Word of God, and it fell among different types of people who gave different responses. The seed that fell among thorns or other plants and was therefore choked stands for those who hear what He says but allow their life to be choked by worries, riches, and pleasures—by the "baggage" of life, if you like.

Why don't you just lay down your load—all of it.

Notes

January

1. Whittier, John Greenleaf (1807–1892), *Child-Songs*.
2. Oxenham, John, *The Day—The Way*. Accessed May 08, 2015. http://–domain-poetry.com.
3. Schuller, Robert, *Tough Times Never Last, But Tough People Do*. New York: Bantam Books, 1984.
4. Arvine, Kazlitt, *Cyclopaedia of Anecdotes of Literature and the Fine Arts*. Boston: Gould and Lincoln, 1852. 532.
5. Used with permission from Charles Harvey.
6. Colson, Charles, *Loving God*. Grand Rapids: Zondervan, 1997. Kobo edition.
7. Source Unkown.
8. Graham, Billy, *Storm Warning*. ©2010 Billy Graham. Used by permission. All rights reserved.

February

1. Margaret Bottome, quoted by Gypsy Smith, *Gypsy Smith His Life and Works*. New York: Fleming Revell, 1902. Chapter 27.
2. Woodrow Wilson, accessed February 17, 2011. http://drpipim.org/bible-Contemporaryissues-54/92-the-bible-a-book-like-no-other.
3. Henry Ward Beecher, accessed February 17, 2011. https://en.wikiquote.org/wiki/Henry_Ward_Beecher.
4. Abraham Lincoln, accessed January 31, 2011. http://quotedb.com/quotes/3681.

March

1. Carroll, Lewis, *Alice in Wonderland* and *Through the Looking Glass*, illustrated by John Tenniel. New York: Grosset & Dunlap Inc., 1996. 221–222.
2. Flint, Annie Johnson, (1866–1932), *What God Hath Promised*.
3. St. Cyprian, Bishop of Carthage, c.258.
4. Used by permission of Dr. Sheila Cassidy.
5. Hadyn, Franz Joseph, *The Family Minstrel*, Vol. 1. New York: James DeVoe, 1836. p56.
6. Christian Biography Resources, *Frances Ridley Havergal*, by J. Gilchrist Lawson, accessed February 11, 2011. http://wholesomewords.org/biography/bhavergal10.html.

NOTES

7. Frances Havergal, (1836–1879), *I am Trusting Thee, Lord Jesus.*

April

1. Smith, Gypsy, *Gypsy Smith, His Life & Work.* Accessed February 19, 2011. http://biblebelievers.com/gypsysmith. Chapter 24.
2. George Savile, Marquess of Halifax, accessed September 26, 2015. http://yquotes.com/quotes/George-savile/.
3. Cheney, Ednah, *Louisa May Alcott: Her Life, Letters and Journals.* 1889. Reprint, Carlisle, Massachusetts: Applewood Books, n.d. 329.
4. McDonell, Chris, compiler, *Shooting From The Lip, Hockey's Best Quotes And Quips.* Richmond Hill, Ontario: Firefly Books, 2008. 76.
5. Gibbon, Edward, *The Decline and Fall of the Roman Empire.* Accessed February 04, 2011. https://bible.org/illustration/fall-roman-empire.

May

1. Linton, William, *Patience.* Accessed February 15, 2011. http://bartleby.com/246/280.html.
2. Source Unknown.
3. Cartoon reference used with permission of cartoonist Brian Gable and the Regina Leader Post.
4. Graham, Billy, *Unto the Hills.* ©1996 Billy Graham. Used by permission. All rights reserved. Used by permission. Copyright. All rights reserved. 255.
5. Dennis DeHaan, *Our Daily Bread.* Copyright 1993 by RBC Ministries, Grand Rapids, Mich. Used by permission. All rights reserved.
6. Vesilind, Pritt "Berlin's Ode to Joy," *National Geographic Magazine.* Washington, DC: National Geographic Society, April 1990. 132.
7. Carmen, Bliss, *Vestigia*, accessed September 19, 2015. http://www.unz.org/Pub/Harpers-1921sep-00428.
8. Goldsmith, Oliver, accessed September, 19, 2015. http://quotationspage.com/quote/30539.html.
9. Paraphrase of *The Little Red Engine,* used by permission of Carlton Books.

June

1. Satchel Page, accessed February 21, 2011. http://great-quotes.com/quote/155883.
2. Hellen Keller accessed September 22, 2015. http://afb.org/info/about-us/helen-keller/quotes/125.
3. John Greenleaf Whittier (1807–1892), *"Dear Lord and Father of Mankind."*

4. Source Unknown.

July

1. Abraham Lincoln, accessed September18, 2015. http://presidentprofiles.com.
2. William Ellery Channing, accessed September 18, 2015. https://books.google.ca/books?id=A-Yd-ICRNXUC.
3. PEANUTS © Peanuts Worldwide LLC.
4. Dorchester, Daniel. *Christianity Vindicated By Its Enemies.* 1896. Reprint, London: Forgotten Books, 2013. 150–151.
5. William Whiting, (1825–1878), *"Eternal Father, Strong to Save."*
6. Courtesy of the Vancouver Sun.
7. John Randolph, accessed September 18, 2015. http://thinkexist.com/quotes/john_randolph/.
8. John Oxenham, *Credo,* accessed February 10, 2011. http://readbookonline.net/readOnLine/48025.

August

1. Used by permission of Ron Evans.
2. Used by permission of Charles Harvey.
3. Muggeridge, Malcolm, *Jesus: The Man Who Lives.* Glasgow: William Collins, 1975. 13.
4. Walter de la Mare, "Poor Jim Jay." Accessed May 21, 2015. http://readbookonline.net/readOnline/33494/.
5. Elizabeth Celphane (1830–1869), *"Beneath the Cross of Jesus."*
6. Source Unknown.
7. Shakespeare, William, The Merchant of Venice. *The quality of mercy is not strained.* Accessed February 10, 2011. http://phrases.org.uk/meanings/297200.html.
8. Van Beethoven, Ludwig, *Heiligenstadt Testament.* Accessed February 10, 2011. http://lvbeethoven.com/Bio?BiographyHeiligenstadtTestament.html.

September

1. Charles Kingsley. Accessed February 11, 2011. http://goodreads.com/quotes/show/92217.
2. Edward Guest. Accessed September 18, 2015. http://yourdailypoem.com/listpoem.jsp?poem_id=660.
3. Plaque information accessed February 11, 2011. http://edinburghmuseums.org.uk/Venues/Monuments/Greyfriars-Bobby.aspx.

NOTES

4. Joseph M. Scriven (1819–1886), *"What a Friend We Have in Jesus."*
5. Source Unknown.
6. Source Unknown.
7. Carroll, Lewis, *Alice in Wonderland* and *Through the Looking Glass*, illustrated by John Tenniel. New York: Grosset & Dunlap Inc. 1996. 66.
8. John Bowring (1792–1872), *"In the Cross of Christ I Glory."*
9. Rudyard Kipling, "Cold Iron." Accessed February 11, 2011. http://poetryloverspage.com/poets/kipling/cold_iron.html.

October

1. Oliver Wendell Holmes, accessed September 19, 2015. https://ministrymagazine.org/archive/1958/11/acknowledging-our-blessings.
2. Robert Burns, "To A Mouse." Accessed February 12, 2011. http://en.wikipedia.org/wiki/To_a_Mouse.
3. Studdert-Kennedy, G. A., *The Word and the Work*. New York: Longmans, Green and Co, 1925. 57–58.
4. Frank Graeff (1860–1919), *"Does Jesus Care?"*
5. Nouwen, Henri, *Seeds of Hope: A Nouwen Reader*. Edited by Robert Durback. New York: Image Books, 1997. 190.
6. Mother Teresa, accessed April 20, 2011. http://brainyquote.com/quotes/quotes/m/mothertere158114.html.
7. John Fawcett (1740–1817), *"Blest Be the Tie that Binds."*
8. *Last Poems by Elizabeth Barrett Browning*. New York: James Miller, 1863. 68–69.
9. Sign quote accessed from *American Imperialism*, collection created & selected by Charles Gregg. Reprint, Arno Press Inc., 1970. 180.
10. Archives de l'Université de Sherbrooke.
11. Anna Elisabeth Hamilton, accessed September 19, 2015. http://bartleby.com/348/534.html.

November

1. Used by permission of Charles Harvey.
2. Source Unknown.
3. *Quiet Heroes: Story of a Forgotten Squadron*. 1995, Avanti Pictures. Used by permission, Tony Papa, Avanti Pictures.
4. Montgomery, Lucy Maud *Anne of Green Gables*. Accessed April 20, 2011. http://gutenberg.org/files/45/45-h/45-h.html.
5. Sir Humphry Davy, accessed September 19, 2015. http://bartleby.com/349/authors/58.html.

NOTES

6. Andrew Carnegie, accessed September 19, 2015. http://preaching-notes.blogspot.ca/2009/10/who-is-going-to-do-work-Andrew-carnegie.html.

7. John Oxenham, *The Ways*, accessed September 19, 2015. http://readbookonline.net/readOnLine/47984.

8. Joseph Conrad, *The Mirror of the Sea*, accessed September 19, 2019. https://en.wikisource.org/wiki/The_Mirror_of_the_Sea/Chapter_XLVII.

9. Cecil Frances Alexander (1818–1895), *"Jesus calls us! O'er the tumult."*

December

1. Roger Babson, accessed September 19, 2015. http://www.middletownbiblechurch.org/greateve/greate11.htm.

2. Source Unknown.

3. From a plaque marking Abraham Lincoln's birthplace near Hodgenville, Kentucky.

4. Osbeck, Kenneth, *101 More Hymn Stories*. Grand Rapids: Kregal Publications, 1985. 46. Used by permission of the publisher. All rights reserved.

5. Gaither, Gloria and William, *"Because He Lives."* Used under Licensing Agreement with Capitol Christian Music Group.

6. Senter, Ruth, Title unknown, *Power for Living*. December 24, 1995.

7. PEANUTS © Peanuts Worldwide LLC.

8. © DaySpring Cards, Inc. and Roy Lessin. Used with permission. All rights reserved.